SUCCESSFUL LEGAL ANALYSIS AND WRITING

The Fundamentals

FOURTH EDITION

Christopher D. Soper
ASSISTANT CLINICAL PROFESSOR OF LAW
DIRECTOR OF LEGAL WRITING
UNIVERSITY OF MINNESOTA LAW SCHOOL

Cristina D. Lockwood
ASSOCIATE PROFESSOR OF LAW
UNIVERSITY OF DETROIT MERCY SCHOOL OF LAW

Bradley G. Clary
CLINICAL PROFESSOR OF LAW
UNIVERSITY OF MINNESOTA LAW SCHOOL

Pamela Lysaght
RETIRED ASSOCIATE PROFESSOR OF LAW
UNIVERSITY OF DETROIT MERCY SCHOOL OF LAW

WEST ACADEMIC PUBLISHING

© West, a Thomson business, 2003, 2006
© 2010 Thomson Reuters
© 2017 LEG, Inc. d/b/a West Academic
    444 Cedar Street, Suite 700
    St. Paul, MN 55101
    1-877-888-1330

West, West Academic Publishing, and West Academic are trademarks of West Publishing Corporation, used under license.

Printed in the United States of America

ISBN: 978-1-63460-621-9

Dedication

To all of the hardworking legal writing teachers
who labor every day to help law students become
accomplished lawyers.
B.G.C.
P.L.
C.D.S.
C.D.L.

To Megan, and in appreciation of your love and support.
C.D.S.

To Anna, William, Scott, and Aiden—my sources of pride and joy.
C.D.L.

To Mary-Louise—for being there.
B.G.C.

To Leon—for eternity.
P.L.

Preface

This is a book about legal analysis and writing for first-year law students. We set out in this preface our fundamental design premise and theme, our fundamental learning outcomes, seven principles that beginning legal writers need to understand, and some features inherent in good legal analysis and communication.

A. THE FUNDAMENTAL DESIGN PREMISE: FLEXIBLE COMPONENTS AND TEMPLATES

Many of the texts currently on the market are comprehensive; that is, they tend to be a form of one-stop shopping. They offer considerable advice on many aspects of analysis and writing. They are very good. But, precisely because of their length and comprehensiveness, they are not always ready-references. Further, they may offer advice that is either beyond a given law school's legal writing program goals or that has to be affirmatively explained away as at least partially inconsistent with the professor's different advice. (This may be inescapable for any text on legal analysis and writing.) Our goal is to minimize significantly this potential problem.

This book adopts a basic component approach to legal writing. Legal writers can assemble a competent analysis and written product by mastering the concepts in this book. They can also mix and match the pieces they want to fit the programs at their own law schools.

B. THE FUNDAMENTAL THEME: PROBLEM SOLVING

We think there is a place for a book on legal analysis and writing that expressly looks at legal writing and analysis through a problem-solving lens. Consider one of the cases in a first-year casebook in contracts, torts, or civil procedure: Does it just drop into place? No, someone's life story was rolling along. A problem developed. "The law" stepped in to solve the problem through the efforts of lawyers and other persons. Those efforts followed a standard sequence: The lawyers first had to learn the facts of the story and identify the legal problem. Then the lawyers had to identify the potentially applicable legal principles and analyze them. Once the lawyers analyzed the principles, the lawyers had to apply them to the facts of the problem. That analysis reached a conclusion as to how "the law" does and/or should resolve the problem. The lawyers then communicated the analysis to one or more audiences—a client, a colleague, a judge, an adversary, or others. In the end, a court picked a resolution among competing choices as to the facts, the law, or both, and the authors of the casebook elected to publish the court's decision to illustrate a legal proposition. This selection occurred far down the line. The lawyers did considerable work long before the court decided the case, and long before the casebook authors decided to include the case in their texts.

This book is about the work of lawyers. We provide fundamental advice and templates for analyzing and discussing legal problems from the standpoint of practicing lawyers who help solve them. For this purpose, we think of lawyers as being on a two-stage expedition, which is reflected in the organization of this book. The first stage is to assemble the material required to solve the legal problem. At this stage, we focus upon a standard road-mapping sequence of identifying the problem with specificity, identifying the key

v

facts in the relevant story that give rise to the problem, identifying with specificity the legal rules that might potentially apply to the problem, analyzing the relevant legal rules and applying them to the material facts, and identifying a solution to the relevant problem. The second stage, once the lawyers have assembled all of the key material, is to communicate the story of the case and the legal analysis in the appropriate context using recognized legal writing conventions. At this stage, we introduce how to create legal documents, such as office memoranda, client letters, trial court briefs, and appellate court briefs.

In this fourth edition, we offer condensed explanatory material on legal rules, condensed explanation of basic citation principles, and a number of new illustrative examples. We have added reference to relevant American Bar Association (ABA) Model Rules of Professional Conduct.[1] Most states have patterned their governing ethical rules on the ABA Model Rules and lawyers as members of the state bar must abide by those rules. In our opinion, it is never too early to become familiar with the types of ethical rules that govern a lawyer's behavior. Further, for each chapter, we have set forth the learning outcomes we envision can be accomplished.

C. THE FUNDAMENTAL LEARNING OUTCOMES: LEGAL ANALYSIS AND REASONING, PROBLEM-SOLVING, AND WRITTEN AND ORAL COMMUNICATION IN THE LEGAL CONTEXT

By practicing the process explained in this book, we expect law students will learn and be able to reliably demonstrate fundamental legal skills. We expect students will be able to identify and analyze legal issues to solve problems, including the ability to interpret and synthesize relevant legal authorities, gather and assess relevant facts, and provide critical analysis of competing legal positions.

We also expect students will be able to communicate effectively in writing and orally. We expect students will learn to communicate with the appropriate tone and sophistication for the relevant audience, and with organization, focus, purpose, and clarity.

Finally, we expect students will be able to conduct themselves professionally and ethically. We expect students will learn the importance of being honest and candid with clients, lawyers, courts, and others.

D. SEVEN KEY PRINCIPLES

1. Legal Analysis and Writing Are Audience-Focused.

Because legal analysis and writing are fundamentally about problem solving, they must be audience-focused. The logic is simple: The relevant story is not the lawyer's story. The relevant problem is not the lawyer's problem. The legal principles are not the lawyer's principles. The ultimate decision-maker is not the lawyer. Instead, the story is the client's. The problem is the client's. The legal principles are the court's, the legislature's, or the agency's. The ultimate decision-makers are the juries and judges (in litigated cases), or the clients (in settled cases and in transactions that do not result in litigation), or other persons or entities such as agencies, colleagues, and adversaries (in various settings). These are all audiences.

---

[1]   ABA Model Rules of Professional Conduct, 2016 Edition. Copyright © 2016 by the American Bar Association, Reprinted with permission. Copies of ABA Model Rules of Professional Conduct, 2016 Edition, are available from www.Shopaba.org. This information or any portion thereof may not be copied or disseminated in any form or by any means or stored in an electronic database or retrieval system without the express written consent of the American Bar Association.

As a result, the writer has to evaluate constantly how his or her analysis and communication will be received by others. And audiences these days are busy. They have too much to do and too little time in which to do it. They want quick answers. They want these answers stated simply and concisely.

We assume that all audiences share some of these characteristics. We provide instruction on how to write concisely and how to state an analysis in a straightforward and simplified manner.

2. Legal Writing Is Hard Work.

Problem solving is not easy. Communicating solutions so that an audience will both understand and adopt the solutions is not easy. This is all true—even with standard sequences and templates—and frustrating.

First-year legal writing courses are fundamentally courses about what it means to be a lawyer. They are not just courses about "writing." They are instead courses about how to piece together a story, how to identify problems, how to think about "the law," how to parse legal rules, how to analyze and apply legal principles, how to determine what legal conclusion will solve a given problem, and how to reach a legal audience in writing. Lawyers spend their entire careers perfecting these skills. There are a lot of moving pieces that have to come together, and putting these pieces together is hard work for even experienced legal researchers and writers.

3. Legal Analysis and Writing Are Learn-by-Doing Tasks.

For the most part, the only way to become good at analyzing and writing about solutions to legal problems is to practice. So what beginning legal writers need the most are a series of steps to follow and a set of simple templates that serve as models. Hard work and feedback are also key ingredients to developing these skills.

Thus, this book is about basic building blocks and the sequence for using them. Readers tend not to absorb detailed nuances that may arise in different configurations unless they can place those nuances in the context of their own specific projects. We count on professors to practice students on the details they think their students need to know to fit their own course designs.

4. Legal Analysis and Writing Require the Ability to Multi-Task.

A good piece of legal writing involves the integration of many tasks—assembling and disassembling facts, assembling and disassembling rules, re-looking at facts, re-looking at rules, applying rules to facts, reaching conclusions, and communicating conclusions. We give a sequence for these tasks, essentially in the order of the chapters in this text. But we do not mean to imply that legal writing and analysis is a linear process. In practice, a lawyer will be engaged in many of the tasks more or less simultaneously, moving back and forth among them.

5. Legal Analysis and Writing Require Living with Ambiguity.

Legal rules are living things. They expand. They change. They contract. They find new application. Even within standard concepts that most persons can accept, reasonable people may differ over what "the law" says, what it should say, and how it should apply to a specific problem.

The same can be said of the process of legal analysis and communication. Some templates and methodologies tend to be more effective than others. We set forth in this book approaches we think will result in consistently competent work product to various audiences. But reasonable legal writing teachers may prefer different advice in a given circumstance. None of them may be affirmatively "wrong." Instead, each professor is making a different judgment about the best alternative among acceptable choices. The key for the legal researcher and writer is to be able to support and clearly explain one's analysis and conclusions in a manner consistent with acceptable legal conventions and ethical considerations.

6. Legal Analysis and Writing Are Messy, but the Final Work Product Cannot Be.

The process of thinking about solutions to legal problems and the process for producing an initial draft of a legal document are messy. There are starts and stops. There are circles and semi-circles. There are reversals of direction. There are detours and unintended wrong turns. A lawyer may think she is dealing with one set of facts, start researching the law, begin applying the law, and discover that there are new or additional facts. Similarly, a lawyer may think that one set of legal principles is relevant, only to find a lead to a new legal argument that heads in a different direction. While drafting a legal document, it is not uncommon for a lawyer to arrive tentatively at one solution to a problem, only to talk herself out of that first solution and into a different solution. Writing helps us clarify our thinking.

All of this is natural. Starting and stopping, thinking and re-thinking, writing and re-writing are all parts of the relevant process. Just make sure, to the extent practical, that there is enough time set aside for the project to allow the full process to play out. Also, remember that the final written work product the audience sees should not be a stream-of-consciousness recitation of the messy analytical and drafting process. Rather, the final written work product the audience sees must be clean, simple, straightforward, logical, and flow irresistibly to a solution to the legal problem at hand.

7. Legal Analysis and Writing Invoke Ethical Considerations.

Lawyers are governed by the ethical rules of the jurisdiction in which they practice. Lawyers as learned professionals are stewards of the legal system. They owe duties to the legal system, to their clients, and to others involved in their practice of law. It is never too soon to recognize that lawyers must make decisions in light of governing ethical rules. It is never too soon to be conscious of a lawyer's unique ability to positively influence the rendering of justice. Any set of rules governing conduct, however, should be seen as a floor not a ceiling. The preamble of the ABA Model Rules of Professional Conduct states, "The rules do not, however, exhaust the moral and ethical considerations that should inform a lawyer, for no worthwhile human activity can be completely defined by legal rules. The Rules simply provide a framework for the ethical practice of law."[2] In other words, although ethical rules will govern, a person's own morals and beliefs must remain as an important guide in making decisions.

Law students' reputations as lawyers begin the day law school starts. Students should familiarize themselves with the governing student code of conduct. Students should aim to be a positive influence in the life of the school, and while working toward their goals, strive to maintain their moral ideals and their ethical standards.

---

[2] MODEL RULES OF PROF'L CONDUCT PREAMBLE (2016).

E. FEATURES OF GOOD ANALYSIS AND WRITING

What are the features, then, of a competent process and a competent final work product? Below are simple ones to keep in mind, no matter what type of legal analysis or communication you may be generating.

1. First, Think.

It is hard to make a point if you have not developed a point to make. Ask yourself:

- ➢ What is the story I am analyzing?

- ➢ What is the problem?

- ➢ What are the potentially relevant legal rules?

- ➢ How do they apply to the problem?

- ➢ What is my solution to the problem?

- ➢ How can I best convey that to a reader?

2. Then, Make Your Point.

Accurately. Accuracy means using honest fact statements, accurate citations to sources, and precision in details.

Clearly. Clarity means eliminating ambiguity; preferring specifics to generalities; using road maps; and following a logical, organized structure.

Concisely. Concision means eliminating excess language, getting to the point, and separating the relevant from the irrelevant.

Responsibly. Responsibility means owning the process and product, acting professionally, following professional ethics rules, and avoiding inappropriate language and name-calling.

In your own way. As a writer, you still have to "be yourself." Otherwise, you are not credible. Incorporate within your own personal style the various processes and templates that will help you best make your point.

3. Work and Rework. Edit and Re-Edit.

The reader of a typical piece of legal writing has to be able to understand the writer's point, be able to easily follow the logic and reasoning that leads to the writer's point, and (especially in the case of persuasive writing) believe what the writer is stating is true.

Editing is not just about checking details of work such as spelling, punctuation, sentence structure, and citation form, although such checking is vital. Editing is also about making sure that you have made a point your reader understands, can easily follow, and believes.

4. Critique Your Work.

Unless you run out of time, do not stop working on your analysis and writing until you are satisfied with your answers to these questions:

➤   Do I understand the relevant story?

➤   Do I understand the problem to solve?

➤   Do I understand the legal principles that might apply?

➤   Have I analyzed and applied those principles to the facts?

➤   Have I reached a conclusion that will solve the problem from my client's standpoint?

➤   Does my writing make the relevant point(s) to my reader?

➤   Will the reader understand?

➤   Will the reader follow?

➤   Will the reader accept?

As these questions demonstrate, the final stages of critiquing require the writer to shift focus—from the writer's perspective to the reader's perspective. In other words, effective self-critique requires evaluating your work product through the lens of the intended audience.

The focus of the rest of this book is on how to use these principles and features to successfully solve legal problems and communicate the analysis to the intended audience.

Christopher D. Soper
Cristina D. Lockwood
Bradley G. Clary
Pamela Lysaght

February 2017

Acknowledgments for the Fourth Edition

We are grateful to Brad Clary and Pamela Lysaght for their guidance and mentorship in our careers. We thank them for allowing us the opportunity to carry their ground-breaking work in this book forward. We are also indebted to Bonnie Karlen, at West Publishing Co., for helping us navigate the publishing process.

Cristina Lockwood thanks Jennifer Pilef for citation work and James Williams for assistance in preparing needed documents. She also thanks her students, who through their learning influenced the instructions in this text.

Finally, Cristina is grateful to her husband, Joe, for his continual support, his encouragement, and most of all for his ability to always find the silver lining.

Chris Soper thanks Allen Barr for his excellent work on the Teachers' Manual and other documents. He also thanks his current and former student teaching partners Adam Lozeau, Jasper Tran, and Alysha Bohanon for making him a better legal writing teacher. He also thanks research assistants Raphael Coburn, Brittany Gefroh, Yesul Lee, and Ronald Waclawski.

Finally, Chris is grateful for the daily inspiration from his daughters, Margaret Hughes Soper and Emeline Day Walsh Soper.

We are indebted to many persons who have helped us along the way in our careers and in the preparation of this book.

We thank Douglas Powell and Pamela Siege Chandler, who had the confidence in us to encourage the publication of this text. We also thank Pam and her colleague Heidi Hellekson for their review of early drafts and their helpful comments and suggestions.

We thank Katherine Donohue for all her dedication and hard work in assisting us with this text; Bethany Tkach Abrams, Maya Parekh, Emily Pruisner, Kevin Toll, and Shaun Godwin for their help in researching and citechecking; Susan Miller for her assistance in formatting portions of the work, as well as helping us keep our senses of humor; and Barbara White and James Williams for their assistance in coordinating the copying and shipping of drafts of this text.

We acknowledge the work of legal writing student instructors Deborah Behles, Rachel Brass, Oliver Kim, and Tara Tilbury in assisting in the original research in the spring of 2000 into the law of the First Circuit and others in the Commonwealth Hospital problem that appears in Chapter 11. A version of this problem was initially conceived in a slightly different form by Author Clary and Professor Susanna Sherry in connection with the work of legal writing sections attached to Professor Sherry's civil procedure class that spring. We additionally acknowledge legal writing students David Klink, Adam Matheson, Madeline Gallo, Elizabeth Reifert, and Cassandra Long for research assistance in the *U.S. v. Anderson* briefs that appear in Chapter 11.

We thank Ryan Kelly, John Hutchinson, Maya Parekh, and Joshua Heggem for their help over the years in researching and drafting variations on the Chris Smith problem found in the Teacher's Manual to this text.

We thank students, Adam Trampe and Joshua Heggem, as well as some colleagues, for their assistance with developing the *U.S. v. Harper* problem in the Teacher's Manual.

Please note that the substantive law discussed in sample letters, memoranda, and briefs in this text is current as of the times those samples were originally prepared. No representation is made that the substantive law is current as of the time a reader may be studying the samples. The samples are presented for methodological purposes only.

Brad Clary thanks former and current student teaching partners Deborah Behles, David Schelzel, Dawn Kim, Jennifer Rogers, Anna Dunbar-Hester, and Nicola Kieves for their help in teaching the small section classes that helped inform his ideas for this book.

Pamela Lysaght thanks her colleagues, Cristina Lockwood, Danielle Istl, Cara Cunningham, Deborah Paruch, Michelle Streicher, Tracy Weissman, Pamela Wilkins, Danton Berube, and Karen Henning for their invaluable insights and support. And she thanks her students who helped inspire many of the ideas in presenting the material for this book.

Finally, Brad and Pam wish to thank Mary-Louise, Ben, Sam, and Leon for their much-appreciated and invaluable support, patience, and grace during the drafting process.

Table of Contents

SUCCESSFUL LEGAL ANALYSIS AND WRITING

The Fundamentals

FOURTH EDITION

CHAPTER 1

An Expedition

LEARNING OBJECTIVES

1. Students will understand that successful legal analysis occurs as a process: a series of steps beginning with a problem and ending with a potential legal solution to the problem.

2. Students will understand that successfully communicating a written legal analysis requires guiding a reader along the legal analysis process, step-by-step.

The process of communicating a legal analysis can be thought of as an expedition.[1] An experienced guide (the lawyer) takes a visitor (the audience, who may or may not be a lawyer) to a destination (the solution to a legal problem). The expedition begins with a set of facts: a "problem" potentially solvable by "the law." The lawyer assesses the facts, identifies and analyzes the legal rules that might apply, and applies them to the material facts. This is the first stage, a messy process full of stops and starts that ends only when the lawyer knows the facts, the law, and the analysis well enough to share her knowledge. The lawyer then shares this knowledge with the audience by bringing the audience along on the journey. This is the second stage, communicating the lawyer's expertise in the facts, legal rules, and analysis to the audience. The expedition ends with a proposed solution to the problem.

You can see that it is not enough to tell the audience the destination without also providing the route. The purpose of an office memorandum, a client letter, a trial court brief, an appellate brief, or a transactional document such as a contract, is to convey the route to the audience. Guiding the audience along the route requires the lawyer to provide directions—a roadmap, a guidebook—from the problem to the solution. When a legal writer is preparing legal documents, the writer should be thinking in terms of conveying information as a tour guide, of giving directions, of guiding the audience along the route.

You can also see that a good guide (the lawyer) will not usually include for the visitor (the audience) the same messy stops and starts the guide had to explore before finding the

---

[1]   Previous editions of this book have referred to the process of communicating a legal analysis as a "roadmap." Two other forms of this concept have previously appeared in BRADLEY G. CLARY ET AL., ADVOCACY ON APPEAL 3D ED. 18–20 (West 2008); Bradley G. Clary & Deborah N. Behles, *Roadmapping and Legal Writing*, 8 PERSP. 134–36 (2000); *see also* Sherri Lee Keene, *Are We There Yet? Aligning the Expectations and Realities of Gaining Competency in Legal Writing*, 53 DUQ. L. REV. 99, 102 (2015); Mark Osbeck, *What is "Good Legal Writing" and Why Does It Matter?*, 4 DREXEL L. REV. 417, 428–30, 434 (2012); Kathy L. Cerminara, *Metaphors Help Students Write More Logically*, L. TEACHER 2 (Spring 1997); Brian S. Williams, *Road Maps, Tour Guides, and Parking Lots: The Use of Context in Teaching Overview and Thesis Paragraphs*, 7 PERSP. 27 (1998). Those of you who may be journalists will recognize the who, what, where, when, why, and how questions from your training in that field. *E.g.* KRISTIE BUNTON ET AL., WRITING ACROSS THE MEDIA 105 (Bedford/St. Martin's 1999).

destination (the solution to the problem). Rather, the guide should provide directions that lead to the destination in the simplest way possible.

To give good directions, a lawyer should think in terms of a standard "where, what, why, who, when, and how" template. Then the lawyer should apply that template in giving directions to the visitor.

A. WHERE, WHAT

Where do you want to take the visitor? *What* are your goals? *What* are your visitor's goals? *What* do you want the visitor to do upon arrival at the destination? *What* does the visitor want to do? We combine the where and what questions for present purposes because they are so closely related in this setting. Those are the first questions you have to ask. To answer them, your analysis of the relevant legal problem, and your proposed solution, must be clear in your mind. You cannot send a visitor to a destination if you do not know what that is or what can be done there. So spend the necessary time to figure out those questions.[2]

B. WHY

Why do you want to take the visitor to *that* destination? Presumably you believe that the destination you have chosen (the proposed solution to the relevant legal problem) is desirable. What good will come from the result? Will the visitor (audience) benefit? If so, how? In the legal context, will the client benefit? If so, how? Will society benefit? If so, how? Will third parties benefit? If so, how?

C. WHO

Who is your visitor (audience)? For example, does your visitor have any prior knowledge of the destination (is your client/the judge/a colleague already familiar with the kinds of legal analyses and solutions that are appropriate in the present matter)? Does the visitor need intricately detailed directions, or just a reminder of the general route (are there already letters/memoranda/briefs in the matter with which the audience is familiar)? And does your visitor follow directions best when there are visual aids (a picture map); when there are numbered steps (first, proceed left out of the parking lot to the second traffic light; second, turn right at the light; third, proceed to . . . .); when there are landmarks (turn left at the traffic light where you see the ABC Supermarket on the corner); or a combination of these? In other words, what kind of a learner is your audience?[3]

D. WHEN

When are you leading your visitor to the destination? Are you going there now (you have a problem whose solution depends upon the law and the facts that currently exist)? Or are you going there in the future (you have a problem whose solution depends upon your prediction as to the law and the facts that will likely exist at some future relevant time)?

---

[2]   Note that you may not fully develop your analysis and proposed solution of a problem until you actually write it out. That is fine. Your first draft of a road map does not have to be, indeed probably should not be, the draft you give your visitor. You may change your mind on the proper destination or the route to get there. Leave yourself enough time to revise the written work product so that it reflects the final version of your analysis and solution, as opposed to the messy interim work.

[3]   Have you and a partner ever attempted to assemble a toy, a piece of furniture, or something similar? Some people need to take out the manufacturer's manual, read all of the directions step-by-step, and then look at the picture of the finished product before commencing any actual assembly. Other people can simply dump the contents of the box on the floor, look at the components, and go to work. Still others will perhaps find a video of the assembly. All will wind up in the end with the same product, but each will have approached assembly in a very different way. Similarly, legal audiences will have different learning styles that need to be recognized and accommodated.

E. HOW

How are you leading your visitor to the destination? There are a variety of possibilities:

> ➤ Are you sending the visitor by a scenic route, or the most direct one?

> ➤ Are you sending the visitor by the most familiar route, or a newer one?

> ➤ Are you sending the visitor by the easiest route, or a more difficult one?

> ➤ Are you sending the visitor by the currently fashionable route, or a more traditional one?

There may not be one single correct answer. The choices likely depend upon the answers to the previous where, what, why, who, and when questions. For example, in a legal writing setting, your visitor (audience) will often be a busy person. So you do not want a leisurely route to the relevant problem's solution. Instead, you want a quick, direct route. Further, if your audience is a conservative client, judge, or colleague, you do not want a risky route that breaks new ground. Rather, you want a familiar, traditional route. The point is that you have to put all of the pieces together to decide what kind of a roadmap you want to prepare in any given expedition.

F. EXAMPLE

Here is a simple example that illustrates the where, what, why, who, when, and how template in the context of an actual expedition from which we will draw some comparisons to legal writing.

Suppose that you have an out-of-town visitor. The visitor would like a tour. You tell the visitor you will happily give her a tour. But ask yourself the where, what, why, who, when, and how questions. You might discover how you could provide a better tour, more in line with what your visitor wants.

What does the visitor want to do on the tour? See local historical landmarks? Any particular landmark, or just whatever happens to be nearby? Visit the local mall? Any mall, or the largest mall in America, which also happens to be in your town? The answers make a difference. If the visitor wants to see the largest mall in the country, and you take the visitor to a historical fort, you have just given your visitor a useless tour. The visitor will be affirmatively annoyed to arrive at an unexpected destination. You must know with some precision what the goal is before you begin the expedition.

Why does the visitor want a tour? Does the visitor simply want to find a way to pass the time on a lazy afternoon? Does the visitor hope to learn something about the history of your town? Do you want to show off the largest mall in America? The answers make a difference because, again, maybe you just directed the visitor to the wrong place. Maybe the visitor who wants to learn something would rather go to a historical landmark with accompanying exhibits or even a museum, rather than a landmark that has no museum attached.

Who is the visitor? Has she visited before? Has she been to the local mall before? Does she already know the history of your town? Even assuming that the local historical landmark is exactly the correct place to send the visitor, will she understand the significance of your visit without explanation of the historical significance?

Turning to the *when* question, you may wonder about timing. If the mall the visitor wants to visit does not open until noon, the local historical landmark opens at 9:00 a.m., and the visitor needs to be back at your house by 2:00 p.m., then sending the visitor to the historical landmark first and the mall second is a good choice. The visitor can go to the landmark in the morning for a couple of hours, then visit the mall when it opens at noon until it's time to return to your house. You might also determine how long it is expected to take from the mall to your house, to ensure the visitor returns home by 2:00 p.m.

Finally, consider the *how* question in the context of directions to the destination. Suppose the expedition involves a trip to the mall, and you write down the following directions:

➢ From my house, go north three blocks to the highway.

➢ Go east on the highway and get off at the Main Street exit.

➢ At the end of the exit, go straight on the frontage road.

➢ In about half a block, turn into the mall parking lot.

This four-point set of directions leaves out information that a clear set of directions should contain. To begin, there is no title. If the visitor puts the directions in a pocket where there are other notes of directions to other places, she will not immediately know which writing tells her how to get to the mall.

The first instruction is ambiguous. It tells the visitor to go "north" three blocks to the "highway." Is north to the right or to the left out of your driveway? Is the "highway" State Highway 56, or County Highway 20, both of which pass through your neighborhood approximately three blocks from your house? A clearer first direction would be, "When you leave my house, turn right (heading north) on my street (Washington St.), and go three blocks to the State Highway 56 entrance ramp."

The second instruction is also potentially ambiguous. It tells the visitor to go "east" on the highway to the Main Street exit. Presumably that means a right turn onto the highway because the visitor has previously been traveling north. But why not make that explicit? And will the Main Street exit be so labeled, or will the exit sign say "Highway 7," because that is another designation for "Main Street"? A clearer instruction would be, "Turn right just after you pass the ABC gas station, and follow the sign for East Highway 56. Go 1.2 miles on Highway 56, stay in the right lane, and go up the exit ramp for Main Street (= Highway 7)."

You can improve even the third instruction. The visitor may not know what you mean by the "frontage road." Spell this out: "At the end of the exit ramp, do not turn on Main Street. Instead, go straight ahead through the Main Street traffic light. You will be on the frontage road that parallels Highway 56."

Finally, you can improve the fourth instruction. The local mall has a name, "Main Street Mall," and a large sign at its entrance. Give the visitor those landmarks by saying, "Go half a block to the large Main Street Mall sign, turn right into the Mall parking lot."

Certain general principles can be distilled from the above example:

➢ Use titles so your reader can tell the destination at the outset.

➢ Do not assume prior knowledge; spell out the terms you are using.

➢ Refer to landmarks as a guide to progress.

➢ Be precise.

➢ Make sure the directions are in proper sequence.

G. COMPARISON TO LEGAL WRITING

Suppose now an assignment to prepare a legal "roadmap" for an expedition in the case of *Bears v. Gold*. The following are the basic facts (adapted from the well-known children's story).[4]

A twelve-year-old girl named Sarah Gold became lost in the woods. She eventually stumbled upon a house as night was falling and nighttime creatures began stirring. She went up to the front door and knocked. When nobody answered, she opened the door, which was unlocked, and went inside after brushing her feet off on the mat on the front porch.

To the right of the entrance hall was the dining room. On the table were three bowls of vegetarian chili. "Wow," said Sarah, "food!" She sat down at the table and began to eat. "That hurt," exclaimed Sarah, as she sampled the first bowl. "Too hot!" Sarah pulled over the second bowl. "Yuck," she said, "too cold." So Sarah turned to the third bowl. "Just right," she said. She gobbled it down because she was ravenously hungry.

Once she had eaten supper, she realized she was frightfully tired. So she lay down on the sofa in the living room and fell fast asleep.

In the morning, she awoke with the sunrise. She did the dishes and left, after leaving a note that said, "Thanks for the food and the good night sleep. I would have paid you, but I am lost and have no money with me. Sarah Gold."

Sarah eventually found her way home. A month later, however, a process server confronted her with a summons and complaint. Robert, Barbara, and Bert Bear are suing Sarah[5] for trespass.

Ignore for the moment whether your expedition roadmap will ultimately take the form of an office memorandum, a client letter, or a brief for a court. We will describe those specific templates in later chapters. Focus instead on the basics.

Assume that Sarah does not have the ability to pay for a lawyer. Further assume that you will represent Sarah on a *pro bono publico* basis. Every lawyer has a professional responsibility to provide legal services to those unable to pay.[6]

You decide that you will argue that Sarah's actions are justified by an "emergency" defense. Further assume that you have conducted research and interviewed Sarah. Here is your roadmap:

---

[4]   One of the authors has previously used a version of the Bears problem at a Minnesota State Bar Association CLE workshop for appellate lawyers.

[5]   Because Sarah is a minor, her parents would assume defense of the case, in the real world. The case caption might read, "Robert Bear, Barbara Bear, and Bert Bear v. Sarah Gold, a minor, by her parents, John Gold and Susan Gold."

[6]   MODEL RULES OF PROF'L CONDUCT R. 6.1(a)(1) (2016). Rule 6.1 does not mandate pro bono services but instead states that a lawyer should provide at least fifty hours of pro bono service a year. *Id*. While in law school seek out pro bono opportunities. Pro bono service is not only personally rewarding, but it helps all individuals, not just the wealthy, have representation and access to the legal system.

Roadmap	Explanation
Robert Bear, Barbara Bear, and Bert Bear *v.* *Sarah Gold, a Minor, by her parents, John Gold and Susan Gold*	Case caption (which in a formal legal document would include the names of the parties, the court, the case number, and the title of the document).
Defense theory for Sarah: Emergency	Title of the roadmap.
Goal: Dismiss the complaint; threshold motion to dismiss for failure of the complaint to state a viable legal claim based on the facts pleaded.	Identification of the destination: the overall *where* and *what* questions and answers.
Basic explanation for why dismissal is proper: Need to encourage assistance to travelers in emergencies; need to encourage assistance to children in emergencies; only nominal "damage" to Bear family in this case; on balance, society's interest in protecting Sarah outweighs interest in protecting Bears under the circumstances.	Identification of the *why* question and answer.
Audience: The client for now; ultimately, the court.	Identification of the *who* question and answer.
Timing: File the motion as soon as possible to hopefully resolve the issue quickly for the client.	Identification of the *when* question and answer.
Basis for the motion in detail:	Identification of the *how* question and answer.
<u>Issue:</u> Whether Sarah can be liable for trespass onto the Bears' property when she entered it in an emergency.	
<u>Conclusion:</u> No, emergency is a complete defense.	
<u>Legal rule:</u> The Moot State Supreme Court has decided six cases involving an emergency defense to a trespass claim. In three cases involving children in trouble, the court upheld the defense and found no liability on the part of the child-trespasser. (In one of those three cases, an eleven-year-old child entered a person's home in a forest to obtain shelter in an electric storm.) In two cases involving adults who were not genuinely in trouble, the court rejected the defense and found liability. In one case involving a child who pretended there was an emergency to gain access to the property for the purpose of playing a prank, the court rejected the defense and found liability.	Within the *how* question, tell the story AND identify the legal rule that will apply.

Factual story: Sarah is twelve years old and still a child. At the time of the "trespass," she was lost in the woods. Night was falling. Dangerous animals, including wolves, prowl the forest at dusk, looking for prey. She entered the Bear family's house across a front porch mat that said, "Welcome." The door was unlocked. She knocked first, but entered upon hearing rustling noises in the bushes behind her. She played no pranks on the Bear family.

Application of the law to the facts: The present case is like the three previous cases in which the court found no liability. It is particularly like the electric storm shelter case. In both the present case and in the electric storm case, a child was in trouble and in need of shelter due to dangerous circumstances arising at night in a forest.

Requested solution: Dismiss the Bears' complaint.

Notice that the factual story in this Roadmap is more detailed than the basic facts set forth above in some ways, and less detailed in other ways. Factual details matter in the law. One of the lawyer's most important tasks is to determine which factual details impact the legal analysis.

H. CONCLUSION

The kind of expedition roadmap provided in this exercise is very helpful in working through a difficult legal question. We encourage you to think about this approach each time you are parsing through a problem that needs a solution.

CHAPTER 2

The Role of Facts in Resolving Legal Problems

> **Just the facts, ma'am, just the facts.**
>
> Jack Webb as Sgt. Joe Friday, *Dragnet*
>
> (NBC 1952–1959, 1967–1970) (TV series).

There was a popular television show in the 1950s and late 1960s known as *Dragnet*. It was a police detective drama, starring Jack Webb. In virtually every episode, or at least the ones we can remember, Webb would knock on the door of a potential witness, typically a woman, who would answer the knock and ask something like, "What would you like to know, officer?" Webb would reply laconically, "Just the facts, ma'am, just the facts."

The writers for the show had the right idea. What matters in police investigations are the facts. Similarly, facts matter first and foremost in legal analysis and writing.

LEARNING OBJECTIVES

1. Students will understand the importance of honestly assessing relevant facts and will learn a holistic approach for gathering all relevant facts.

2. Students will learn that they must listen and engage with clients to gather relevant facts in order to identify client objectives, interests, and potential legal positions.

Facts are the driving force behind legal problems. If you do not understand the relevant factual story with which you are dealing, then you do not really understand which legal principles might, will, or should apply to the problem you are addressing. Facts are also the driving force behind the law. The common law develops through a series of individual court decisions, each one of which addresses a single problem for a single set of parties. **It is by looking at the material fact patterns across the relevant decided cases that a lawyer predicts how a court will view the problem in the client's present case.** Similarly, statutory law develops through a series of legislative enactments, each one of which addresses a category of fact problems confronting multiple persons (civil rights issues, employment difficulties, environmental concerns, etc.). **It is by looking at the facts behind the legislative problem that a lawyer predicts how a court will apply the statute to the client's present case.**

Curiously, this concept can be easy to forget. It is easy to become embroiled in learning "the law" (read: rules), without considering that legal principles serve to solve problems, and problems arise because of facts. From a practicing lawyer's standpoint, "the law" is not an abstract set of rules. Lawyers do not simply look up a legal rule in a book, provide the rule to the relevant audience, and then expect to get paid large sums of money. If that were all there was to the practice of law, then courts, clients, and adversaries would just look up the rules themselves. No, a practicing lawyer must investigate and analyze both the law and the facts. The rest of this chapter focuses on the identification of the facts that give rise to legal problems.

We will cover legal rules in common law and statutory contexts in subsequent chapters of the book. You can see already that sequencing facts and rules in legal analysis is not easy. One might take the position that a lawyer should study and analyze the legal rules first. (Note that understanding legal rules necessarily requires analyzing the facts behind court decisions and legislative enactments, so that even if a lawyer were to begin with "the law" that would require some factual analysis.) But how will the lawyer know which rules to analyze, which rules will apply to the client's situation, without knowing first the client's facts? In this sense the process of legal analysis requires the lawyer to move back and forth between developing and understanding the facts and researching and analyzing the law.

We cover facts before legal rules in this book because that is generally the sequence in which a lawyer works: the client comes to the lawyer with a set of facts, the lawyer develops additional relevant facts, researches and analyzes the law, and proposes a solution. And it is not the case that every lawyer is a blank slate when it comes to the law. Lawyers are expected to know general principles of law that will serve as a starting point before investigating facts and researching additional law.

A. STORY IDENTIFICATION

At the outset, remember that a lawyer is not analyzing or writing fiction. She does not get to make up the facts.[1] She gets to discover them. That is a digging process. The lawyer reads. The lawyer talks to people. The lawyer searches for data. The lawyer does what a good investigative reporter does: She looks for "who, what, where, when, why, and how."

And do not assume that all of the facts will be readily available or come tumbling out of sources such as the lawyer's client. Sources do not always recognize the materiality of specific facts. Sometimes, even when the source does recognize the materiality, the source does not want to volunteer the facts because the source perceives they are unfavorable. It is the lawyer's job to investigate, and to investigate hard.

Let's break out the factual analysis in the *Bears v. Gold* case to illustrate the process. Recall the basic story from Chapter 1: A twelve-year-old girl named Sarah Gold became lost in the woods, stumbled upon the house of the Bear family, where she spent the night. The Bears are suing Sarah for trespass.

Sarah and her parents have now hired you to represent Sarah in the lawsuit. They want to know if this is a frivolous case. Before you answer, what would you need to know?

Your first instinct might be to look up the current rules of the law of trespass in your jurisdiction. Undoubtedly, you will want to research those rules, and undoubtedly once you research those rules you will want to relook at the facts, and then probably relook at the

---

[1]   There is a quasi exception to this statement: A client may come to a lawyer to seek assistance in connection with events that are still unfolding. For example, the client may be negotiating a transaction that has not concluded. Or the client may be jockeying for position in a potential dispute that has not yet fully matured. In these kinds of settings, the lawyer is not creating fiction, but the lawyer is helping to create the real facts of the story as events move forward. Most first-year law students will be working on problems where the material facts already exist, and the students are to identify and analyze them. But rejoice if you get the chance to work on a scenario in real time, where you get to help create the story proactively as it unfolds.

rules. But before you begin looking up "the law," think about the material facts you know and the ones you do not know.

First, what do you know and what do you not know so far about the *who* in the story? You know that your client is twelve years old. Trespass is an intentional tort. Can a twelve-year-old form the requisite intent? How precocious is Sarah? Did *this* twelve-year-old form the requisite intent?

By the same token, *who* is the Bear family? Do the Bears run a bed and breakfast place? Is there a sign on the front door that reads, "Bear B & B; Welcome all visitors"? Or did Sarah wander into the Bears' private home? Does the sign on the front door read, "Beware of Bears"?

Do the Bear family and Sarah know each other? Is there any prior history of animosity? Alternatively, is there any prior history of accommodation?

Second, what do you know and what do you not know about the *when* in the story? You know that night was falling at the time of the house entry. Were the woods getting dark? Were the house lights on? What kinds of animals roam this forest at night? Did Sarah become afraid for her safety? Did nightfall create an emergency in her mind? Was she under duress?

Third, what do you know and what do you not know about the *where* in the story? You know that Sarah came upon the house in the middle of the forest and that the house door was unlocked. Did Sarah take the unlocked door as an indicator of consent to enter? Did Sarah have to climb over a locked fence gate to get to the porch in the first place? Is there a common understanding in the forest relating to the freedom of visitors to enter buildings to rest?

Fourth, what do you know and what do you not know about the *what* in the story? You know that Sarah knocked on the front door, entered the building, ate some vegetarian chili, slept on the sofa, did the dishes, and departed without leaving cash. Was the knock a sign of respect, a polite act, or a sign that Sarah knew she needed permission to enter the building? And what about the dishes? Did Sarah intend to offer doing the dishes as a form of payment for the chili and the night's sleep, in lieu of cash? Does the note she left help in that regard or does it hurt? What else did she do? For example, did she drop the hot bowl on the floor when she picked it up from the table? Did the bowl break? Did she leave a mess on the floor for the Bears to clean?

Fifth, what do you know and what do you not know about the *why* in the story? What motivated Sarah? Fear? Exhaustion? Hunger? For that matter, what is motivating the Bears? Saving face among the other bears? Greed? Frustration?

Finally, what do you know and what do you not know about the *how* in the story? How did Sarah act? She seems to have been respectful. Was she really?[2]

Without knowing the answers to the above fact questions, you do not know which legal principles might be relevant to solving the client's problem, namely ending the lawsuit favorably. You do not know how to compare your case to others that have involved trespass. You might conceivably be interested in a number of different potential legal defenses, including lack of relevant intent, existence of an emergency, duress, consent, and payment. The facts come first, then the law.

---

[2]   Notice, by the way, that after becoming a law student, you may never look at life the same way again. We suspect that many of you have not previously thought of children's stories as involving potential lawsuits.

B.   ADDITIONAL STORY IDENTIFICATION PRINCIPLES

As you formulate an understanding of the who, what, where, when, why, and how facts of a story, you should also have in mind the following related principles.

1.   While gathering the facts, make sure to assemble the beginning, the middle, and the end to the story. Think about the relationships among the *who, what, where, when, why,* and *how* pieces. Do they fit together? Do they make sense as a whole? Are they clear? Can a person begin in place x, travel through place y, and wind up in place z when you put all of the pieces side-by-side? At the end of the day, can you put together a coherent solution to the problem presented by the story?

2.   Recognize and account for all the material facts in the story. It is hard to assemble a good story with incomplete facts. It is especially hard to solve a legal problem when operating with incomplete facts. Test and retest your understanding to make sure you are finding and accounting for all material information. And if you have to offer a tentative solution to a legal problem before you believe you have all the material facts, consider how you will tell your audience what is missing that might affect your solution.

3.   Lawyers must live with the facts they have. Lawyers can and should work hard to uncover all of the relevant truthful facts. In doing so, they may be given false or fictitious information. Lawyers have an ethical obligation to be truthful to the court and to others involved in the litigation or legal matter.[3] Lawyers cannot write fiction. In fact, if a lawyer knows that a false material fact was presented to the court, the lawyer must rectify the situation.[4]

4.   Think about what in the story makes it interesting. Legal stories are inherently interesting because by definition they involve some kind of clash among people or ideas. No need to write fiction. Focus on the facts that produced the clash. Ask yourself: As I assemble the *who, what, where, when, why,* and *how* pieces of the story I am analyzing, what about each piece makes it intriguing?

5.   Think about the context for the story. Legal problems do not exist in a vacuum. They arise in the context of a society that has a history, customs, values, attitudes, and policies. Legal stories are inextricably intertwined with all of those. Do not forget to think about the *who, what, where, when, why,* and *how* of your specific story within the broader context in which that story takes place.

C.   CONCLUSION

In Chapters 10 and 11, you will see some examples of fact statements for different audiences. For now, we want you simply to understand how important it is for you to dig for and analyze the facts giving rise to legal problems. Those facts drive everything else.

---

[3]   A lawyer cannot knowingly provide a tribunal false facts, MODEL RULE OF PROF'L CONDUCT R. 3.3(a)(1) (2016), or false evidence. *Id.* at 3.3(a)(3). Further, while representing a client, the lawyer cannot knowingly make a false statement of material fact to a third party. MODEL RULE OF PROF'L CONDUCT R. 4.1 (2016).

[4]   MODEL RULE OF PROF'L CONDUCT R. 3.3(a)(1).

CHAPTER 3

The Role of Rules in Resolving Legal Problems

To resolve legal problems, lawyers must be able to identify the appropriate rules that will be applied to the facts—or the story of the case. To identify the appropriate rules requires an understanding of the sources of rules and the hierarchy of these sources. Discussions of sources as authority necessarily involve jurisdictional issues, which can be a complex area of the law. An in-depth discussion of jurisdiction is more properly taken up in such courses as civil procedure, conflicts of laws, and federal jurisdiction. The purpose in this chapter is two-fold: first, to acquaint you with the basic sources of rules and hierarchy of authority; second, to provide you with enough detail to convey the potential complexity of jurisdictional issues.

LEARNING OBJECTIVES

1. Students will know the sources of primary legal authority, enacted law and case law, and will understand what each encompasses.

2. Students will understand the differences between primary and secondary authority.

3. Students will understand the federal and state court systems, their relationships, and will know that each system has trial courts and at least one level of appellate court.

4. Students will be able to identify when a source can be used as precedent and when a source is binding, persuasive, or not applicable.

A. THE SOURCES OF RULES: ENACTED LAW AND CASES

Broadly speaking, the rules that lawyers identify and apply to resolve a legal problem come from primary authority. Primary authority consists of enacted laws and cases. *Enacted law* is defined here to include constitutions (which are more typically adopted by representative bodies), statutes (which are enacted by legislative bodies), and rules and regulations (which are promulgated by administrative agencies and courts). *Cases* are the written reports of decisions by judicial bodies—or courts. Case law is further divided into cases that interpret enacted law and common law cases. These sources of law exist at the federal and state levels.

Sources of Primary Authority	
Federal	**State**
Constitution	Constitution
Statutes	Statutes
Rules and Regulations	Rules and Regulations Local: Municipal Charters and Ordinances
Cases: 　Interpretive (of enacted law) 　Common Law	Cases: 　Interpretive (of enacted law) 　Common Law

1. Enacted Law

The United States Constitution is the source of our federal system of government. The Constitution is the highest law in the United States. In other words, legislative bodies—federal and state—may not enact rules that are inconsistent with the federal constitution. Courts determine whether a statute or regulation is unconstitutional.[1] The United States Supreme Court is the highest and final authority on federal constitutional issues. The individual states also have constitutions, and the state's court of last resort (usually, but not always, the state's Supreme Court) is the highest authority with respect to interpreting that state's constitution. If, however, there is a federal constitutional challenge to a provision in a state constitution, the United States Supreme Court would have final authority with respect to whether that provision violated the federal constitution.

Statutes are typically more specific than constitutions, although some constitutional provisions can be quite specific. Statutes are general statements of the law and usually prescribe or proscribe specific conduct in a particular area across a class of persons. There are several reasons why a legislative body may decide to enact statutes. For example, there may be a generic problem that the legislature wants to address, such as environmental protection, or a specific problem, such as permitting electronic signatures. Additionally, the legislature may want to provide a framework of rules for the conduct of certain activity, such as the sale of goods, which is governed in forty-nine states by their enactment of Article 2 of the *Uniform Commercial Code*. Further, the legislature may want to clarify an ambiguity created by case law or enact legislation to change—or abrogate—the common law.

Statutes often need to be interpreted by courts. For example, sometimes the court must determine the meaning of a particular statutory provision. At other times, the court must determine if the statute is constitutional—either under the federal or a state constitution. There often is a wealth of legislative history material available to the lawyer when advocating a particular meaning or construction of a federal statute because of the vast

---

[1] The doctrine of judicial review was first announced by the United States Supreme Court in Marbury v. Madison, 5 U.S. (1 Cranch) 137 (1803).

number of documents created in passing the legislation. There are fewer documents at the state level when interpreting state statutes, but some exist.[2]

For our purposes, it is important to note that courts routinely interpret statutes. As discussed above, the United States Supreme Court is the final authority on the federal constitutionality of any federal or state statute. The state court of last resort is the highest authority with respect to interpreting a state statute in accordance with state law.[3] In fact, if a federal court is interpreting a substantive state law in a diversity action, the federal court must look to how that state's highest court has interpreted the provision.[4] If the state's highest court has not spoken on the issue, then the federal court must try to discern how the state court would decide.[5] And if the state court subsequently addresses the same issue, it is not bound by the federal court opinion, although the federal opinion typically would be persuasive.

At this point, it is important to understand that the lawyer as problem solver must master two systems of government—federal and state. There are federal statutes created by Congress, and each state legislature enacts statutes. The federal and state governmental systems are at times parallel; at other times they overlap and the lawyer must determine which jurisdiction's rule applies. (This can also be said of determining which state's rule applies in some situations.) As a general principle, if there is a conflict between a federal statute and a state statute, the federal statute trumps the state statute, assuming that Congress intended to preempt that area of law and that Congress has the constitutional authority to govern that subject.[6]

Regulations are generally promulgated by federal and state administrative agencies. They are typically more specific than statutes. Administrative law—at the federal and state level—is complex. The weight given to a regulation, as well as to the agency's interpretation of the regulation, can vary. When confronted with an administrative law problem, it is important to read the statute that created the specific agency and gather background information regarding the agency and its procedures, as well as determine the governing agency regulations.

Where a problem involves a federal statute, federal administrative regulations may be relevant. In certain circumstances, courts look to agency regulations to help interpret the statute. Although when a court is required to give deference to the agency interpretation is nuanced, a couple of general points will help to understand the interrelationship between statutes and regulations. Initially, Congress can delegate authority to an agency to implement a statute. A federal administrative agency charged with implementing a federal civil statute will often issue regulations interpreting that statute. Subsequently, if a court determines that the statute is ambiguous, a court may be required to give deference to a reasonable agency interpretation.[7] Although questions will arise, such as whether the

---

[2]   Learning how to find these documents and the relative value of each of them in relation to each other will likely be taken up in the research component of your research and writing course. Learning how to use these documents as a problem solver is the subject of Chapter 5.

[3]   State courts do address the federal constitutionality of state statutes, but they are not the final authority. The U.S. Supreme Court is the final authority.

[4]   Erie R.R. Co. v. Tompkins, 304 U.S. 64 (1938). More specifically, a federal court sitting in diversity must apply state substantive law—either statutory or common law.

[5]   West v. AT&T Co., 311 U.S. 223, 236–37 (1940). State courts ascertaining federal law in the absence of a United States Supreme Court decision have not been uniform in their approaches. Donald H. Zeigler, *Gazing into the Crystal Ball: Reflections on the Standards State Judges Should Use to Ascertain Federal Law*, 40 WM. & MARY L. REV. 1143, 1143 (1999).

[6]   This is an overly simplified discussion of this topic. We assume it will be explained in greater detail in the research component of your research and writing course, or in your civil procedure and constitutional law courses.

[7]   *See generally*, Chevron U.S.A., Inc. v. Natural Resources Defense Council, Inc., 467 U.S. 837 (1984); United States v. Mead Corp., 533 U.S. 218 (2001).

statute is ambiguous and whether the agency was interpreting the statute in performing its delegated duties, the point is that administrative law intersects with statutory law in this context.

> **Example**: Congress passed the Family and Medical Leave Act in 1993. This federal law is codified in Title 29 of the U.S. Code. The law has many subdivisions, numbered from §§ 2601, 2611 to 2619, 2631 to 2636, and 2651 to 2654.
>
> Congress also passed a law authorizing the Department of Labor, an agency, to "prescribe such regulations as are necessary to carry out" the Family and Medical Leave Act. That law is codified within the FMLA, at 29 U.S.C. § 2654.
>
> The Department of Labor has issued regulations implementing the Family and Medical Leave Act. Those regulations are codified in Part 825 of Title 29 of the Code of Federal Regulations. The regulations also have many subdivisions.

Other rules are promulgated by courts themselves. Federal and state courts are authorized, usually by statute, to prescribe general rules of procedure, rules of evidence, and rules governing lawyers' professional conduct, for example. These rules generally have the force of law when approved by the relevant court, as long as the relevant legislative body does not enact legislation rejecting the rules as promulgated.

2. Cases

> There are two categories of cases:
>
> interpretive and common law

Cases, like enacted laws, are primary authority. There are two categories of cases: interpretive and common law. *Interpretive cases* are court decisions in which the court interpreted enacted law. Interpretive cases also include those cases in which courts apply enacted law by ruling on how the law should—or should not—be applied to a particular set of facts. For example, if the statute states, "Where a tender has been accepted . . . the buyer must within a reasonable time after he discovers or should have discovered any breach notify the seller of the breach or be barred from any remedy . . . ,"[8] and the buyer did not notify the seller, then the court would apply the rule. The buyer would be precluded from pursuing a remedy for a breach by the seller.

If the buyer sent notice, then there may be an issue as to whether the notice was sent in a reasonable time. Before it could apply the rule, a court would be required to determine what is reasonable in the specific situation. The court would likely engage in a fact-specific analysis. It would compare and contrast the facts of the case currently before it with the facts of similar cases in which notice was sent to determine what constitutes reasonable notice. Perhaps three days was "reasonable" in a case between two local merchants who had previously done business together and communicated by email, whereas one month was "reasonable" in a case between two merchants communicating across the country by letter. The court would determine whether the case before it was more similar to two local merchants, familiar with each other, communicating by email, or more similar to far-flung merchants communicating by letter. Having reached a determination based on similar cases, the court would apply the rule and reach a conclusion.

Sometimes a term is ambiguous. The court cannot apply the statute, because it is not clear what the legislature intended the term to mean. For example, if the statute states, "No

---

[8] U.C.C. § 2–607(3)(a) (2014).

vehicles allowed in the park," how should the term "vehicles" be interpreted? What type of transportation would be included in that term? Would the word "vehicle" include a moped or a motorized wheelchair? Would it include a fire truck? The court may then rely on canons of statutory construction, the legislative history, or administrative regulations to interpret the ambiguous word. Thus, interpretive cases apply and may interpret enacted law.

Another form of case law is the *common law*. The common law consists of court decisions where the rule is created by judges.[9] In other words, there is no enacted law. The common law evolves from precedent. Precedent can be described as coming from custom or habit.[10] Courts will look to previous cases that involve the same issue and similar facts to help decide the current case. The United States is considered a common law country, having a system of law brought by the first settlers from England. English common law was, and continues to be, albeit much less so, precedent for the courts in this country.[11]

Interpretive cases also use precedent. In the previous example where the court was determining what is "reasonable" notice, we stated that the court would look to previous cases with similar facts that interpreted the same statutory notice provision. The similar or like cases that the court relied upon are precedent. Thus, regardless of whether the rule comes from enacted law or common law, judges will look to precedent to help resolve the case before them.

Like cases should be treated alike

The doctrine of precedent has a strong ethical component that dates back to Aristotle: Like cases should be treated alike.[12] This idea is furthered by the doctrine of *stare decisis*. Under this judicial policy, a court should adhere to its own precedent and also to the precedent developed by higher courts in its jurisdiction. The doctrine of *stare decisis* and precedent help to create stability in the common law system by advising courts to treat similar cases alike. Although followed as a matter of practice, these doctrines are not absolute. For example, a court can overturn one of its previous decisions.

Common law cases are resolutions to specific problems between specific parties. These cases tend to be fact specific. In time, however, when later courts apply a case as precedent to subsequent cases on the same issue with similar—or seemingly similar—facts, general common law rules evolve. The common law rule that the acceptance must be the mirror image of the offer in contract law is but one example.

Sometimes common law rules become codified as statutes. For example, the contract damages rules announced in *Hadley v. Baxendale*, 156 Eng. Rep. 145 (Ex. 1854), were codified when legislatures enacted Sections 2–714 and 2–715 of the *Uniform Commercial Code*. Or legislatures may enact laws that abrogate—or displace—the common law. For example, a legislature may enact Section 2–207 of the *Uniform Commercial Code*, which abrogated the common law mirror-image rule mentioned above. And here is an important point to remember when working with authority: statutes trump the common law within a specific jurisdiction. Even though courts are the mechanism for interpreting and applying enacted law, legislatures have the power to enact laws that abrogate the common law.

---

[9]   Some have said that the common law, or the precedent, is discovered—not created. In fact, judges do create law while applying precedent to resolve a particular legal problem. J. MYRON JACOBSTEIN ET AL., FUNDAMENTALS OF LEGAL RESEARCH 4–5 (7th ed., Found. Press 1998).

[10]   KARL N. LLEWELLYN, THE BRAMBLE BUSH: THE CLASSIC LECTURES ON THE LAW AND LAW SCHOOL 65 (Oxford Univ. Press, Inc. 2008).

[11]   For example, you will read a number of now-famous English cases in your contracts and criminal law courses.

[12]   *See* ARISTOTLE, NICOMACHEAN ETHICS b. 5, ch. 4.

> Predictability is critical for the problem solver.

Just as facts are the driving force in identifying legal problems, primary authority is the driving force in resolving legal problems. The complex system of enacted law and case law promotes predictability and provides for needed change. Predictability is critical for the problem solver. Without some degree of stability, we would be unable to conduct our lives and business affairs in an orderly, rational fashion. Without some degree of stability, lawyers would not be able to advise clients. The stated rules in enacted law and the doctrines of *stare decisis* and precedent allow for some degree of predictability. Predictability in the law, however, is not the same as a guaranty. Sometimes the law is so clear that you can predict with a high degree of certainty, but often it is not.[13]

At the same time, the system allows for needed change. Legislatures repeal unnecessary legislation and enact necessary legislation. Courts narrow—even overrule—precedent as conditions change that once made that particular precedent useful or desirable. And in this system, the lawyer often has room to make arguments regarding how the law should apply to a certain set of facts. Much of your first year in law school will be devoted to learning how to interpret a case broadly and narrowly to support such arguments.

B. BASIC PRINCIPLES FOR UNDERSTANDING PRIMARY AUTHORITY

Primary authority is classified as mandatory, persuasive, or not applicable. Not knowing when the authority is mandatory or persuasive or not applicable could lead to disastrous results. You may give your client the wrong advice, or you may argue rules or cases that have no applicability to your problem even though they are on point. This section provides some basic principles for understanding how to classify authority. The key is understanding the role jurisdiction plays. But first, some definitions. *Mandatory* means the courts within that jurisdiction are bound by the enacted rule or precedent. *Persuasive* means the courts may look to the source in helping them to decide a particular issue. *Not applicable* means just that. For example, the source may be a statute that resolves the issue or a case applying that statute with similar facts, but this authority cannot be applied in the governing jurisdiction because the jurisdiction has not enacted that statute. Or, the authority may be from the relevant jurisdiction, but it is not applicable because the facts are dissimilar or the authority does not address the legal problem you are solving.

1. State constitutions and statutes are either mandatory or not applicable. The constitution and statutes from one state are mandatory—or binding—on the state law problems and claims arising in that state. They have no persuasive value in other states. In other words, it would be impermissible to argue in a case involving Michigan law that the Michigan Supreme Court should apply a statute from Wyoming.

However, and this is a big however, if a jurisdiction has the same or a very similar statute as other jurisdictions, the *cases* from other jurisdictions interpreting those provisions can be persuasive to courts in the initial jurisdiction. (The same would be true of constitutional provisions.) To illustrate, assume State A and State B have both enacted Article 2 of the *Uniform Commercial Code*. Further assume that the courts of State A have not interpreted a particular provision that is at issue in a case before a court in State A. The

---

[13] Caveat: a client should always be advised in terms of predictabilities; do not guarantee an outcome. Juries and judges occasionally misapply the law—that is, they act irrationally or inconsistently with the stated rule or precedent.

judicial opinions of State B (and any other state that has interpreted the same enacted provision) are persuasive authority.[14]

The same is true between federal and state legislation, i.e., state constitutions and statutes do not resolve federal legal questions, and vice versa. But assume that State A has enacted rules of evidence that closely mirror the federal rules of evidence. If the courts of State A must interpret a particular rule, the opinions of the federal courts interpreting the same rule in the federal system will be highly persuasive.

2.   **Enacted law trumps the common law within a specific jurisdiction.** As mentioned above, the legislature of a specific jurisdiction can modify or abrogate a common law rule. This is because legislation is an expression of the will of the people in that state. Consequently, if you are resolving a problem in a specific jurisdiction, which in practice you would be, you must first determine if there is enacted law that governs the problem. If the legislature in your jurisdiction has not spoken, then you would determine if the highest court of that jurisdiction has addressed the issue. If the highest court and the inferior appellate courts have not addressed the issue, then you would search the common law from other jurisdictions. But statutes from other jurisdictions are not applicable. The common law is said to belong to everyone, and judges can choose to adopt rules articulated by other judges. Thus, a state court is free to look to the common law of other states, but it is not free to adopt legislation that other jurisdictions have enacted. Courts do not enact legislation.

3.   **Cases can be mandatory, persuasive, or not applicable.** The only part of a mandatory case that is mandatory—or binding—is where the court is announcing the rule of law with respect to the dispute before it—the holding—and even then it is only binding on that court and the inferior courts in that jurisdiction. All other parts of the court's opinion are considered persuasive. This includes dicta (general statements by the court not necessary to the holding but which may be highly persuasive), concurring opinions, and dissenting opinions. These parts of the case may be cited as authority, but they must be properly attributed and treated as only persuasive.

To determine whether the rule of a case is mandatory requires first asking whether the case was decided by a court in the jurisdiction that governs your problem and if so, asking whether that case is binding under the doctrine of *stare decisis.* As to all cases that are binding under the doctrine, it is then necessary to further question whether any of these cases concern the same legal issue and have similar facts. In other words, can any of the binding cases be used as precedent?

As an illustration of the doctrine of *stare decisis,* under the federal system involving a federal issue, the Federal District Court for the Eastern District of Michigan is bound by the decisions of the Court of Appeals for the Sixth Circuit and the decisions of the United States Supreme Court. Decisions from other federal courts of appeal, such as the Ninth Circuit, are persuasive, but not mandatory. Similarly, the Sixth Circuit Court of Appeals is bound by the decisions of the United States Supreme Court on federal issues. But the opinions of its sister courts of appeal are not mandatory, only persuasive.

At the state level, the inferior courts are bound by all the decisions of the highest state court on matters of state law.[15] However, on matters of federal law, the state courts are

---

[14]   There are, of course, some nuances to this basic principle. For example, greater weight is usually given to states whose courts routinely address this type of issue.

[15]   Some state appellate courts are bound by the decisions of other appellate panels within that state. Therefore, it is always important to check that state's court rules regarding whether courts are bound by other courts or panels operating at the same level.

bound by the decisions of the United States Supreme Court.[16] And the federal courts are bound by the decisions of the highest state courts on purely state issues. Knowing which court decisions are binding, you would then search for precedent—cases with similar facts where the court issued a holding on the same legal issue.

> Secondary authority is never binding.

4.   If the authority is not primary, then it is secondary, which may be persuasive but is never binding. Secondary authority includes all other expressions of the law, such as Restatements, treatises, law review articles, and monographs. These are all sources to use in resolving the problem and communicating the analysis. Other sources such as legal dictionaries, legal encyclopedias, *American Law Reports*, and various case-finding tools, such as digests, are often useful in helping to locate or identify the potentially appropriate rules. Courts do not treat all secondary authority equally. Some secondary sources are considered to have more persuasive value, which is often based on the credibility of the author or institution generating the source. Moreover, a court is always free to ignore secondary authority.

C. CONSIDERATIONS WHEN WORKING WITH STATUTES AND CASES

Being able to resolve a legal problem requires understanding not just the sources of rules, but how to work with them. Below we provide general considerations in working with statutes and cases, followed by a basic template for organizing your approach to identifying the correct sources to resolve a legal problem.

Working with Statutes
First, statutes regulate human conduct. Identify when the conduct is always regulated and when it is regulated only at specified times.
Second, statutes are best understood as imperative statements that command, prohibit, or permit specific conduct.
Third, courts presume when interpreting statutes that the drafters intended to create a consistent and coherent body of law. Therefore, courts will resist any interpretation of one portion of a statute that negates or contradicts another section of the statute.
Fourth, statutes have a discernable structure. Pay close attention to the definitions, the language used, the punctuation, and how the parts of the statute relate to one another.

---

[16]   There is a split of authority among the state courts as to whether they are bound by lower federal court decisions on issues of federal law. Amanda Frost, *Inferiority Complex: Should State Courts Follow Lower Court Precedent on the Meaning of Federal Law?*, 68 VAND. L. REV. 53, 56 (2015).

Working with Cases

First, understand that there are two ways to read a case as a lawyer. One is as a historical event where the court resolved a specific dispute between specific parties involving specific facts. The second is to determine its viability as precedent for predicting how a court would decide a case involving the same issue on similar facts. It is the latter with which you will be most concerned as a problem solver. So, read the cases thinking about the problem you are trying to resolve.

Second, appreciate that each case tells a story. Determine which facts of the story the court relied on in its reasoning and in arriving at its conclusion. Determine the factual similarities and dissimilarities between relevant decisions and their importance to the court's reasoning and its outcome.[17]

Third, formulate the rule from the case or cases broadly and narrowly. Ask how much the case or cases can be made to stand for and how little.[18] (Much more will be said about how to formulate rules from cases in Chapters 4 through 6.)

Basic Template for Identifying Sources to Resolve Legal Problems

Organize your approach to a legal problem based on the source(s) of law that will govern the result:

First, ask: Is the problem one of federal law or state law (or both)?

Second, ask: In the category of federal or state law, is the problem governed by enacted law or common law?

Third, ask: If enacted law governs, then in the category of federal enacted law or state enacted law, what kind of enacted law applies—a constitution? A statute? An administrative regulation? All of the above?

Fourth, ask: If enacted law governs, and court decisions interpret the enacted law, which cases are binding in your jurisdiction and can be used as precedent? (Cases that are not binding in your jurisdiction can never be more than persuasive.)

Fifth, ask: Within the binding cases interpreting the enacted law, what parts of the opinion are mandatory and what parts are merely persuasive?

Sixth, ask: If common law rather than enacted law governs, then which common law cases are binding in your jurisdiction and can be used as precedent? (Cases that are not binding in your jurisdiction can never be more than persuasive.)

Seventh, ask: Within the binding common law cases, what parts of the opinions are mandatory and what parts are merely persuasive?

Eighth, ask: If there is no binding authority, which jurisdictions' common law treatment of the problem will you select as most persuasive?

---

[17]   Llewellyn, *supra* note 10, at 50.

[18]   *Id.* at 73–74; SOIA MENTSCHIKOFF & IRWIN P. STOTZKY, THE THEORY AND CRAFT OF AMERICAN LAW xxxi–xxxii (Matthew Bender 1981).

D. ETHICAL CONSIDERATIONS

At a fundamental level, the ABA Model Rules of Professional Conduct require that lawyers be competent. "Competent representation [of a client] requires the legal knowledge, skill, thoroughness and preparation reasonably necessary for the representation."[19] Knowing the sources of legal rules and authority in the American legal system and understanding their interrelationships is fundamental to achieving the competence required of every lawyer.

Working hard in law school to acquire legal knowledge and skills in a broad range of legal subject areas is also part of the process of gaining competency to represent clients. Specifically, in your legal writing and research courses, you will learn skills, such as how to identify legal issues, how to research the law, how to interpret the law, and how to communicate a legal analysis. These fundamental skills are just the beginning. You will gain more knowledge and skills throughout law school, and after you are admitted to practice, you will need to familiarize yourself with each new area of law involved in your clients' representation. The Model Rules anticipate that all lawyers, even newly admitted lawyers, can become competent through study.[20]

Thus, lawyers can take on matters if they can become competent through study and preparation. But if, as part of the process, a lawyer realizes that the legal issues are too complex, he can associate with an experienced attorney, who can help him navigate the difficult terrain. After the representation is complete, having gained experience and knowledge in that area of law, the lawyer would likely handle the next similar case on his own. Recognize also that diligently preparing for the tasks required to move the representation forward will go a long way toward handling the matter competently.

---

[19] MODEL RULES OF PROF'L CONDUCT R. 1.1 (2016).

[20] *Id.* at cmt. 2.

CHAPTER 4

Determining the Rule in Typical, Simple Scenarios: Enacted Rules and Single Cases

Lawyers spend their entire careers working with rules. In Chapter 3, we discussed the role of rules in resolving legal problems. In this chapter, we discuss how to disassemble and assemble rules.

LEARNING OBJECTIVES

1. Students will learn how to identify legal rules from an enacted law provision and a single court decision.

2. Students will be able to analyze legal rules by identifying and interpreting component parts of a legal rule.

3. Students will begin to critically analyze competing legal rules.

A. PULLING APART AN ENACTED RULE

We begin by breaking apart one of the Minnesota Rules of Professional Conduct (2015) comprised of elements.[1] The same process of parsing applies equally to those common law and statutory rules that are composed of elements.

Minnesota Rule of Professional Conduct 3.7(a):

(a)   A lawyer shall not act as an advocate at a trial in which the lawyer is likely to be a necessary witness unless:

1. the testimony relates to an uncontested issue;

2. the testimony relates to the nature and value of legal services rendered in the case; or

3. disqualification of the lawyer would work substantial hardship on the client.

---

[1]   The Minnesota Rules of Professional Conduct are similar if not identical to the American Bar Association Model Rules. Accordingly, readers in other jurisdictions can likely find the same basic rule in their own state. Careful readers will notice that this book cites to a number of Minnesota and Michigan authorities as examples. The authors are familiar with the illustrative value of those authorities after many years of practice and teaching. You can find similar authorities in other jurisdictions.

How many elements does this rule contain? One potential answer would be three, but that is an understatement. There are at least twenty-five elements.

Outline of the Elements of Rule 3.7(a):	Commentary on the Outline of the Elements of Rule 3.7(a):
➤　A lawyer ➤　shall not act ➤　as an advocate ➤　at a trial ➤　in which ➤　the lawyer ➤　is likely to be ➤　a necessary ➤　witness ➤　unless: ➤　the testimony ➤　relates to ➤　an uncontested ➤　issue; 　　　OR ➤　the testimony ➤　relates to ➤　the nature and ➤　value of ➤　legal services ➤　rendered in the case; 　　　OR ➤　disqualification ➤　of the lawyer ➤　would work substantial ➤　hardship ➤　on the client.	The introductory language to Rule 3.7(a) contains nine discrete elements. You need all nine of those elements present *or you never get to* "unless (1)," "unless (2)," or "unless (3)": The rule only applies to lawyers. It involves a prohibition. The lawyer cannot act as an advocate. When? At trial. What kind of a trial? One in which the lawyer will be a witness. What kind of a witness? A likely one. Is that all? A likely, necessary witness. So you are into *who, what, where, when, why,* and *how* questions again. If your problem does not involve a lawyer, Rule 3.7(a) is not applicable. If your problem does not involve a trial, the rule is not applicable. If the lawyer is not going to be a witness in the trial, the rule is not applicable. If the lawyer is not likely to be a witness in the trial, the rule is not applicable. If the lawyer is likely to be a witness, but not a necessary witness, the rule is not applicable. Assume that all nine of the predicate elements are present. You can tell there are three exceptions to the prohibition in the rule. Each of the exceptions contains several elements. In the first exception, the testimony must relate to something—an uncontested issue. In the second exception, the testimony must relate to something—the nature *and* value of legal services rendered in the case in which the lawyer is testifying. The third exception refers to the disqualification of the lawyer to be his client's advocate in the case covered by the general prohibition. That disqualification must do something—work substantial hardship.

Why is parsing a rule important? Because one of the easiest ways, perhaps the single easiest way, for a lawyer to go astray at the outset of legal analysis is to overlook elements of the potentially relevant legal rules. It is easy to miss valuable lines of analysis if a lawyer does not make the threshold effort to break apart (*really* break apart) all (*every single one*) of the components of the legal standards.

In the case of Minnesota Rule 3.7(a), for example, assume you represent a trust created by a now deceased member of a family. Over the last twenty years, you have been the lawyer who has given advice to the trustee who administers that trust, and you have represented the trustee in court six different times on issues relating to the interpretation of the document creating the trust. From time to time, you also have given personal legal advice to family members who are beneficiaries of the trust. That legal advice has been on matters unrelated to the trust. Now a dispute has arisen between the trustee and certain family members relating to interpretation of the trust document. That dispute is about to go to trial (trial number 1). You expect to try the case in court. One of the family members is objecting to your participation as an advocate for the trustee because you are expected to be a witness for that family member in the trial (trial number 2) of an unrelated matter on which you have given her legal advice in the past. How would you contest the objection?

Consider this sequence of questions:

➢   Are you a lawyer? Yes.

➢   Do you plan to act as an advocate? Yes.

➢   At a trial? Yes, trial no. 1.

➢   In which you are likely to be a witness? No. You are going to be a witness in a different proceeding, trial no. 2.

➢   The rule does not apply to your circumstances.

Does that make sense from a public policy standpoint? Yes. One purpose of the rule is to preserve the integrity of proceedings by not having lawyers appear before a judge and/or jury simultaneously as advocates and as sources of facts. Another purpose is to avoid conflicts among lawyers and clients when the lawyers must zealously advocate cases at the same time that, as witnesses, they are sworn to tell the truth as to facts that might hurt the clients. When a lawyer is not acting as an advocate in the same trial as she is acting as a material witness, then the policy reasons behind the rule are not violated (although there still may be an unhappy client). So the lawyer can feel reasonably comfortable that her logic in parsing the rule is correct.

Does the lawyer have to break apart all of the elements if she already thinks one is controlling? The answer is yes.

In the Rule 3.7(a) problem, for example, keep going through the elements even though you think there is a dispositive argument that the rule simply does not apply. Assume, hypothetically, that trial number 1 and trial number 2 were going to be the same, single trial. (Perhaps the trial judge decided to consolidate the two trials into one.) *Even if* you were going to be a witness in that trial, are you likely to be a necessary witness? The answer is unclear on the known facts. *Even if* you were likely to be a necessary witness in that trial, might you be testifying on an uncontested issue? The answer is unclear on the known facts. *Even if* you were likely to be a necessary witness in that trial, might you be testifying about the nature and value of the services you rendered? The answer is unclear on the known facts. *Even if* you were likely to be a necessary witness in that trial, might your disqualification as trial counsel work substantial hardship on the trustee for the trust? The answer is likely yes. You have been the trust's counsel for twenty years, as well as its advocate in court six previous times on matters of trust interpretation. The rule seeks to preserve the integrity of court proceedings and to avoid placing lawyers in potential conflict situations with clients; but the rule also seeks to preserve a client's choice of counsel to avoid hardship. What should you do? You now may assert a second, subsidiary argument against the objection to your serving as advocate: *Even if* trial number 1 and trial number 2 *were* the same, the family member's objection should still be denied because your disqualification would work substantial hardship on the trustee within the meaning of the "unless" clause (3).

Working through all of the elements of Rule 3.7(a) has enabled you to adopt a classic two-pronged analysis of the relevant rule: First, the family member's objection should be denied because Rule 3.7(a) does not apply, i.e., you are not going to be a witness in the same trial in which you are acting as an advocate. Second, even if Rule 3.7(a) did apply, your disqualification as counsel would work a substantial hardship on the trustee, and thus the court should reject the disqualification attempt.[2]

Note, of course, that there may be debate about how courts have applied such terms in the rule as "substantial hardship." Like the word "reasonable," which was discussed in Chapter 3, determining what is a "substantial hardship" likely will involve a fact-specific analysis, i.e., comparing and contrasting the facts of your case to those of other cases in which courts have applied the term.

B. COMMON MISTAKES IN PARSING A RULE

Try to avoid the following mistakes in parsing rules.

1. Common Mistake No. 1: Sloppy Reading

It is easy for a reader in a hurry to run through a rule too quickly and miss components or important structural features. Consider Rule 3.7(a), for example. The word "unless" modifies all three of the exceptions, which are "either/or" clauses. When you construct your outline of Rule 3.7(a), do not associate the word "unless" only with the very first exception. Similarly, do not treat the three exceptions as cumulative instead of alternative.

2. Common Mistake No. 2: Imprecise Paraphrasing

Be careful when paraphrasing the language of rules for your own interpretation or when you are explaining the rule in writing. For example, suppose in Rule 3.7(a) that you substituted the word "proceeding" for the word "trial." That paraphrase may have actually changed the meaning of the rule. "Proceeding" may well be a broader term than "trial." Your change of words may actually cause you to give mistaken advice. Begin your analysis with the actual text of the rule. Only then is it permissible to paraphrase the text in explaining the rule.

3. Common Mistake No. 3: Converting Negative Language into Positive

It is tempting to convert "shall not" negatively phrased rules into "may" positively phrased rules. From the standpoint of language flow, this conversion is appealing. But watch out: Conversions can be dangerous because they can be tricky to accomplish without accidentally changing the rule. For example, you might think about changing Rule 3.7(a) from a "shall not" structure to a "may" structure: "A lawyer MAY act as an advocate at a trial in which the lawyer is likely to be a necessary witness WHEN . . . ."

Notice three things about what this change does: First, each of the three exceptions to the "shall not" rule now becomes a predicate for the "may" rule. Second, you happen to be

---

[2]   You may be able to construct additional arguments by digging for more facts relating to the questions for which the answers are currently unclear.

lucky: the conversion process with Rule 3.7(a) can be accomplished without changing an explicit or implicit "or" clause to an "and" clause. The conversion can also be accomplished without inserting the word "not" into the three exception/predicate clauses. But do not assume this is always conveniently true. Third, you have created a new and different bottom-line standard: In the original rule, the assumption is that there are only three circumstances when a lawyer can both testify and advocate in the same trial. In the new converted rule, the assumption is that the lawyer may both testify and advocate in the same trial under each of three circumstances, but do you actually know what the lawyer should do in other circumstances? The answer is probably no, you do not know what the lawyer should do. So do you have to add the word "ONLY" in front of the word "WHEN," to make the meaning of the rule clearer? That kind of additional conversion can be easy to forget, which is why conversions are dangerous.

4. Common Mistake No. 4: Assuming Your Detailed Outline of the Rule Elements Is for Public Consumption

Your detailed outline for breaking apart a rule is for your own use, to help make sure that you are not overlooking material components of the rule that might bear on the answer to the legal problem you have to solve. The outline would not typically be provided to a court, a client, a colleague, or other audiences. When you prepare a rule analysis for persons other than yourself, you will begin with the actual text, but you will then be able to cluster the components because some will be irrelevant or undisputed for purposes of the problem you are solving. The focus for now, however, is on your own personal understanding of the nuances of the rule bearing upon your problem. So err on the side of making your outline of the material elements of the rule as detailed as possible for your own use.

5. Common Mistake No. 5: Assuming You Never Have to Consult Case Law, or That You Always Must Consult Case Law

Recall that Minnesota Rule 3.7(a) included a term, "substantial hardship," that likely requires looking to case law to determine which facts have risen to the level of "substantial hardship," and which have not. Sometimes it will be clear that a legislature, for example, intended to leave the detailed meaning of an enacted provision to the decision of the courts in light of the courts' reason and experience. In this situation, the problem solver must synthesize a series of cases where courts have applied the language to understand what the words likely mean. This synthesis is accomplished by looking at the spectrum of case authority (using the techniques for reading cases described below and in Chapter 6) and by using analogical reasoning (discussed in Chapter 7 and exemplified in Chapters 10 and 11).

Alternatively, there will be times when the language of an enacted provision of law is clear on its face. In that setting, a review of court decisions will initially be less important. As is typical in legal settings, therefore, "never" and "always" can be dangerous mind-sets. As you gain experience, you will be able to ascertain when research is necessary to properly interpret statutory language.

C. ASSEMBLING A RULE FROM A SINGLE COURT DECISION

In the Minnesota Rule 3.7(a) example, we gave you the rule and asked you to break it apart. But what if you are not given a rule? What if you have to figure out what the rule is before you can begin disassembling it? This is a typical problem when working with court decisions as opposed to enacted law, model rules, codes, and the like. We will start with the simplest version of the task—assembly of a rule from the language in a single court decision.

Assume that you are a lawyer for a gigantic company in the pharmaceutical industry. Your client wants to sue a competitor for theft of a trade secret, namely the chemical formula for a prototype of a drug that will cure a dreaded disease. The competitor likely will counterclaim that the lawsuit is predatory, designed simply to distract the competitor from its efforts to develop its own similar drug and to maintain your client's dominant position in the industry. The evidence in your possession indicates that your client put elaborate security precautions into place to protect the relevant formula. The competitor, nonetheless, was able to obtain the details from a disgruntled former employee of your client's research department, who violated the confidentiality provision in his employment agreement. You also know that your client is locked in a desperate race with the competitor to be the first company to bring the relevant drug to market, and the client's files are replete with minutes of brainstorming sessions in which your client's employees have discussed how to impede the competitor's efforts. The client wants your advice as to the viability of the likely counterclaim.

You find the United States Supreme Court opinion in *Professional Real Estate Investors v. Columbia Pictures*, 508 U.S. 49 (1993). You already know the following basic information: The federal antitrust laws regulate the competitive process in the United States. One of those laws is the Sherman Act, 15. U.S.C. § 1 *et seq.* Section 1 of the Act prohibits contracts, combinations, and conspiracies in (unreasonable) restraint of trade.[3] Section 2 of the Act prohibits monopolization, attempts to monopolize, and conspiracies to monopolize.[4] At the same time, the United States Constitution, through the Bill of Rights, preserves the right of the people to petition the government, and the Sherman Act is meant to regulate business activity, not political activity.[5] The courts are considered part of the "government."[6] So a genuine effort to obtain law enforcement through a lawsuit filed in court cannot be a Sherman Act violation.[7] But what if the lawsuit is just a "sham," a disguised effort simply to hurt a competitor? That is the question that *Professional Real Estate Investors* addressed.

Read the majority opinion excerpts below (from which we have omitted footnotes, a number of citations, and other materials for the sake of brevity).[8] See if you can describe the "rule" from the case.

Professional Real Estate Investors, Inc. v. Columbia Pictures
508 U.S. 49 (1993)

This case requires us to define the "sham" exception to the doctrine of antitrust immunity first identified in *Eastern Railroad Presidents Conference v. Noerr Motor Freight, Inc.*, . . . as the doctrine applies in the litigation context. . . . We hold that litigation cannot be deprived of immunity as a sham unless the litigation is objectively baseless. The Court of Appeals for the Ninth Circuit refused to characterize as sham a lawsuit that the antitrust defendant admittedly had probable cause to institute. We affirm.

I

Petitioners Professional Real Estate Investors, Inc., and Kenneth F. Irwin (collectively, PRE) operated La Mancha Private Club and Villas, a resort hotel in Palm Springs, California. Having installed videodisc players in the resort's hotel rooms and assembled a library of more than 200 motion picture titles, PRE rented videodiscs to

---

[3]   *E.g.*, Bd. of Trade of City of Chi. v. U.S., 246 U.S. 231 (1918).

[4]   *E.g.*, Spectrum Sports, Inc. v. McQuillan, 506 U.S. 447 (1993).

[5]   *E.g.*, E. R.R. Pres. Conf. v. Noerr Motor Freight Co., 365 U.S. 127 (1961).

[6]   *E.g.*, Cal. Motor Transport Co. v. Trucking Unlimited, 404 U.S. 508 (1972).

[7]   *E.g.*, MCI Commun. Corp. v. AT&T Co., 708 F.2d 1081 (7th Cir. 1983).

[8]   For present purposes, we have chosen to use ellipses to denote all omissions. We note, however, that some citation rules require special treatment for omitting footnotes and citations from opinions.

guests for in-room viewing. PRE also sought to develop a market for the sale of videodisc players to other hotels wishing to offer in-room viewing of prerecorded material. Respondents, Columbia Pictures Industries, Inc., and seven other major motion picture studios (collectively, Columbia), held copyrights to the motion pictures recorded on the videodiscs that PRE purchased. Columbia also licensed the transmission of copyrighted motion pictures to hotel rooms through a wired cable system called Spectradyne. PRE therefore competed with Columbia not only for the viewing market at La Mancha but also for the broader market for in-room entertainment services in hotels.

In 1983, Columbia sued PRE for alleged copyright infringement through the rental of videodiscs for viewing in hotel rooms. PRE counter-claimed, charging Columbia with violations of §§ 1 and 2 of the Sherman Act .... In particular, PRE alleged that Columbia's copyright action was a mere sham that cloaked underlying acts of monopolization and conspiracy to restrain trade.

The parties filed cross-motions for summary judgment on Columbia's copyright claim and postponed further discovery on PRE's antitrust counterclaims. Columbia did not dispute that PRE could freely sell or lease lawfully purchased videodiscs under the Copyright Act's "first sale" doctrine, ... and PRE conceded that the playing of videodiscs constituted "performance" of motion pictures .... As a result, summary judgment depended solely on whether rental of videodiscs for in-room viewing infringed Columbia's exclusive right to "perform the copyrighted work[s] publicly." ... Ruling that such rental did not constitute public performance, the District Court entered summary judgment for PRE.... The Court of Appeals affirmed on the grounds that a hotel room was not a "public place" and that PRE did not "transmit or otherwise communicate" Columbia's motion pictures....

On remand, Columbia sought summary judgment on PRE's antitrust claims, arguing that the original copyright infringement action was no sham and was therefore entitled to immunity under *Eastern Railroad Presidents Conference v. Noerr Motor Freight, Inc., supra.* Reasoning that the infringement action "was clearly a legitimate effort and therefore not a sham,".... the District Court granted the motion ....

. . .

II

. . .

In *California Motor Transport Co. v. Trucking Unlimited*, 404 U.S. 508 (1972), we elaborated on *Noerr* in two relevant respects.... We left unresolved the question presented by this case—whether litigation may be sham merely because a subjective expectation of success does not motivate the litigant. We now answer this question in the negative and hold that an objectively reasonable effort to litigate cannot be sham regardless of subjective intent.

. . .

... Our recognition of a sham in [*California Motor Transport*] signifies that the institution of legal proceedings "without probable cause" will give rise to a sham if such activity effectively "bar[s] ... competitors from meaningful access to adjudicatory tribunals and so ... usurp[s] th[e] decision making process."

. . .

III

We now outline a two-part definition of "sham" litigation. First, the lawsuit must be objectively baseless in the sense that no reasonable litigant could realistically expect success on the merits. If an objective litigant could conclude that the suit is reasonably calculated to elicit a favorable outcome, the suit is immunized under *Noerr*, and an antitrust claim premised on the sham exception must fail. Only if challenged litigation is objectively meritless may a court examine the litigant's subjective motivation. Under this second part of our definition of sham, the court should focus on whether the baseless lawsuit conceals "an attempt to interfere *directly* with the business relationships of a competitor," . . . through the "use [of] the governmental *process*—as opposed to the *outcome* of that process—as an anticompetitive weapon." . . . This two-tiered process requires the plaintiff to disprove the challenged lawsuit's *legal* viability before the court will entertain evidence of the suit's *economic* viability.

. . .

IV

. . .

The existence of probable cause to institute legal proceedings precludes a finding that an antitrust defendant has engaged in sham litigation. The notion of probable cause, as understood and applied in the common law tort of wrongful civil proceedings, requires the plaintiff to prove that the defendant lacked probable cause to institute an unsuccessful civil lawsuit and that the defendant pressed the action for an improper, malicious purpose. . . . Probable cause to institute civil proceedings requires no more than a "reasonabl[e] belie[f] that there is a chance that [a] claim may be held valid upon adjudication. . . ." . . . Because the absence of probable-cause is an essential element of the tort, the existence of probable cause is an absolute defense. . . . Under our decision today, therefore, a proper probable cause determination irrefutably demonstrates that an antitrust plaintiff has not proved the objective prong of the sham exception and that the defendant is accordingly entitled to *Noerr* immunity.

The District Court and the Court of Appeals correctly found that Columbia had probable cause to sue PRE for copyright infringement.

What is the rule announced in *Professional Real Estate Investors*? You actually have several different possibilities. In the opening paragraph of the excerpted majority opinion, the Court stated that "[w]e hold that litigation cannot be deprived of immunity as a sham unless the litigation is objectively baseless." But then the Court also stated that "[w]e . . . hold that an objectively reasonable effort to litigate cannot be sham regardless of subjective intent." Are the concepts of "[not] objectively baseless" and "objectively reasonable" the same? They both purport to be "holdings" of the Court.

And what are the roles of two other parts of the opinion—the two-part definition of sham litigation and the discussion of probable cause? In the two-part definition, the Court explained that, to be a sham, a "lawsuit must be objectively baseless in the sense that no reasonable litigant could realistically expect success on the merits." Then, *if* the lawsuit is objectively baseless, it may be a sham when the litigant's subjective motive is *additionally* anticompetitive (as when the litigant intends the lawsuit itself to interfere with a competitor's business regardless of the ultimate outcome of the case). Is the two-part definition designed to explain what "objectively baseless" means, or what "objectively reasonable" means, or both? And what if a litigant files a lawsuit against a competitor, knowing that (a) the litigant has a fair chance of winning on the merits; (b) the costs of the litigation will outweigh the value of the victory; but (c) the litigant will inflict severe litigation costs, regardless of outcome, on the competitor who has fewer financial resources? Under the definition in *Professional Real Estate Investors*, is that "sham litigation"?[9]

What about the "probable cause" discussion? The Court wrote that "[t]he existence of probable cause to institute legal proceedings precludes a finding that an antitrust defendant has engaged in sham litigation." Is that simply a second way of characterizing the two-part definition of sham litigation? Or is it really an alternative test?

There are really no perfect answers to the above questions.[10] Assuming multiple choices exist for assembling a rule from a court opinion, however, you would pursue the following six steps.

Step 1: Look for the words, "we hold that . . . ." These words may signal the announcement of the legal rule in the case, although they may instead simply signal the announcement of the outcome rather than the legal principle adopted by the court. So watch out. There are two "we hold that" statements in *Professional Real Estate Investors*, and one reasonable formulation of the legal rule from the case would involve combining the two statements—i.e., "litigation is not 'sham' if the litigation is objectively reasonable on its merits without regard to the subjective motivations of the person filing the suit."

Step 2: Look for the result in the case. Whatever the rule is, it must be consistent with, as well as explain, the result. For example, suppose you read a court opinion and tentatively conclude that the relevant rule in the case is composed of four elements. You then look at the result in the case and read that the plaintiff has won. You then look back at the facts in the case and notice that, given the facts, plaintiff could not have prevailed if element 3 in your proposed four-part rule is actually part of the equation. By definition, assuming that you have correctly identified the result and the material facts from the case, your proposed formulation of the rule must be incorrect, at least as to proposed element 3.

In *Professional Real Estate Investors*, you might conclude that the winner (Columbia Pictures) won because it had reasonable cause to believe that Professional Real Estate Investors was violating Columbia's copyright on movies. Thus, you might formulate the relevant legal rule as being that "litigation is not 'sham' if the person filing the litigation has reasonable cause to believe that the sued party is violating the legal right that the person seeks to enforce in the litigation." You would not formulate the rule as being that "litigation may be sham when a subjective expectation of success does not motivate the litigant" because there is no indication that Columbia could have prevailed on summary judgment if subjective intent alone were the rule.

Step 3: In selecting or formulating the succinct explanation, start with the narrowest statement that fully explains the resolution of the problem the court addressed. **The true legal rule of the case does not include any statements about the law that are unnecessary to the resolution of the problem before the court.** By the same token, your succinct explanation of the rule of the case is *too* succinct if you cannot fully explain the outcome from it.

---

[9]   If you were actually giving client advice, you would read the concurring opinion of Justice Stevens (not reprinted here) for additional insight.

[10]   The fact that we are even asking the questions illustrates the helpfulness to your audience of saying something once, and not re-characterizing it multiple times unless you absolutely have to do so. Sometimes re-characterization language can be explained by the existence of multiple persons who must sign off on the text of a document before it is issued. Also, sometimes re-characterization language can be explained by the need to reconcile your writing with the approach taken by a previous writer (as in the case of an appellate court reviewing a lower court's decision in the same case). But still strive to say what you mean once clearly, and then move on. Or at a minimum use consistent terminology.

In *Professional Real Estate Investors,* you might conclude that much of the language in the majority opinion is unnecessary. You might conclude that much of the language is not the narrowest statement that fully explains the resolution of the problem the Court addressed. You might conclude that the second part of the Court's two-part test (the subjective motivation part of the objective reasonableness/subjective motivation standard) for analyzing a "sham" lawsuit was irrelevant to the facts at hand in the case. Columbia Pictures had a reasonable chance of winning its copyright claim on the merits, even if ultimately it did not prevail on that claim. Whether Columbia was subjectively motivated by a desire to hurt Professional Real Estate Investors competitively was ultimately irrelevant. Thus, you might conclude that the legal rule in the case should resemble the one in Step 2 "look for the result" discussion above, but not the rule formulated in Step 1 "we hold that" discussion.

Step 4: If there appear to be multiple, appropriate formulations of the legal rule in the case after you apply the three previous steps, then put all of the potential formulations side-by-side and do two things: First, look for elements of the rule that are common to more than one of the formulations. You can be reasonably sure that common elements are part of the court's definition of the relevant rule. Second, in choosing among multiple, appropriate formulations, opt for the version that is most helpful to your preferred resolution of the problem in your client's case.

Applying Step 4 to *Professional Real Estate Investors,* you might put "[not] objectively baseless," "objectively reasonable," and "having probable cause" side-by-side and notice that the word "objectively" appears more than once and is thus likely part of the relevant definition of genuine lawsuits. You might also conclude hypothetically that "[not] objectively baseless" and "objectively reasonable" are equally viable legal definitions of a lawsuit that is not a "sham," in which case you should pick the one that favors your client's circumstances.

Step 5: Go back and compare the results you obtain from all four of the above steps to try to ensure that your selected rule formulation is consistent with the thrust of the court's opinion. It is perilous to zero in on a snippet of language in a court's opinion as being the rule in the case if your selection of language appears inconsistent with the outcome, or inconsistent with the majority of the rules produced by your efforts under Steps 1 through 4 above.

Step 6: Consider the policy implications of your rule formulation, and ask yourself if your construction of the rule is consistent with the policies that the court expressly or impliedly is seeking to uphold. In the *Professional Real Estate Investors* opinion, the Court was seeking to balance two competing considerations. On the one hand, the Court wanted to make sure that litigants are free to exercise their right to seek relief in court for perceived legal violations. Otherwise, the system would encourage people to engage simply in self-help to remedy perceived wrongs. On the other hand, the court system should not be a pawn for misuse by businesses. So the Court sought to formulate a quasi-objective test for differentiating between genuine and "sham" lawsuits.

Template for assembling a rule from a case:

➢   Look for the words, "we hold that . . . ."

➢   Look for a formulation that is consistent with the result in the case.

➢   Look for the narrowest statement that explains the resolution.

➢   Compare the potential formulations side-by-side.

> ➤ Look for a formulation that is consistent with the thrust of the court's opinion.

> ➤ Consider the policy implications.

So what advice would you give your client in our hypothetical pharmaceutical problem? If the formula for the proprietary drug has indeed been well guarded, and the competitor has indeed stolen the formula by causing a former employee of your client to divulge the secret formula in violation of a confidentiality agreement, then your client's proposed lawsuit against the competitor appears to have an objectively reasonable basis. If it does, then your client's interest in slowing down the competitor is ultimately irrelevant. Under *Professional Real Estate Investors*, an antitrust counterclaim likely should fail.

D. ETHICAL CONSIDERATIONS

The lawyer-as-advocate problem and the pharmaceutical company problem discussed above concern how the lawyer will recommend that the clients proceed to solve their legal problems. Giving clients advice can invoke multiple ethical considerations and requires communication between the lawyer and the client.

As you can imagine, a client will have overall objectives that he or she would like to accomplish through the representation. When representing a client, a lawyer must determine the client's objective and consult with the client regarding how the lawyer will pursue those objectives.[11] For example, in the lawyer-as-advocate problem, although the lawyer knows that the goal is to block the family member's objection to the lawyer's participation, the lawyer must consult with the client regarding how best to achieve that objective. The lawyer would share the lawyer's interpretation of the governing Minnesota ethics rule (based on the lawyer's careful parsing of the rule) and discuss the lawyer's recommendations regarding how to stop the family member from blocking the lawyer's participation.

---

[11] Model Rules of Prof'l Conduct R. 1.2(a), 1.4(a)(2) (2016).

CHAPTER 5

Determining the Rule in Typical Complex Scenarios: Statutory Law

---

In Chapter 4, we explained how to parse the elements of Rule 3.7(a) of the Minnesota Rules of Professional Conduct, a simple, enacted legal rule. We then posed a problem: Suppose you are not given a rule's text. Suppose instead that you must determine what the rule is before working with it. And we identified this problem as "typical" when analyzing rules developed by court decisions rather than rules presented by enacted law, such as statutes. We now turn to an issue unique to enacted statutory law—how to determine the meaning of the enacted language. To see the principles outlined in this chapter put into practice, review the sample memos and briefs in Chapters 10 and 11 involving issues of statutory interpretation.

LEARNING OBJECTIVES

1. Students will learn how to craft a legal rule from statutory law.

2. Students will learn how courts interpret statutory language and the various sources that courts use.

A. INTERPRETING STATUTORY LANGUAGE

Sometimes a statute states what it means in unmistakable language. If so, you as a problem solver will apply that language to the particular problem and recommend a solution. Ultimate decision makers will do the same thing to reach a conclusion on your recommended solution.

Sometimes, however, you are faced with statutory language that is not clear. In other words, the wording or the grammatical structure of the statute appears to create an ambiguity. One reading helps your client; a contrary reading does not. To solve the client's problem, you must first interpret the statute before applying it. The sources for interpretation that you rely on will determine the structure and types of arguments available to you, the other interested advocates, and the decision makers.

Courts look to two sources in interpreting a statute—canons of statutory construction and legislative histories. While these sources will be discussed more thoroughly when you are learning legal research, we provide a very brief overview here. A canon of statutory construction is a tool that helps a court give meaning to the statute. There are many canons, and some contradict each other.[1] The most fundamental canon, the one that courts turn to first, is the "plain meaning rule." In applying this canon, the courts assume the legislature intended that words used in the statute be given their ordinary meaning.

---

[1] Karl Llewellyn, *Remarks on the Theory of Appellate Decision and the Rules or Canons About How Statutes are to be Construed*, 3 VAND. L. REV. 395 (1950).

When the plain meaning rule leads to illogical results or unintended consequences, then the courts will turn to other canons.[2] For example, one canon states that where general words follow specific words, then the general words should be read to include objects of a similar nature or class. To illustrate, if the statutory text refers to "cars, trucks, recreational vans, and other vehicles," the general term "other vehicles" would be read in the context of the preceding, more specific terms. Applying this canon, "other vehicles" would include any motorized vehicle, but would likely exclude non-motorized vehicles like bicycles.

What sometimes happens, however, is that even after the application of simple, threshold canons, statutory language is still ambiguous. The courts often will then turn to the legislative history of the statute to determine what the legislature intended when it enacted the statute. A legislative history is composed of the various documents created by the legislative body when it drafted and enacted the statute. These documents include various versions of the bill, committee and conference committee reports, and transcripts of hearings and debates.[3]

B.   UNDERSTANDING STATUTORY INTERPRETATION IN THE LEGISLATIVE CONTEXT

To help understand how these sources are used to interpret statutory text and its meaning, assume you are involved in the following case: The United States has charged your client, Mr. Gerving, with illegal possession and manufacturing of Chemical X. Chemical X has various hallucinogenic properties, and Mr. Gerving has been telling friends they can get "high" on the chemical. The United States charged Gerving with violations of 21 U.S.C. §§ 841, 844, 856, 813, and 802(32)(A). Section 813 provides:

> A controlled substance analogue shall, to the extent intended for human consumption, be treated for purposes of any Federal law as a controlled substance in schedule I.

Section 802(32)(A) defines the phrase "controlled substance analogue" as:

> The term "controlled substance analogue" means a substance—
>
> (i)   the chemical structure of which is substantially similar to the chemical structure of a controlled substance in schedule I or II;
>
> (ii)   which has a stimulant, depressant, or hallucinogenic effect on the central nervous system that is substantially similar to or greater than the stimulant, depressant, or hallucinogenic effect on the central nervous system of a controlled substance in schedule I or II; or
>
> (iii)   with respect to a particular person, which such person represents or intends to have a stimulant, depressant, or hallucinogenic effect on the central nervous system that is substantially similar to or greater than the stimulant, depressant, or hallucinogenic effect on the central nervous system of a controlled substance in schedule I or II.

---

[2]   One of the more widely used resources on statutory construction is the multi-volume treatise originally authored by Jabez Gridley Sutherland. NORMAN J. SINGER & J.D. SHAMBIE SINGER, SUTHERLAND STATUTORY CONSTRUCTION (7th ed. 2007).

[3]   For a more detailed discussion of the documents that comprise a legislative history, as well as the difficulties in compiling and relying on legislative histories, see Chapter 4 in CRISTINA D. LOCKWOOD & PAMELA LYSAGHT, MICHIGAN LEGAL RESEARCH, THIRD EDITION (Carolina Academic Press 2016).

Assume the construction of § 802(32)(A) is the sole question before the court. The government concedes that Chemical X lacks a substantially similar chemical structure to any scheduled controlled substance and that, therefore, element (i) of § 802(32)(A) is not met on the present facts. However, the government urges a disjunctive reading of the statute; i.e., the government argues that the statute requires only that (i) *or* (ii) *or* (iii) be satisfied for the substance to constitute a controlled substance analogue. From the government's perspective, because either (ii) or (iii) is present, the absence of element (i) is irrelevant to its case against Gerving.

In contrast, you, on behalf of Gerving, urge a conjunctive reading of the statute, arguing that the statute requires the government to prove (i) *and* either (ii) or (iii). Your theory is that the word "which" in each of elements (ii) and (iii) links those elements back to element (i). Under your reading of the statute, therefore, the conceded absence of element (i) — a substantially similar chemical structure to a scheduled controlled substance — is fatal to the government's case against him.

Read the following excerpt from *United States v. Forbes*. Identify which sources the court relied on and think about how to apply them in developing your argument.

> **United States v. Forbes**
> 806 F. Supp. 232, 234–36 (D. Colo. 1992)
>
> Defendants contend that this section requires a two-pronged definition. The first prong requires a substantially similar chemical structure. The second prong requires either a substantially similar effect on the human nervous system or the intent to have such an effect. The government argues that a substance may be an analogue if it satisfies any of the three clauses. I agree with defendants.
>
> The goal of statutory construction is to effectuate the intent and purpose of Congress. *Rocky Mountain Oil & Gas Assoc. v. Watt*, 696 F.2d 734, 745 (10th Cir. 1982). Where the language of the statute itself is unambiguous, it is presumed that it expresses congressional intent and the language is controlling. *Id.* If the statutory language is unclear after resort to traditional tools of statutory construction, courts look to the legislative history to glean the intent and purpose of Congress. *Blum v. Stenson*, 465 U.S. 886, 896, 104 S.Ct. 1541, 1547, 79 L.Ed.2d 891 (1984); *Rocky Mountain Oil*, 696 F.2d at 745.
>
> The government's reading of the analogue definition has superficial appeal. As a matter of simple grammar, when an "or" is placed before the last term in a series, each term in the series is usually intended to be disjunctive. Under this reading, AET would be an analogue if it satisfies any of the three clauses. However, this reading ignores other grammatical principles that apply in favor of defendants' construction. The operative segments of clauses (ii) and (iii) both begin with the word "which", signaling the start of a dependent relative clause modifying a precedent noun. In each case, the precedent noun is "chemical structure" found in clause (i). Because both clauses (ii) and (iii) can be read to modify clause (i), the statutory language can be fairly read as requiring the two-pronged definition asserted by defendants. *See, First Charter Financial Corp. v. U.S.*, 669 F.2d 1342, 1350 (9th Cir. 1982), (Modifying phrases generally refer to immediately preceding phrase). At best, the statute is ambiguous.
>
> Defendants' reading is also bolstered by a deeply rooted rule of statutory construction. A statute must be construed to avoid unintended or absurd results. *American Tobacco Co. v. Patterson*, 456 U.S. 63, 71, 102 S.Ct. 1534, 1538, 71 L.Ed.2d 748 (1982); *Ewing v. Rodgers*, 826 F.2d 967, 970 (10th Cir. 1987). If I adopt the government's construction and read clause (ii) independently, alcohol or caffeine would be controlled substance analogues because, in concentrated form, they can have depressant or

stimulant effects substantially similar to a controlled substance. Likewise, if I read clause (iii) independently, powdered sugar would be an analogue if a defendant represented that it was cocaine, effectively converting this law into a counterfeit drug statute. In both cases, a defendant could be prosecuted for selling a controlled substance analogue even though the alleged analogue did not have chemical structure substantially similar to a schedule I or II controlled substance. Therefore, to prevent this unintended result, clause (i) must apply to any substance that the government contends is a controlled substance analogue.

Further, defendants' construction is supported by legislative history. In July, 1985, the Senate began consideration of the "Designer Drug Enforcement Act of 1985" (S.1417, later redesignated the "Controlled Substance Analog Enforcement Act of 1985," S.1437). The bill's stated purpose was "to prohibit persons who specifically set out to manufacture or to distribute drugs which are substantially similar to the most dangerous controlled substances from engaging in this activity." S.Rep. No. 196, 99th Cong., 1st Sess. 5 (1985). The Senate Judiciary Committee reported that law enforcement authorities find themselves one step behind underground chemists who slightly alter the molecular structure of controlled substances to create new drugs. *Id.* at 1–2. The Senate proposed a two-part definition of the term analogue: either the substance has a substantially similar chemical structure or it was "specifically designed" to produce an effect substantially similar to schedule I or II drugs.

In July, 1986, the House of Representatives considered the Designer Drug Enforcement Act of 1986 (H.R. 5246). As with the Senate, the House bill focused on underground chemists who seek to evade the drug laws by slightly altering a controlled substance. H.R.Rep. No. 948, 99th Cong., 2d Sess. 4 (1986). The House proposed a two-pronged definition of analogue that is virtually identical to the construction advocated by defendants here. The House bill contained the same three clauses as the current statute, but added the word "and" after clause (i).

> The term "controlled substance analogue" is defined to conform as closely as possible to the policy of the Controlled Substances Act by requiring a chemical relationship to a substance which is controlled . . . and either the existence of some stimulant, depressant, or hallucinogenic effect on the central nervous system, or a representation or intent that the substance have a stimulant, depressant, or hallucinogenic effect substantially similar to, or greater than, such effect of any controlled substance.

Id. at 2, (emphasis added). The report illustrates the point with coffee. "Coffee, for example, has a stimulant effect on the central nervous system, but it is not chemically substantially similar to a controlled substance." *Id.* at 7.

Congress ultimately adopted the analogue statute as part of the comprehensive "Anti-Drug Abuse Act of 1986" (H.R. 5484). Inexplicably, the analogue definition enacted by Congress dropped the word "and" after clause (i). Otherwise, that definition and the two-pronged definition considered by the House are virtually identical. I consider the House report to be persuasive legislative history as to Congress' intent underlying its definition of a controlled substance analogue.

The legislative history thus clearly supports defendants' construction. The analogue statute is directed at underground chemists who tinker with the molecular structure of controlled substances to create new drugs that are not scheduled. If a substance could be an analogue without a substantially similar chemical structure, Congress' stated purpose would be significantly expanded. Moreover, by essentially adopting the House definition, Congress evidenced its intent to require a two-pronged definition.

. . .

Finally, courts must construe criminal statutes narrowly in favor of lenity to the accused. *United States v. Enmons*, 410 U.S. 396, 411, 93 S.Ct. 1007, 1015, 35 L.Ed.2d 379 (1973); *Mahn v. Gunter*, 978 F.2d 599 (10th Cir.1992), (Rule of lenity is a doctrine of last resort in statutory construction). Although it is not necessary to apply this rule as a last resort, its application yields a result entirely consistent with defendants' construction. The two-pronged definition not only promotes lenity in this prosecution, but narrows future analogue prosecutions to only those cases where the substance has a chemical structure substantially similar to a schedule I or II controlled substance. Therefore, I hold that a substance may be a controlled substance analogue only if it satisfies clause (i) and clauses (ii) or (iii).

The court in *Forbes* was engaged in a classic statutory construction analysis. When you develop statutory arguments, consider this sequence.

Step 1: Determine if the questionable words can be given their plain, ordinary meaning. In *Forbes*, the court looked to the ordinary meaning as well as the grammatical structure of the statute. It ruled, after this "plain meaning" analysis that the statute was ambiguous.

Step 2: Search for other canons that support your client's interpretation. In *Forbes*, the court used the canon that states "A statute must be construed to avoid unintended or absurd results."[4] Pay particular attention to which canons the courts in your jurisdiction apply to ambiguous statutes. Even if those canons help your adversary, chances are, that you will be able to distinguish the canon or find others that support your position. If in doubt, just scan the examples identified by Karl Llewellyn.[5]

Step 3: Canvass the documents that comprise the legislative history. Determine which ones support your interpretation and which do not. Some sources are more persuasive — various drafts of the bill and committee and conference committee reports. Emphasize those persuasive sources that favor your interpretation, and distinguish those that do not.

Step 4: Determine whether there is an administrative agency interpretation of the statute. There was not an applicable administrative agency regulation in *Forbes*. If there is not a relevant administrative regulation, move to Step 5. If such a regulation exists, your analysis will include a discussion of the regulation or regulations. This part of statutory interpretation is discussed in the next section.

Step 5: Look for the underlying policy considerations that motivated the legislature to create the legislation. What problem was the legislature intending to address? In *Forbes*, the court noted Congress's desire to reach underground chemists who molecularly alter controlled substances to create new designer drugs. Focusing on these policy considerations is a way to distinguish between legislative history sources that offer competing interpretations.

Step 6: When interpreting criminal statutes, note that there is an additional canon that can be raised as a final argument — the rule of lenity. The *Forbes* court invoked this rule to support its holding. But note if you are the government, not all is lost. The rule is not

---

[4]   U.S. v. Forbes, 806 F. Supp. 232, 235 (D. Colo. 1992).

[5]   *See supra* note 1.

consistently applied. Thus, as the government, you would discuss those cases in which the rule was not applied or was rejected.

Does your client, Gerving, have a strong argument, based on the canons, legislative history, and policy considerations? Certainly, under *Forbes*, he does. Of course, a thorough analysis would require reading any binding case where the court interpreted the statutory section before reaching a final conclusion. When there are no cases, however, you will need to go through these steps, searching the canons and the legislative history to develop your position.

C. USING ADMINISTRATIVE REGULATIONS TO INTERPRET STATUTORY LANGUAGE

As discussed in Chapter 3, when a statute is ambiguous, courts may also look to an administrative agency's interpretation of the statute. Congress often delegates authority to an administrative agency to administer federal statutes. In doing so, the administrative agency may issue regulations interpreting that statute. There are, however, varying levels of deference that federal courts give to agency interpretations of statutory language. Such deference mainly occurs in the federal context. State courts do not regularly defer to state agency interpretations of state statutes.

If you are faced with an agency interpretation of a federal statute, you will set forth rules regarding the appropriate level of deference the court should give to the agency interpretation. You will also likely make arguments regarding how the court should interpret those rules.

Courts recognize two possible standards of review for evaluating agency statutory interpretations and determining the deference due them. The first, articulated by the United States Supreme Court in *Chevron U.S.A. Inc. v. Natural Resources Defense Council, Inc.*, 467 U.S. 837 (1984), requires a two-step evaluative process. First, the reviewing court assesses the clarity of the relevant statute. If the statute's meaning is clear, that is the end of the inquiry, for both agencies and courts must abide by clearly expressed congressional intent, and the court must reject an alternative agency determination. If the statute is ambiguous, however, then the second step of the *Chevron* standard calls upon reviewing courts to defer to the agency's reasonable interpretation thereof.

The second standard that courts sometimes use to evaluate agency statutory interpretations is that articulated by the Supreme Court in *Skidmore v. Swift & Co.*, 323 U.S. 134 (1944). *Skidmore* and its progeny call upon reviewing courts to consider various factors in determining the degree of deference that is appropriate for a given agency statutory interpretation, including "the thoroughness evident in its consideration, the validity of its reasoning, its consistency with earlier and later pronouncements, and all those factors which give it power to persuade, if lacking the power to control." *Id*. at 140.

So how do courts determine whether to apply *Chevron* or *Skidmore* deference? *United States v. Mead Corp.*, 533 U.S. 218 (2001) provides the typical test for what level of deference, if any, a court will give to an agency interpretation of a statute. First, the reviewing court asks whether Congress has given the agency in question the authority to bind the regulated parties with "the force of law." *Id*. at 226–27. If Congress has made such a delegation, then the reviewing court must determine whether the agency has "exercise[d] . . . that authority." *Id*. Where the answers to both of *Mead*'s questions are affirmative, then *Chevron*'s two-part standard of review applies. If the answer to either of *Mead*'s questions is negative, however, then *Skidmore* offers the appropriate standard of review.

Consider the following excerpt from *Si Min Cen v. Attorney General*, 825 F.3d 177 (3d Cir. 2016) where the court examined a federal agency regulation interpreting a federal statute. It is presented to demonstrate the intersection between the type of statutory interpretation in *Forbes* and a statutory interpretation involving an administrative regulation where the regulation was properly promulgated under authority Congress delegated to the agency. It is the Third Circuit Court of Appeals' interpretation of this intersection relying on the *Chevron* standard discussed above.

Si Min Cen v. Attorney General
825 F.3d 177 (3d Cir. 2016)

Under the familiar two-step *Chevron* analysis, we first determine under Step One if Congress has "directly addressed the precise question at issue," and if so, we strike down a regulation that is contrary to Congress's "unambiguously expressed intention." *Chevron*, 467 U.S. at 842–43, 104 S.Ct. 2778. At Step One, we consider the statutory text, as well as "traditional tools of statutory construction," including canons of construction and the broader statutory context. *Shalom Pentecostal Church v. Acting Sec'y U.S. Dep't of Homeland Sec.*, 783 F.3d 156, 164–65 (3d Cir. 2015); *United States v. Geiser*, 527 F.3d 288, 292–94 (3d Cir. 2008). If, however, "the statute is silent or ambiguous with respect to the specific issue," we move on to Step Two, where "the question for the court is whether the agency's [regulation] is based on a permissible construction of the statute." *Chevron*, 467 U.S. at 843, 104 S.Ct. 2778. . . . Step Two affords agencies considerable deference, and "where Congress has not merely failed to address a precise question, but has given an 'express delegation of authority to the agency to elucidate a specific provision of the statute by regulation,' then the agency's 'legislative regulations are given controlling weight unless they are arbitrary, capricious, or manifestly contrary to the statute.' " *Zheng*, 422 F.3d at 112 (quoting *Chevron*, 467 U.S. at 843–44, 104 S.Ct 2778). But deference under Step Two is not absolute, and the regulation must still "harmonize[ ]" with the statutes, *id*. at 119 (quoting *O'Leary*, 93 F.3d at 110), and be "reasonable in light of the legislature's revealed design," *NationsBank of N.C., N.A. v. Variable Annuity Life Ins. Co.*, 513 U.S. 251, 257, 115 S.Ct 810, 130 L.E.d2d 740 (1995).

As indicated by the court in *Si Min Cen*, where there are properly promulgated agency regulations, Step One of a *Chevron* analysis requires that courts examine the text of the statute, using "traditional tools of statutory construction."[6] The court does so to determine whether Congress has spoken directly and unambiguously on the issue. Consequently, Step One can involve all of the statutory interpretation steps that were exemplified in *Forbes*. Then, if the statutory ambiguity is not resolved, the regulations are examined consistent with Step Two of a *Chevron* analysis.

In *Si Min Cen*, the court determined that it could not resolve the case under Step One of the *Chevron* analysis. The court ultimately determined under Step Two that the regulation, although clearly stated, was inconsistent with the purpose of the statute and declared it invalid.[7] There can, however, be a situation where not only is the statute ambiguous, but the regulation interpreting the statute is also ambiguous.[8]

In a statutory analysis, when a statute is ambiguous, the courts often look to the statute's legislative history. The excerpt from the *Forbes* opinion gives an example of such an analysis. Administrative regulations are not created in the same manner as statutes.

---

[6]   The U.S. Supreme Court has used the language "the ordinary tools of statutory construction" to describe the tools courts use to determine if Congress has spoken directly to the issue in Step One of the *Chevron* analysis. *See e.g.*, City of Arlington, Tx v. F.C.C., 133 S. Ct. 1863, 1868 (2013). There is some debate over whether legislative history is one of the ordinary tools of statutory construction that courts can use in Step One of *Chevron* to determine if Congress has spoken directly.

[7]   Si Min Cen v. Attorney General, 825 F.3d 177 (3d Cir. 2016).

[8]   *See* Auer v. Robbins, 519 U.S. 452 (1997); Bowles v. Seminole Rock & Sand Co., 325 U.S. 410 (1945).

Courts, however, may look to procedural information an agency creates in promulgating a regulation. Specifically, many federal regulations that are binding law are created through the notice and comment procedure set forth in the Administrative Procedure Act.[9] In interpreting administrative regulations, courts may look to procedural information that is created and required by that process.

Sometimes, the administrative agency has stated an interpretation of an administrative regulation, or it operates according to a certain understanding of the meaning of the regulation. Where there is an agency interpretation of its regulation, a court will generally give that agency interpretation some level of deference. Although what that level of deference is exactly and how it should be determined can be the subject of much debate.

Thus, statutory interpretation can require several levels of analysis. Courts will first look to the plain meaning and if necessary to other canons of construction, the legislative history, and the policy underlying the statute. Where there are regulations interpreting the statute, then courts will still look to determine whether the statutory language is clear. If it is, then the court uses the plain language of the statute, just as it would if there were no regulations. If the court determines, however, that the statute is ambiguous, the focus of the analysis turns to the relevant regulations.

Where the text of the administrative regulation is clear, then this analysis involves determining whether the agency acted within its authority and the level of deference to afforded the regulation. If the text of the regulation is also ambiguous, then the court must interpret the ambiguous regulation. The structure of this analysis and the sources used to interpret administrative regulations vary considerably. The point is that the interpretive analysis of the regulation can become a sub-analysis within the interpretive analysis of the statute.

Thus, in terms of the Steps listed previously, Step 4 requires that you determine whether there are agency regulations interpreting the statute. If the statute is clearly worded, then analysis of the regulation may not be required. If there is an argument, however, that the statute is not clearly worded, an additional analysis applying and possibly interpreting the regulation may also be required.

D. WHAT TO AVOID IN STATUTORY INTERPRETATION

First, even if you have a strong plain meaning argument, do not stop there. The opposing party likely will argue that the plain meaning leads to illogical or unintended results. You should make additional arguments that support your plain meaning interpretation. For example, if interpreting a statute, you can also argue that the legislative history supports your plain meaning interpretation. You should include these additional arguments, even though technically the court should not look to additional sources if the plain meaning resolves the issue. By developing these "even if" arguments, you are countering your opponent's position.

Second, and somewhat inconsistently, appreciate that not *all* judges favor delving into legislative histories or other information created in the drafting process. For example, some judges will resist turning to legislative histories because they do not believe it is possible to determine a singular intent of a legislative body or because it is too easy for lawyers to select only bits of legislative history that favor their own clients instead of representative

---

[9]   When learning legal research, your professor will discuss, in more depth, the Administrative Procedure Act, equivalent state administrative procedure acts, and how administrative regulations are created.

legislative history as a whole. Some judges prefer to focus on the words used in the enacted law.

E. ETHICAL CONSIDERATIONS

When lawyers make rule interpretation arguments based on documents created in the legislative or administrative process, they are often making arguments based on inferences. The information in the document may not directly state what the drafters intended, but the lawyer argues that the drafters' intent can be inferred from that information. Thus, creative arguments are possible. A lawyer, however, must be careful that his zeal in representing his client does not overshadow his role as an officer of the court. These two roles that a lawyer engages in simultaneously can conflict. Lawyers should zealously represent their clients taking the necessary steps to accomplish their clients' objectives.[10] During representation, a lawyer should make arguments, in good faith, based on existing law and facts, or the lawyer can argue, in good faith, for an extension, modification, or reversal of existing law.[11] But the lawyer cannot assert or take positions that are without merit[12] or for purposes of embarrassment, harassment, or delay.[13]

Also recognize that zealous representation does not justify uncivil conduct towards opposing counsel or require "press[ing] for every advantage."[14] If opposing counsel needs an extension due to unforeseen life circumstances, unless it would cause determent to your client's position, think seriously about granting such a request. Refusing the request sets a precedent that might result in hardship for you in the future if you were to need leniency on an issue.

F. CONCLUSION

In resolving problems that are governed by statutes, courts must apply the law to the facts of the problem, but to do so, often the court must first interpret the meaning of that statute. If the statute is stated clearly, then the court's responsibility is to apply that clear statute as stated. When faced with statutory language that is not clear, the problem solver must then look to other canons of statutory construction, the legislative history, and the policy supporting the statute. If there is a relevant regulation that interprets the ambiguous statute, the court will need to engage in an additional analysis. This additional analysis can involve determining whether the regulation is a valid exercise of the agency's authority, what level of deference the court should give the regulation, and how the court should interpret and apply it.

---

[10]   MODEL RULES OF PROF'L CONDUCT R. 1.3 cmt. 1 (2016).

[11]   MODEL RULES OF PROF'L CONDUCT R. 3.1 (2016).

[12]   *Id.*

[13]   MODEL RULES OF PROF'L CONDUCT R. 3.2, 4.4(a) (2016).

[14]   MODEL RULES OF PROF'L CONDUCT R. 1.3 cmt. 1.

CHAPTER 6

Determining the Rule in Typical Complex Scenarios: Court Decisions

You have worked through how to determine the rules from a simple enacted rule and from a single court decision (Chapter 4). You have worked through how to determine a complex rule from an enacted statute (Chapter 5). Now you will work through how to determine the rule from a typical, complex set of cases.

What if there are multiple court decisions from which you must assemble a rule? The rule assembly becomes more complex. You have to reconcile different cases that discuss the same basic legal concept and make sense out of the language.

LEARNING OBJECTIVES

1. Students will learn how to identify variations on a legal rule as stated by multiple court opinions.

2. Students will learn how to analyze and synthesize multiple court opinions.

3. Students will learn how to reconcile court decisions in conflict.

4. Students will learn how to address a legal issue of first impression in a particular jurisdiction.

A. ASSEMBLING A RULE FROM MULTIPLE COURT DECISIONS

Assume that your client, a real estate agency, presents you with the following problem. The client wishes to recruit and hire a sales agent who works for a competing company. The agent has a contract with the competitor that allows either the agent or the competitor to terminate the contract at will on thirty days notice. The client has heard that the competitor is aggressive about retaining its sales agents and looks for excuses to sue real estate agencies that try to hire away the agents. The client wants your advice as to the likelihood of a legitimate claim.

Read the four excerpts below (from which we have omitted footnotes, a number of citations, and other materials for the sake of brevity). See if you can describe the rule from the cases.

RJM Sales & Marketing, Inc. v. Banfi Products Corp.
546 F. Supp. 1368 (D. Minn. 1982)

[Authors' note: Defendant Banfi Products Corp. ("Banfi") was a manufacturer of beverages and an importer of wines. RJM Sales & Marketing, Inc. ("RJM") was a broker

---

for beverage manufacturers. Banfi contracted with RJM to be a broker of Banfi's products. The contract included a termination clause, which stated: "Either party to this agreement may terminate it by giving thirty (30) days written notice to the other party." Fifteen months after contracting with RJM, Banfi terminated the agreement. Shortly after that, Banfi hired a former employee of RJM to become Banfi's broker. That employee, Howard Mourer, had tendered his resignation at RJM on April 6, 1981, effective on May 1, 1981, and was hired by Banfi on May 1. These events caused RJM to sue Banfi on a number of causes of action, which included a claim that Banfi tortiously interfered with Mourer's employment at RJM by hiring him away.]

Counts 9 and 10 of RJM's amended complaint are based on Banfi's alleged hiring away of Howard Mourer, RJM's employee for North and South Dakota, to be Banfi's broker for those states. RJM alleges that Banfi tortiously interfered with RJM's contract with Mourer by procuring Mourer's resignation, and that this activity constituted unfair competition.

Mourer's employment contract with RJM was terminable at will. The prevailing rule in Minnesota and elsewhere is that one is not liable for interfering with the rights of parties to a contract that is terminable at will. . . . In some jurisdictions a cause of action nevertheless exists "if either the defecting employee or the competitor . . . is guilty of some concomitant, unconscionable conduct" . . . such as misappropriation of trade secrets, . . . enticing away the employer's customers, . . . or intending to cripple the employer's business . . . .

Counsel for RJM attempted to take advantage of this exception by arguing that Banfi's hiring of Mourer was part of a larger conspiracy or plot to terminate RJM. By hiring Mourer, counsel argued, Banfi would obtain a broker experienced in the North and South Dakota markets and be in a position to terminate its relationship with RJM. Even assuming that this was Banfi's purpose, Banfi's conduct can still not be considered "unconscionable" since, under the contract, Banfi had the right to terminate RJM as its broker at any time upon 30 days notice. . . . The Court concludes that RJM has no cause of action under Counts 9 and 10 of its complaint.

Hough Transit, Ltd. v. National Farmers Organization
472 N.W.2d 358 (Minn. Ct. App. 1991)

[Authors' note: Hough Transit, Ltd. ("Hough") was a trucking service hauling milk from farmers to creameries. National Farmers Organization ("the co-op") was a farmer cooperative. The co-op had a practice of using Hough to transport its milk. In 1988, the co-op became dissatisfied with Hough and approached one of Hough's truck drivers about the possibility of starting his own milk hauling business. The driver did so, taking over the co-op's milk routes. In subsequent litigation, Hough claimed, among other things, that the co-op had tortiously interfered with the relationship between Hough and its former driver.]

[T]he co-op cannot be liable in tort for interfering with the rights of the driver and Hough because their contract was terminable at-will. . . . Even if Minnesota were to recognize a cause of action for tortious interference with an at-will relationship, there is no evidence the co-op improperly enticed the driver away from Hough's employment. Instead, the record shows the co-op members simply asked the driver to haul the co-op routes and the driver agreed. This job offer did not rise to the level of an improper interference with Hough's relationship with the driver. . . . Under these circumstances, the trial court properly granted summary judgment [for the co-op].

Oak Park Development Co., Inc. v. Snyder Brothers of Minnesota, Inc.
499 N.W.2d 500 (Minn. Ct. App. 1993)

[Authors' note: Oak Park Development Co., Inc. ("Oak Park") owned the St. Croix shopping mall. Snyder Brothers of Minnesota, Inc. ("Snyder Brothers") was a tenant in the mall. The lease agreement required Snyder Brothers to subordinate its lease to any mortgage on the property. In connection with a mall expansion that would involve adding a Herberger's store to the mall, Oak Park asked Snyder Brothers to sign a subordination agreement, expressly subordinating the Snyder lease to a mortgage that would secure financing for the Herberger store construction project. Snyder Brothers eventually produced the subordination agreement, but not before Herberger's decided to locate in another mall after the closing on the mortgage financing had to be delayed for lack of Snyder's subordination document. Oak Park then sued Snyder Brothers, alleging that Snyder Brothers unreasonably delayed signing the subordination agreement in order to extract concessions from Oak Park on Snyder's own lease, and that this tortiously interfered with Oak Park's prospective deal with Herberger's.]

The elements of interference with contract are: (1) the existence of a contract; (2) the alleged tortfeasor's knowledge of the contract; (3) the intentional interference with the contract; (4) without justification; and (5) damages resulting from the interference. . . .

. . .

Although the Oak Park/Herberger's lease was terminable at will, a binding contract was still in existence, and thus any interference was actionable. *See, e.g., Michaelson v. Minnesota Mining & Mfg. Co.*, 474 N.W.2d 174, 180 (Minn.App. 1991), *aff'd*, 479 N.W.2d 58 (Minn.1992). In *Michaelson*, this court stated: "A person may be held liable for interference with a contract, however, *even if the contract is terminable at will.*" *Id.* at 181 . . . .

We do agree, however, with the trial court's analysis that Snyder Brothers did not intentionally interfere with the Oak Park/Herberger's contract. There is no evidence that Snyder Brothers did anything to intentionally induce Herberger's to terminate its contract with Oak Park. Rather, Herberger's simply terminated its contract with Oak Park after receiving a superior offer from [the other mall]. . . .

Many of the delays in this case resulted from Oak Park's actions or inaction. . . . In light of all the facts, it is not plausible to presume the Herberger's store was not built due solely to Snyder Brother's delay in delivering the subordination agreement. . . .

. . .

The trial court did not err in granting summary judgment for Snyder Brothers . . . .

J.N.R. Enterprises, Inc. v. Frigidaire Co., No. C5–98–2281
1999 WL 377747 (Minn. Ct. App. June 1, 1999) (Unpublished Opinion)

[Authors' note: J.N.R. Enterprises ("JNR") was a distributor of Frigidaire Company ("Frigidaire") appliances to commercial users. In early 1997, JNR and Frigidaire entered into an agreement requiring JNR to maintain an adequate sales and service staff, as well as to maintain suitable office and warehousing facilities. In late 1997, Frigidaire terminated JNR as a distributor. Frigidaire cited JNR's alleged failure to comply with the distribution agreement. JNR in turn commenced a lawsuit against Frigidaire and ALL, Inc. ("ALL"), one of JNR's competitors. JNR alleged, among other things, that ALL wrongfully procured the termination through tortious interference with JNR's relationship with Frigidaire. JNR further alleged that ALL accomplished the interference, at least in part, by defaming JNR because ALL falsely had told Frigidaire employees that JNR was not fulfilling its contract obligations to Frigidaire. The district court granted summary judgment to ALL on the tortious interference claim (and a separate defamation claim), and JNR appealed.]

A cause of action for wrongful interference with a contractual relationship requires (1) a contract, (2) knowledge of that contract by the wrongdoer, (3) intentional interference with the contract, (4) without justification, and (5) damages. . . . To establish the third element of the cause of action, a plaintiff may show that the defendant induced a third party to breach the contract or that the defendant intentionally interfered with the plaintiff's contractual rights by committing an independent tort. . . . A party may be held liable for interference with a contract even if the contract is terminable at will. . . .

. . . This court has held that interference with a binding contract terminable at will is actionable, even if the contract is not breached. . . .

Because JNR alleged no other independent tort, the only tort upon which JNR can base its tortious interference claim is defamation. . . . JNR's defamation claim was not properly dismissed on summary judgment. Accordingly, the defamation claim may properly serve as a basis for JNR's tortious interference with contractual relations claim. . . . For the foregoing reasons, the district court erred in granting summary judgment dismissing JNR's tortious interference claim.

How would you describe Minnesota's tortious-interference-with-contract rule if the above four cases were the only ones you had available? The following template is one possible way of approaching the assembly of the relevant rule.

Step 1: Start by identifying the most recent, most authoritative case. Let's examine the available possibilities. The *RJM* decision is the oldest of the four cases (1982) and, in addition, is a federal court opinion. Federal courts may use state legal rules to resolve problems in cases properly before them, but federal courts do not authoritatively make state law.

The *Hough Transit* decision is more recent (1991), and it is a published decision of the Minnesota Court of Appeals. In the absence of a Minnesota Supreme Court opinion in our hypothetical group of only four opinions, the Minnesota Court of Appeals is the most authoritative court in the pool. But there are two more recent opinions from the same court available to us, so *Hough Transit* is not the most recent, most authoritative case.

The *Oak Park Development* decision (1993) is a later case from the court of appeals, and it is published. The *J.N.R* decision (1999) is the most recent case from the court of appeals, but it is not published. Minnesota Statute 480A.08, subdivision 3(c), provides that "[u]npublished opinions of the Court of Appeals are not precedential." Thus, the most recent, most authoritative decision is *Oak Park Development*.[1]

---

[1] In Minnesota, although unpublished opinions are not precedential, they may nonetheless be cited by lawyers, provided the lawyers in a litigation context give copies to the relevant court and other counsel. Moreover, the reasoning in the opinions may be deemed persuasive and adopted. Ge Lee v. Hunt, 642 N.W.2d 57 (Minn. Ct. App. 2002). This will become relevant to our rule formulation steps at a later point down the line. You should always look at the procedural rules in your own jurisdiction to determine what use, if any, you may make of unpublished opinions. Different jurisdictions adopt different rules. In some courts, for example, unpublished court opinions are considered to have no precedential value and may not be cited.

Step 2: Determine what the most recent, most authoritative decision says the relevant legal rule is (using the six-step process from the "assembling a rule from a single court decision" discussion in Chapter 4), and look at the result in the case. The *Oak Park Development* court stated three key things about tortious interference with contract that produced a victory for Snyder Brothers. First, the "elements of interference with contract are: (1) the existence of a contract; (2) the alleged tortfeasor's knowledge of the contract; (3) the intentional interference with the contract; (4) without justification; and (5) damages resulting from the interference." Second, there can be tortious interference with a terminable-at-will contract. These appear to be statements of legal rules. Third, the court explained the definition of "intentional" by stating that Snyder Brothers did nothing to procure Herberger's move to a different mall. Note that and tuck it away for possible further use.

Step 3: Ask yourself how the selected authoritative court's statement of the rule squares with the statements and the results in the other available cases. Let's turn to the other three decisions in our pool. *RJM* is the early federal court decision. It held that there is no such thing as tortious interference with a terminable-at-will contract. That does not appear to be a current statement of the law, however, because subsequent Minnesota appellate decisions (*Oak Park Development* and *J.N.R.*) hold otherwise. *RJM* may thus be discounted on the terminable-at-will point. The *RJM* court did, however, offer an aside that a cause of action might exist in some jurisdictions if a defendant engages in "concomitant, unconscionable conduct," and it identified three examples: misappropriation of trade secrets, enticing away customers, and intending to cripple the plaintiff's business. Make a note of that and tuck it away to see if any similar concept shows up in the other cases. Notice also the result in *RJM*—the defendant won.

Hough Transit is the next case. The *Hough Transit* court stated there is no such thing as tortious interference with a terminable-at-will contract. *Hough Transit* does not appear to be a current statement of the law, given *Oak Park Development* and *J.N.R.* The *Hough Transit* decision thus can be discounted on the terminable-at-will point. It did, however, offer an aside that, even if Minnesota recognized a cause of action for tortious interference with a terminable-at-will contract, there would be no legal violation in *Hough Transit* because the co-op never did anything improper. All the co-op did was ask whether Hough Transit's truck driver would haul Hough Transit's routes. Make a note of that and tuck it away to see if any similar concept shows up in the other cases. Also notice the result in *Hough Transit*— the defendant won.

J.N.R. Enterprises is the last case. It postdates *Oak Park Development*. It is an unpublished case, but you know that unpublished opinions of the court of appeals may be cited in Minnesota (with proper notice), and their reasoning may even be persuasive and later adopted in published decisions. So it matters what *J.N.R.* holds.

What does *J.N.R.* hold? First, it stated that a cause of action for "wrongful interference with a contractual relationship requires (1) a contract, (2) knowledge of that contract by the wrongdoer, (3) intentional interference with the contract, (4) without justification, and (5) damages." This is almost identical language to *Oak Park Development*, strongly suggesting that there are currently five elements to the cause of action. Second, the case stated that there can be tortious interference with a terminable-at-will contract. This is consistent with *Oak Park Development*, indicating that contrary statements in *RJM* and in *Hough Transit* are no longer good law. Third, in commenting upon the "intentional interference" element of the cause of action, the *J.N.R.* court stated that a plaintiff may show that "the defendant induced a third party to breach the [relevant] contract, *or* that the defendant intentionally interfered with the plaintiff's contractual rights by *committing an independent tort.*" (Emphasis added.) The court stated that the presence of the defamation claim in the case meant the plaintiff might go forward.

Can you now predict with some reasonable certainty what the rule of law is regarding the elements of a tortious-interference-with-contract claim, assuming the relevant universe of cases consists of the four with which we have been working? Yes. You can say with some confidence that there is such a cause of action that currently consists of five defined elements. The cause of action is likely available even in cases involving terminable-at-will contracts. You can predict, again with some confidence, that a Minnesota court will permit an action to go forward, even in a case where the defendant technically does not procure an actual breach of a terminable-at-will contract, so long as the defendant's conduct is independently wrongful. Examples of such independently wrongful conduct likely include defamation and theft of trade secrets. In our one case where the cause of action did go forward, there was such alleged improper conduct (defamation). In our three cases where the defendant won, there was not.

Step 4: Test your conclusions against the reasoning of the authorities and common-sense policy considerations. Does our extraction of the relevant rules from the above cases make sense? Yes. In the rough-and-tumble commercial arena, all kinds of activities by competitors may "interfere" with existing contracts involving other players in business. If the courts called all of the interferences "tortious," the courts would be deluged with claims, and legitimate competition would be discouraged. What, then, do the courts really seek to prevent? They seek to prevent persons from inducing breaches of contract. They also seek to discourage independently wrongful conduct such as defamation and theft. Therefore, the claim elements should mirror those concerns. In our formulation of the legal rules, they do.

Template for assembling a rule from multiple cases:

➤ Start with the most recent, most authoritative case.

➤ What does that case say the relevant legal rule is, and what result occurred?

➤ Square the rule and the result with the other cases.

➤ Test your conclusions against the reasoning of the authorities and common-sense policy considerations.

Some lawyers find it helpful to create a chart to reflect the analysis. This gives them a visual picture of the development of the law. Consider what a chart might look like in the abstract, and then we will apply it to the tortious interference scenario in particular.

1.   Sample Hypothetical Cases Chart

Assume a matter that you will resolve by applying the law from four hypothetical precedents in a given state. Two of the precedents are state supreme court opinions from 1999 and 2004, respectively. The other two precedents are intermediate court of appeals opinions from 2002 and 2005, respectively. Assume that the opinions all discuss a legal rule containing three elements. You plot the opinions in a chart that looks something like the following:

	CASE 1	CASE 2	CASE 3	CASE 4
Court	State Supreme Court	State Court of Appeals	State Supreme Court	State Court of Appeals
Year	1999	2002	2004	2005
Result	Defendant wins	Defendant wins	Plaintiff wins	Defendant wins
Legal Rule	A claim for relief exists if: Element 1 Element 2 Element 3	A claim for relief exists if: Element 1 Element 2 Element 3	A claim for relief exists if: Element 1 Element 2 Element 3	A claim for relief exists if: Element 1 Element 2 Element 3
Facts	Facts favor the plaintiff on Elements 2 and 3, but not Element 1	Facts favor the plaintiff on Elements 1 and 3, but not Element 2	Facts favor the plaintiff on Elements 1, 2, and 3	Facts favor the plaintiff on Elements 1 and 2, but not Element 3

What does the chart indicate? It suggests that the legal rule to resolve your problem is well settled—all of the four existing precedents identify and apply the same three-element legal test. It indicates that each of the three elements is a necessary part of the test. In the one case where the plaintiff won, the facts supported the plaintiff on each of the three elements of the test. On the other hand, in each and every other case where the plaintiff lost, the facts favored the defendant on one of the three elements. The logical conclusion is that the legal elements are connected by "ands." The plaintiff needs to prove Element 1 *and* Element 2 *and* Element 3. The matrix is simple, and it provides a convenient picture of how the rule operates. At this point, you would go back and insert "*ands*" into the chart of the legal rule, if you had not already placed them in the outline.

Now, to give you a sense of how such a chart might be helpful in a more complex scenario, suppose a different set of five precedents. All of the precedents are state supreme court opinions. Each is from a different year. Assume that the opinions all discuss a legal rule containing three elements but do not clearly state whether all of the elements are required. You plot the opinions in a chart that looks something like this:

	CASE 1	CASE 2	CASE 3	CASE 4	CASE 5
Court	State Supreme Court	State Supreme Court	State Supreme Court	State Supreme Court	State Supreme Court
Year	1998	1999	2002	2004	2005
Result	Plaintiff wins	Plaintiff wins	Defendant wins	Plaintiff wins	Defendant wins
Legal Rule	A claim for relief exists if: Element 1 Element 2 Element 3	A claim for relief exists if: Element 1 Element 2 Element 3	A claim for relief exists if: Element 1 Element 2 Element 3	A claim for relief exists if: Element 1 Element 2 Element 3	A claim for relief exists if: Element 1 Element 2 Element 3
Facts	Facts favor the plaintiff on Elements 1, 2, and 3.	Facts favor the plaintiff on Elements 1 and 2. Facts favor the defendant on Element 3.	Facts favor the plaintiff on Elements 2 and 3. Facts favor the defendant on Element 1.	Facts favor the plaintiff on Elements 1 and 3. Facts favor the defendant on Element 2.	Facts favor the plaintiff on Element 1. Facts favor the defendant on Elements 2 and 3.

Using your chart, what would you conclude? All of the cases recite that the relevant legal rule contains three elements. So the "law" appears well-settled. And yet it looks as if not all of the elements have the same import.

Let's consider each element in turn. Element 1 is an important component of the rule. That element was discussed in all five cases. The facts favored the plaintiff on Element 1 in all three cases where the plaintiff won. And the only time the facts favored the defendant on Element 1, the defendant won the case even though both of Elements 2 and 3 favored the plaintiff. Element 1 is materially important to the results. Plaintiff must prove it to win.

Is winning on Element 1 sufficient by itself to produce an overall victory for the plaintiff? No. In every case in which plaintiff won, the facts also favored the plaintiff on at least one other additional element. Moreover, defendant won the case where the facts favored plaintiff on Element 1 but the facts favored the defendant on the other two elements.

What about Elements 2 and 3? They do appear to be part of the rule. They are discussed in all five cases. And plaintiff cannot win unless the facts favor plaintiff on at least one of those two elements. If defendant prevails on both of Elements 2 and 3, defendant wins.

So how do you explain what you see in the chart, for purposes of solving the client's problem? The legal rule appears to be a kind of balancing test. Element 1 is materially significant. Plaintiff needs to satisfy Element 1 to win. In addition, plaintiff needs one more of the two other elements, thereby prevailing on a majority of the three elements. You now need to insert an *"and"* after Element 1 in the chart, and then to indent the two other elements and insert an "or" between them, if you have not already placed the connectors in the outline.

2. Tortious Interference Cases Chart

How might a chart look in the tortious interference cases? One possibility follows:

	RJM SALES	*HOUGH*	*OAK PARK*	*J.N.R. ENTER.*
Court	D. Minn.	Minn. App.	Minn. App.	Minn. App. (unpublished)
Year	1982	1991	1993	1999
Result	Defendant wins	Defendant wins	Defendant wins	Plaintiff wins (against summary judgment)
Legal Rule	No tort liability for interference with terminable at will contract. Hint: Possible liability for concomitant, unconscionable conduct.	No tort liability for interference with terminable at will contract. Hint: Possible liability for improper enticement.	A claim for relief exists if: 1. a contract 2. tortfeasor knowledge of contract 3. intentional interference 4. without justification 5. damages Possible claim if terminable at will contract.	A claim for relief exists if: 1. a contract 2. wrongdoer knowledge of contract 3. intentional interference 4. without justification 5. damages Possible claim if terminable at will contract. Claim if D. procures breach or commits independent tort.
Facts and Reasoning	D. hires away one of P.'s terminable at will employees.	D. hires away one of P.'s terminable at will drivers.	D. delays signing agreement. But not clear delay caused	D. mfr. terminates P. as distributor. Co-D. other distributor

	No bad conduct.	No improper conduct.	third-party to walk away from terminable at will lease with P.	allegedly defames P. Causes termination? No breach of contract because contract terminable at will, but possible independent tort of defamation?

So now, what advice do you give your real estate agency client? Likely you state something along these lines: In theory, hiring away the competitor's sales agent could constitute "tortious interference" with contract under current law. The two latest cases recognize there may be interference with a terminable at will contract, and one of the cases allowed a claim by a plaintiff to proceed. However, because the agent's contract with the competitor is terminable at will by either party, the hiring of the agent does not procure a breach of the contract. When the hiring does not procure a breach of an existing contract, there is no tortious interference unless the hiring is accompanied by other wrongful conduct, such as theft of trade secrets. So if the agency hires the competitor's agent, the agency must make sure that in the employment agreement and in practice the agency takes visible steps to ensure that the new agent does not reveal to the agency any information that the competitor might consider a trade secret, such as information about specific prospective clients or about proprietary computer systems.

B. COMMON MISTAKES IN ASSEMBLING A RULE FROM MULTIPLE CASES

Try to avoid the following mistakes when assembling rules.

1. Common Mistake No. 1: Assuming That a Legal Rule Is Consistent Across Multiple Cases

Look for subtle (and sometimes not-so-subtle) additions to and subtractions from legal rules—even where courts say nothing expressly about those. It is important to take the multiple cases, place them side-by-side, and compare their facts, their rule statements, and their results. If the winner in case number 2 could not have won under the elements of the rule announced in case number 1, then the rules in the two cases *are* different, whether the courts have bothered to say so or not.

2. Common Mistake No. 2: Failing to Focus on the Dates of Decisions

In general, recent authority trumps older authority. But note that pairing an older decision with a recent decision can be an effective way to demonstrate the continued vitality of a long-standing, venerable rule.

3.   Common Mistake No. 3: Failing to Focus on Court Hierarchy

In general, supreme court authority trumps intermediate appellate court authority, which in turn trumps trial court authority.[2]

4.   Common Mistake No. 4: Failing to Focus on Binding Authority

Recall from Chapter 3 that only the decisions of the courts in your jurisdiction can be mandatory authority. The decisions of the courts in other jurisdictions are merely persuasive. If the question you are analyzing is a matter of state law, only the decisions of the state courts in that state can be binding. If the question you are analyzing is a matter of federal law, only the decisions of the United States Supreme Court, federal court of appeals for your circuit, and the federal district court in your district can be binding. You cannot ignore binding authority merely because you like a particular persuasive authority better.[3]

Instead, as a competent advocate for your client, you will provide the judge the binding authority that supports your client's position. Recognize, however, that most jurisdictions also require lawyers to notify the judge of controlling authority that supports the opposing position. A lawyer is required to disclose to the court "legal authority in the controlling jurisdiction known to the lawyer to be directly adverse" to the position the lawyer is advocating, even if the opposing counsel has not cited to this authority.[4] Thus, adverse authority in the controlling jurisdiction must be mentioned and addressed. Often when the lawyer's role as an advocate and as an officer of the court are in conflict, the lawyer's duty to the court will prevail. The overarching principle is the need to protect the integrity of the judicial process.[5]

C.   ASSEMBLING RULES IN CASES OF FIRST IMPRESSION

As you have already seen, courts often announce slightly different legal rules when resolving a case. Usually, this difference represents the evolution of the law over time. Because every case involves different facts, a court's application of the law to the facts will be different in every case. But you can still determine the rule by following the four steps and the template for assembling a rule from multiple cases discussed above. Sometimes, however, you may face a legal issue on which there is no prior authority in your jurisdiction.[6] If so, you must formulate a proposed rule from persuasive authorities in other jurisdictions. The court's decision in *Horner v. Rowan Companies, Inc.*, 153 F.R.D. 597 (S.D. Tex. 1994), is a good example of the kind of analysis you will need to prepare and communicate.

Assume that you are a lawyer representing a client in a car accident case. Your client wants you to interview the doctor who examined the other party for injury. Your client wants you to conduct the interview ex parte, meaning that the other party's lawyer will not

---

[2]   The terminology can be confusing. In New York, for example, the name of the highest court is the New York Court of Appeals. New York Supreme Court, General Term, is actually the name given to trial courts. So you need to become familiar with the terminology in the specific jurisdiction whose law you are analyzing.

[3]   Note that the question of mandatory versus persuasive authority can become quite complex in various circumstances. For example, assume that a client wants you to analyze a Minnesota contract. You find a Minnesota Supreme Court case involving similar facts that applied Michigan contract law to an agreement between a Minnesota resident and a Michigan resident. Is the Minnesota Supreme Court decision mandatory authority for your problem? Not really, in the sense that, although the question involved a matter of state law, and the Minnesota Supreme Court is the highest court in the state, the decision applied Michigan law, and is thus merely persuasive authority for your problem.

[4]   MODEL RULES OF PROF'L CONDUCT R. 3.3(2) (2016).

[5]   *Id*. at cmt. 2.

[6]   For example, either the court must interpret a statutory provision for the first time, or the court has never addressed an issue governed by the common law.

be present. You are uneasy about doing this, and you research the law in your jurisdiction to see if any court decisions address the propriety of this type of interview. You find no cases. How would you advise the client?

Review the excerpted *Horner* opinion below (from which we have omitted various footnotes, citations, and other materials). The court employed the basic template for analyzing a case of first impression.

Horner v. Rowan Companies, Inc.
153 F.R.D. 597 (S.D. Tex. 1994)

[Authors' note: The issue in *Horner* was whether and when defense counsel, in litigation conducted under the Federal Rules of Civil Procedure, may engage in an ex parte interview of a plaintiff's treating physician. The plaintiff filed his case under the Jones Act and federal maritime law for personal injury. The plaintiff had signed a broad medical release form. Relying on that form, the defendant's lawyers cancelled depositions of the plaintiff's treating physicians, and instead conducted ex parte interviews of them without informing plaintiff's lawyers of the latter. The plaintiff's lawyers filed a motion for sanctions against the defendant's lawyers. The federal magistrate judge assigned to the case had to decide the motion for sanctions.]

[T]he propriety of ex parte interviews of a plaintiff's treating physician by defense counsel is an unanswered question in this Circuit. The question, however, is not a new one, and of the numerous courts that have dealt with it there is no consensus. Accordingly, in its quest to establish the appropriate rule, while this Court lacks Circuit authority, it is not without the guidance and counsel of other jurists.

While the Federal Rules of Civil Procedure provide certain specific discovery devices, it is clear that no federal procedural rule explicitly permits or prohibits ex parte interviews between defendants and plaintiff's treating physicians. . . . [F]ederal courts that have dealt directly with this issue seem to be split. . . .

. . .

In reviewing and evaluating the various decisions, this Court has come to the conclusion that the appropriate rule should prohibit private ex parte interviews between defense counsel and plaintiff's treating physicians unless, with advance notice thereof, plaintiff specifically and unconditionally authorizes same; this is the only way in which physician patient privilege can be held inviolate.

The physician/patient privilege is recognized by Texas Rule of Evidence 509 and is adopted for use in this forum pursuant to Federal Rule of Evidence 501. . . . Quite candidly, case law and Texas Rule 509(d)(4) create an exception, or statutory waiver, of the privilege, but only as to communications or records *relevant* to the issue of a plaintiff's medical condition when litigation relative to that condition is instituted. Therefore, while there is conflicting authority, in order to preserve the integrity of the physician/patient privilege, a defendant must be limited to the formal methods of discovery enumerated by the Rules of Civil Procedure, absent the plaintiff's *express* consent to counsel's ex parte contact with his treating physicians. . . .

Unacceptable problems are inherently attendant to a contrary view. When a treating physician is interviewed ex parte by defense counsel, there are no safeguards against the revelation of matters irrelevant to the lawsuit and personally damaging to the patient, and the potential for breaches in confidentiality can have a chilling effect upon the critically important underlying relationship. Such interviews also create situations which invite questionable conduct. . . .

In answering your own question, consider the following reasoning sequence.

Step 1: Determine that the relevant jurisdiction has not previously decided the legal issue. You always begin, of course, with the binding authorities in your own jurisdiction. In *Horner*, there were relevant procedural rules codifying physician-patient privilege, and cases interpreting waiver of that privilege, but none directly on point as to the interface between privilege waiver and ex parte interviews.

Step 2: Canvass the authorities in other jurisdictions. The authorities are merely persuasive in your setting, but they are nonetheless informative. As you canvass the authorities in other jurisdictions, pay special attention to the reasoning those authorities used to support "the rule" they chose and applied. For your purposes, the reasoning is at least as important as "the rule" because, in your jurisdiction, there is no rule (or interpretation of a rule) on point. Thus, a rule choice (that you are predicting a court will follow or advocating that a court ought to adopt) and the reasoning supporting that rule choice will need to be discussed fully.

Step 3: Determine whether there is a split of authority. Sometimes, it appears that the jurisdictions have adopted different rules or different interpretations of the same rule. First, consider whether the apparent conflict in the rules announced in the cases is a real conflict. There is a possibility, for example, that one (or more) of the courts in an apparent direct conflict did not consider the relevant rule in question to be central to the decision. Another possibility is that the cases can be distinguished upon their material facts. Thus, the apparent conflict in rules is not a genuine one. Rather, one rule applies in one fact setting, and a different rule applies in a different fact setting. (In general, facts drive the law.)

Step 4: If there is a genuine, direct conflict, then is one opinion more deliberate and reasoned on the relevant point than the other is? The discussion in one decision may be more extensive, explore policy to a greater degree, compare and contrast more authority from other jurisdictions, and generally demonstrate a fuller analysis than the other.

Step 5: If there is a genuine, direct conflict, then which opinion announces a rule that is more favorable to the resolution of your client's problem? If there is a genuine, direct conflict in authority in other jurisdictions that cannot easily be explained away, you should identify and discuss the split. That is the honest way to proceed. It also gives credibility to your ultimate suggestion as to what the relevant legal rule to resolve your problem should be. But then propose as the correct rule the formulation that most helps your client. You are not obligated to vote against yourself, as long as you are honest about the potential debate.

Step 6: Analyze policy considerations. The law exists to balance policy choices in resolving problems. Legal rules are always backed by policy considerations. So, in the case of two directly competing legal rule choices, which one of the formulations makes the most policy sense? Especially in a case of first impression, your formulation of the relevant legal rule has to make sense from a policy standpoint. You cannot just say, "Apply the rule that our court of appeals tells us to apply." There is no such rule yet. Note that this may require you to review earlier decisions for explanations of relevant policies. The earlier decisions may give you insight into changing legal conditions, trends, and the like.

Step 7: Balance the policy considerations to articulate a rule. In *Horner*, for example, the court struggled to balance two competing concerns. On the one hand, the court wanted to protect doctor-patient relationships by not opening the door to defense lawyers prying into sensitive information irrelevant to a given lawsuit. On the other hand, the court wanted to preserve the right of a defendant to obtain information to defend itself. The legal compromise the court reached was to hold that a defendant can use formal discovery devices to obtain information and informal interviews if the plaintiff consents. Without the plaintiff's consent, informal interviews are forbidden.

Template for assembling rules in cases of first impression:

➢ Determine there are no cases on point in your jurisdiction.

➢ Canvass the authorities in the other jurisdictions.

➢ Is there a split of authority?

➢ Is one opinion more deliberate and considered?

➢ Which case is more favorable? In persuasive writing, focus on why the court ought to adopt a particular rule.

➢ Analyze the policy considerations.

➢ Balance the policy considerations to articulate a rule.

Thus, in your circumstances, advise your client that the courts are split. Advise your client that, in light of no direct precedent in your jurisdiction, reasonable lawyers may reach different conclusions concerning the propriety of ex parte interviews of treating physicians. Advise your client that the conservative approach would be for the questioning of the doctor in your case to proceed through formal procedures.

D. CONCLUSION

The steps in Chapters 4, 5, and 6 will help you understand how to assemble and disassemble legal rules. The steps are useful in a wide variety of contexts, and are the building blocks of legal analysis.

CHAPTER 7

Basic Organizing Principles in Legal Analysis and Writing

There are several ways to structure your thinking about legal problems to facilitate solving the problems and presenting the analysis to readers. One approach is well known under the acronym IRAC, which stands for Introduction, Rule, Application, and Conclusion.[1] Properly understood and executed, the IRAC formula: introduces the issue and the conclusion, identifies the governing rules, analyzes the problem in light of the rules and the client's facts, and concludes the analysis. This formula helps to communicate the solution and the analysis because it provides a basic framework that is audience focused and reader friendly.[2]

Moreover, the IRAC formula is consistent with the syllogism paradigm so common to legal argument.[3] As you may recall from your undergraduate education, a syllogism 삼단논법 consists of a major premise, a minor premise, and a conclusion that flows as a logical consequence from the premises. One of the most classic examples of a syllogism is the following:

Major Premise:	All men are mortal.
Minor Premise:	Socrates was a man.
Conclusion:	Therefore, Socrates was mortal.

In the legal context, the major premise is the rule; the minor premise consists of the facts; and the resolution is the conclusion. This is oversimplified. But syllogisms can be

---

[1]   Because so many legal writing professionals have written about the IRAC formula and similar analytical paradigms, much of our discussion in this chapter is necessarily derivative. We gratefully acknowledge those colleagues whose discussions of IRAC and IRAC-type formula helped shape and refine our own views: CHARLES R. CALLEROS, LEGAL METHOD AND WRITING (7th ed. Wolters Kluwer 2014); LINDA HOLDEMAN EDWARDS, LEGAL WRITING: PROCESS, ANALYSIS, ORGANIZATION (6th ed. Wolters Kluwer 2014); RICHARD K. NEUMANN, JR., LEGAL REASONING AND LEGAL WRITING (7th ed. Wolters Kluwer 2013); DIANA V. PRATT, LEGAL WRITING: A SYSTEMATIC APPROACH (5th ed. 2015); NANCY L. SCHULTZ & LOUIS J. SIRICO, JR., LEGAL WRITING & OTHER LAWYERING SKILLS (6th ed. Wolters Kluwer 2014); and CHRISTINA KUNZ & DEBORAH SCHMEDEMANN, SYNTHESIS: LEGAL READING, REASONING, AND WRITING (4th ed. Wolters Kluwer 2014).

[2]   The IRAC formula is not the exclusive device for thinking about and presenting a legal analysis, nor is it without controversy. Critics complain that it is too formulaic, overly simplistic, rigid, and misleading; advocates claim it is flexible, adaptable, and a powerful organizing tool. Christina Kunz & Deborah Schmedemann, *Point/Counterpoint: Use of IRAC-type Formulas—Desirable or Dangerous?*, 10 THE SECOND DRAFT 1–20 (Nov. 1995) (bulletin of the Leg. Writing Inst.).

[3]   For an in-depth and informative discussion of how syllogistic reasoning is similar to legal reasoning, see Steven D. Jamar, *Aristotle Teaches Persuasion: The Psychic Connection*, 8 SCRIBES J. LEG. WRITING 61 (2001–2002). *See also,* Amy E. Sloan, *Erasing Lines: Integrating the Law School Curriculum*, 1 J. ALWD 3, 3–4 & n. 4 (2002) (discussing how syllogisms and the IRAC formula are taught as a problem-solving methodology). For a discussion of how to use syllogistic reasoning in crafting all legal arguments, see JAMES A. GARDNER, LEGAL ARGUMENT: THE STRUCTURE AND LANGUAGE OF EFFECTIVE ADVOCACY (2d ed. 2007).

expressed through an IRAC structure. Syllogisms are discussed in more detail later in this chapter.

An additional benefit of the IRAC formula is that it is suitable for both predictive and persuasive writing. Predictive writing is often used in memoranda and client letters to predict to another lawyer or a client how a court is likely to rule on a particular issue. Persuasive writing is often used in documents submitted to a court, usually to persuade the court to rule favorably. The IRAC formula can be used for both types of writing because both involve arguments. Predictive writing presents the arguments objectively, and arguments in persuasive writing are presented through advocacy.

Finally, the IRAC formula works at macro and micro organizational levels. The IRAC formula is best explained at the macro level in the context of the more common types of documents lawyers prepare: office memoranda, client letters, and trial and appellate briefs.[4] In each of these documents, the lawyer must introduce the problem to be resolved, explain the relevant rule that governs the problem, apply the rule to the client's facts, and provide the conclusion. In this respect, the analysis section of a memorandum, the body of a client letter, and the argument sections of a trial brief and an appellate brief contain a macro IRAC.

Often, however, there are multiple problems—or issues—that must be addressed. Each discrete issue, sub-issue, or element can usually be presented in a micro IRAC formula. Discrete IRACs must be carefully meshed together using guides for the reader. More will be said later about these micro IRACs.

All of these reasons account for the IRAC formula's continued vitality. A key to its proper use is to know the basic IRAC components and how to adapt them for different types of legal reasoning and legal problems. It is also important to remember that the IRAC formula is an organizational tool that should embody your analysis. It does not determine your analysis. With these points in mind, you can capitalize on the IRAC formula's strengths while minimizing its limitations. The remainder of this chapter discusses how to work with the IRAC formula in both predictive and persuasive writing.

The basic components described below are intended to apply to the analysis section of a memorandum, body of a client letter, and argument sections of trial and appellate briefs. Although we discuss below the IRAC components and how to adapt them, the discussion is unavoidably abstract, even with simple examples. You must practice working with the IRAC components in the context of solving legal problems. Mastering the IRAC formula, like much of legal analysis and writing, is an acquired skill. If you would like to see a picture of what an IRAC might look like in practice before you read the discussion below, review the outline on page 73 of this chapter, and review the examples in Chapters 10 and 11.[5]

LEARNING OBJECTIVES

1. Students will know how to structure their legal analysis using the IRAC formula.

2. Students will understand how deductive reasoning, as a type of syllogism, can be used in their legal analysis.

---

[4]   There are many other types of documents that lawyers prepare, including transactional documents like contracts, but our focus is on the most typical documents explored within a first-year legal writing course as vehicles to communicate the resolution to a problem.

[5]   You may also want to refer back to Chapter 1, which covers road mapping. Note the use of an IRAC formula in constructing the overview of the analysis in *Bears v. Gold*.

3. Students will understand how analogical reasoning can be used in their legal analysis.

4. Students will learn how to incorporate counter arguments into their legal analysis using the IRAC structure.

A. IRAC: THE BASIC COMPONENTS

1. Introduction

The first step in analyzing and presenting a legal analysis is to identify the issue—the problem that must be solved. The introductory section also states a conclusion to the issue, unless there is a specific reason not to do so. The legal reading audience *does not want to wait* in suspense to see how the analytical story ends—or how the problem is resolved. Sometimes this purpose is accomplished by combining the issue and conclusion into a thesis statement. Either way, the audience wants to know the answer. Identifying the problem without identifying a solution is less than fully satisfactory.

There is also a practical reason for including the conclusion. You want your reader to *understand* where your analysis is headed. By stating your conclusion in your introduction of the issue, the reader can more easily follow the reasoning you present later in the application section of the IRAC.

Introductions in both predictive and persuasive legal writing may also contain general background information for context. Additionally, for a multi-issue analysis, the introduction may include a basic overview of the analysis or argument that follows. In developing your introductions, consider the following questions.

➢   Is the problem you are analyzing clearly stated, either as an issue or as a thesis statement?

➢   Is the conclusion stated, either separately from the issue or in the thesis statement?

➢   If a fairly lengthy analysis will follow, is a brief factual background discussion required to provide context for understanding the analysis that follows?

➢   Are there several rules or elements that will be provided, explained, and applied in the rule and application sections, requiring a general overview of the analysis?

➢   Is there any other reason to expand the introduction so as to assist the reader in following your analysis?

The following examples demonstrate the basic composition of each section of the IRAC formula. They are based on an office memorandum analyzing whether a dog owner will be liable for a dog bite under Michigan Compiled Laws § 287.351, where the applicable rule is "not at issue." "Not at issue" means that the parties agree as to the matter. Here, they agree that the dispute is governed by § 287.351.

Further assume that the following facts are undisputed: Mr. Wade Smith owns a mixed breed dog. The dog has a mild disposition and has not previously bitten anyone. A month ago, Mr. Smith invited the Johnson family over for a barbeque. Both Mr. Smith and the Johnsons have two young children. The four children were playing tag in the yard. One of the Johnson children, Selena, accidentally stepped on the dog while it was sleeping. The dog jumped up and bit Selena on the calf.

Assume that you are a summer associate at a law firm and a partner has asked that you research whether Mr. Smith will likely be liable for Ms. Johnson's injuries. After your research, you conclude that Mr. Smith is not liable.[6] Your thesis statement might look something like this:

> Mr. Wade Smith, the dog owner, is not liable to Selena Johnson for her dog-bite injuries.

In the above example, the introduction captures the issue (Is Mr. Wade Smith liable for the injuries caused by his dog) and the conclusion (No). But as the reader do you want to know why? The statement in the example above is a thesis statement. It states a conclusion to the issue. It could be followed by a very brief reason why, which would also give some factual context for the reader.

> Mr. Wade Smith, the dog owner, is not liable to Selena Johnson for her dog-bite injuries because Ms. Johnson provoked the dog. Ms. Johnson inadvertently stepped on the sleeping dog when she was playing tag.

The above example is a thesis statement with a statement of factual context that expands the thesis statement. But how was it determined that provoking the dog matters? A thesis statement often incorporates the relevant part of the rule. To craft an informative thesis statement, the writer must know and understand the governing rule. Sometimes, a writer will first draft the issue to ensure that the writer understands the legal issue. The writer will wait to draft the conclusion or thesis statement after drafting the rest of the IRAC, when the writer has a better understanding of how the problem is resolved under the rule.

2. Rule

The legal writer must next provide the governing rule. This sounds simple enough in theory, but it can be fairly complex in practice because there are a number of considerations. In predictive and persuasive legal writing, the legal writer must demonstrate why the rule governs the problem and must provide an explanation of how the rule works. The former can sometimes be done through citation to the rule, especially when the rule is mandatory in the jurisdiction. At other times, a discussion of the source of the rule, and its persuasive value, may be necessary.

In general, when there is a statutory or common law rule to apply, but it is "not at issue," then the rule section of the IRAC template may be short. All that may be required is a quotation or a paraphrase of the relevant rule and a citation demonstrating that it governs the problem. But often an explanation of the rule is necessary. The rule explanation can be fairly straightforward, discussing one or more courts' interpretation of the rule. Or, the explanation can be quite elaborate, involving synthesizing various cases to determine the scope and the proper interpretation of the rule.

a. Quote the Rule

In crafting a rule section, it is best to begin with a general statement of the rule and then move to more specific statements of the rule. For this dog-bite hypothetical, the writer

---

[6] We recommend that before proceeding you read the full IRAC for this hypothetical provided as a sample memorandum in Chapter 10. Seeing the full IRAC will help you better understand the component parts and their relationship to each other.

would first quote the relevant statutory section. Here is what the rule looks like on the Michigan Legislature website[*]:

LIABILITY OF OWNER FOR DOG BITE (EXCERPT)
Act 73 of 1939

287.351 Person bitten by dog; liability of owner.

Sec. 1.

(1) If a dog bites a person, without provocation while the person is on public property, or lawfully on private property, including the property of the owner of the dog, the owner of the dog shall be liable for any damages suffered by the person bitten, regardless of the former viciousness of the dog or the owner's knowledge of such viciousness.

(2) A person is lawfully on the private property of the owner of the dog within the meaning of this act if the person is on the owner's property in the performance of any duty imposed upon him or her by the laws of this state or by the laws or postal regulations of the United States, or if the person is on the owner's property as an invitee or licensee of the person lawfully in possession of the property unless said person has gained lawful entry upon the premises for the purpose of an unlawful or criminal act.

History: 1939, Act 73, Imd. Eff. May 4, 1939 ;-- CL 1948, 287.351 ;-- Am. 1988, Act 142, Eff. Mar. 30, 1989

© 2015 Legislative Council, State of Michigan

The following is an example of how this rule could be quoted in a rule section of an IRAC:

> Michigan Compiled Laws Annotated § 287.351(1) (West 2003) governs when a dog owner will be liable for injuries caused by his or her dog. This statute states, in part, "If a dog bites a person, without provocation while the person is . . . lawfully on private property, including the property of the owner of the dog, the owner of the dog shall be liable for any damages suffered by the person bitten . . . ." *Id.*

It is a good idea to quote the legal rule. Quotations are discussed more fully in Chapter 9, but a couple of quick points can be mentioned here in context. First, you only have to include the body of the rule, so no title is needed. Second, you only have to quote the relevant portion of the rule. This point leads to the next. Once a quote begins, you must quote the original *exactly* or indicate any omission. So, you can delete any information from the beginning of a quote without indicating that omission, but once the quote begins you must use an ellipsis to indicate any deleted information.

The above quote contains two examples where information was deleted—in the middle of the quote and at the end. Under the facts of the hypothetical, there is no need to discuss being on public property because Ms. Johnson was on Mr. Smith's property when the dog bit her. Thus, the information about public property was deleted, and this omission was indicated with an ellipsis. Also, an ellipsis was included at the end of the statute because information regarding the viciousness of the dog was deleted. In the hypothetical, there was no indication that the dog was vicious (i.e. deliberately cruel or violent). Deleting this information would be a matter of preference. You could choose to keep it because you believe it leads to a better understanding of the rule. If you are uncertain whether information is relevant, it is generally better to quote more than less.

---

[*] Portions of this work are reproduced with permission of the copyright holder, the Michigan Legislative Council.

b.   Break Down the Rule

After quoting the rule, you would next break the rule down for the reader into its elements or otherwise explain the rule further to the reader as was explained in Chapters 3, 4, and 5. There are several elements to the Michigan dog-bite statute. There must be a lack of provocation. The person must lawfully be on the property when bitten, and there must be a dog owner. These elements come from the rule itself. Sometimes, however, courts interpret rules differently than an initial reading might suggest. It is required that you read cases interpreting the rule. Further, if possible, read a treatise or other trusted secondary source that discusses the rule.

When breaking the rule down for the reader, you can provide the elements in any order. Often it is best to list the elements in the order that they appear in the rule. But there are other possibilities. It may be that you set forth the elements by quoting or paraphrasing a case that lists the elements. In that situation, the elements would be listed in the order stated in the case law. Or you may want to first list those elements that are undisputed, listing the disputed element or elements last. After deciding the order, you may decide that two elements are so related that they should be viewed as one element. The example below treats the requirement of a dog bite and being lawfully on the premises as one element.

> To recover from a person for dog-bite injuries under this statute, the injured party must establish that the defendant owned the dog, that the dog bite occurred while the injured party was lawfully on the property, and that the dog was not provoked.

This example lists the undisputed elements first. Doing so facilitates moving to the next step—the discussion of the undisputed elements. So after providing the required elements of the rule, the legal writer would next use deductive reasoning to explain which elements are met under any undisputed facts.

c.   Explain the Undisputed Parts of the Rule

Deductive reasoning is similar to a syllogism. Where the rule (the major premise) is binding and where the relevant facts (the minor premise) are undisputed, then they are similar to true premises in a syllogism. In a syllogism, where the premises are true, then the conclusion can logically follow. In legal writing, where the rule is binding and the facts are undisputed, deductive reasoning can be used to support a conclusion.

Deductive reasoning can be seen as an additional step in explaining the rule because it demonstrates that some parts of a rule are not at issue. If, however, there is a question as to what the rule states, what the facts are, or how the rule applies to the facts, then deductive reasoning cannot be used. The premises would not necessarily be true, which is required for the conclusion to logically follow. In that situation, the reader must use analogical reasoning.

Analogical reasoning involves comparing and contrasting the current case with precedent cases where the court has applied the rule to a set of facts. This comparison is used to determine the scope of the rule and how it should be applied to the current facts. If possible, the legal writer starts with deductive reasoning.

In the dog-bite hypothetical, the rule is not at issue. Further, it is undisputed that Mr. Smith owned the dog, that Mr. Smith invited the Johnsons over for a barbeque, and that the dog bit Selena Johnson. In the following example, we repeated the elements of the rule so that the deductive reasoning is easier to see.

> To recover from a defendant for dog-bite injuries under this statute, the injured party must establish that defendant owned the dog, that the dog bite occurred while the injured party was lawfully on property, and that the dog was not provoked. The first element is met because Defendant Mr. Smith admits that he is the owner of the dog.

This deductive reasoning example is not in the order of a syllogism, but it supports the conclusion. To demonstrate the first element of the Michigan dog-bite statute in syllogism form:

1. Major premise (rule): Dog owners can be liable if their dogs bite.

2. Minor premise (facts): Mr. Smith owns the dog that bit Ms. Johnson.

3. Conclusion: Mr. Smith can be liable for Ms. Johnson's dog bite.

Recognize that all this syllogism or deductive reasoning establishes is that Mr. Smith is possibly liable because being a dog owner is only one of several elements. All of the remaining elements must be proven before he can be held liable. This point can be seen by crafting the following syllogism fallacy:

1. Major premise (rule): A dog owner *can* be liable if his or her dog bites.

2. Minor premise (facts): Mr. Smith owns the dog that bit Selena Johnson.

3. Conclusion: Mr. Smith *is* liable for Selena Johnson's injuries.

This is a syllogism fallacy because the conclusion is incorrect. Not only do the premises have to be true, but the conclusion must not deviate from the premises. Here where the major premise, the rule, states "can," the conclusion cannot state "is." Thus, the syllogism shows that the deductive reasoning would be unconvincing.

Having provided valid deductive reasoning for one element, the legal writer should continue to move the rule section forward by using deductive reasoning for all undisputed elements. Sometimes to do so, it will be necessary to reference other rules.

The second element of the Michigan dog-bite statute requires an injury that occurred while the injured party was lawfully on the property, and requires referencing other rules. The deductive reasoning could be presented as follows:

> The second element of the statute requires that the dog-bite occurred while the injured person was lawfully on the property. Michigan Compiled Laws Annotated § 287.351(2) defines when a person is lawfully on the property. It states, in part, "A person is lawfully on the private property of the owner of the dog within the meaning of this act . . . if the person is on the owner's property as an invitee or licensee of the person lawfully in possession of the property . . . ." Under Michigan law, a licensee "is a person who is privileged to enter the land of another by virtue of the possessor's consent." *Stitt v. Holland Abundant Life Fellowship*, 614 N.W.2d 88, 91 (Mich. 2000). It is undisputed that Mr. Smith gave the Johnsons permission to be on the property when he invited the Johnson family to his home for a barbeque. Consequently, Ms. Johnson was a licensee and was lawfully on Mr. Smith's property. Further, it is undisputed that Mr. Smith's dog bit Selena while she was on the property. Thus, the second element has also been met. The remaining element concerning provocation is the element that is at issue.

Notice a couple of things about this example. This deductive reasoning analysis required not only citing to the definition in the statute, but also citing to a case that defines a licensee in Michigan. Thus, while deductive reasoning can be straight forward, as it was for the first element, it can also require additional layers of analysis.

As previously stated, deductive reasoning can be used as long as there is no dispute as to the facts and the rules as stated. In other words, where the writer believes that there is no possible argument against using certain rules or facts, then deductive reasoning can be used to move the analysis forward to the part of the rule that is "at issue." "At issue" means that the parties disagree. Where the premises (the rule or the facts) are at issue and deductive reasoning cannot be used, analogical reasoning will be required.

Reviewing the examples given to this point, we started with a general statement of the rule and continued to move the analysis forward with more specific statements of the rule. Specifically, we quoted the rule, broke it into elements, and then used deductive reasoning to narrow the analysis to the element of the rule at issue. Now we are discussing a specific part of the rule—the element of provocation. Whether this element is met where the child accidently stepped on the dog is not clear under the rule. The rule does not define provocation. It is not clear whether provocation must be intentional or whether it can also be accidental. Consequently, analogical reasoning is required.

d.   Explain the Disputed Parts of the Rule

First, we must define provocation. We need a more specific statement of this element of the rule. There is no statutory definition, so we turn to the case law. The Michigan courts have defined provocation under this statute. Because a Michigan court, a primary authority, has defined the term, there would be no need to look for the term in secondary sources. The following is a screen shot from Westlaw's publication of a Michigan Court of Appeals case[*], *Brans v. Extrom*, in which the court stated,

> 5 6 7 8 The term "provocation" is not defined in the dog-bite statute. If the statute does not define a term, it is appropriate to consult a dictionary for definitions of statutory terms. *Peters v. Gunnell, Inc.*, 253 Mich.App. 211, 220, 655 N.W.2d 582 (2002). Black's Law Dictionary (4th ed) defines "provocation" as "[t]he act of inciting another to do a particular deed. That which arouses, moves, calls forth, causes, or occasions." The definition of "provocation" does not take into account the intent of the actor; rather, the definition focuses on the nature of the act itself and the relationship between that act and an outcome. Thus, an unintentional act could constitute provocation within the plain meaning of the statute because some actions, **166 regardless of intent, may be more than sufficient to relieve a dog owner of liability. Had the Legislature intended only an intentional act to bar recovery it could have so specified. See, e.g., MCL 287.321(1)(d) (for the purposes of the dangerous animal statute, " '[p]rovoke' means to perform a willful act or omission that an ordinary and reasonable person would conclude is likely to precipitate the bite or attack by an ordinary dog or animal"). Instead, it imposed liability on an owner of a dog who would attack or injure someone without provocation. The intent of the victim is immaterial.

701 N.W.2d 163, 165–66 (Mich. Ct. App. 2005). Thus, the Michigan Court of Appeals has defined the term, but you would not want to include this big block quote in your document. Big block quotes interrupt the flow of the text. Instead, paraphrase and quote some language. Here is one possibility:

---

[*]   Reprinted with permission from Thomson Reuters.

> The Michigan Court of Appeals has defined the term "provocation" in this statute as " '[t]he act of inciting another to do a particular deed. That which arouses, moves, calls forth, causes, or occasions.' " *Brans v. Extrom*, 701 N.W.2d 163, 165–66 (Mich. Ct. App. 2005) (quoting Black's Law Dictionary (4th ed.)). Using this definition, the court determined that intentional as well as unintentional acts could constitute provocation. *Brans*, 701 N.W.2d at 165.

Note a couple of things regarding this example. First, the Michigan Court of Appeals relied on Black's Law Dictionary, a secondary source. Once the court incorporates the definition into its analysis, that definition now comes from a primary source, the Michigan court opinion, as opposed to a secondary source. Second, if you quote language that is quoting another source, you must indicate that fact and list that source in your citation. Third, when you paraphrase, you still must provide a citation and a pinpoint cite to where that information is located in the original.

We would continue providing specific information regarding the term, "provocation" if it were available from other binding sources. There is a subsequent Michigan Court of Appeals opinion that agreed with the *Brans* court's definition of provocation. One more sentence might be added to the rule explanation paragraph above:

> A subsequent Michigan Court of Appeals decision agreed with this interpretation of provocation. *Koivisto v. Davis*, 745 N.W.2d 824, 827 (Mich. Ct. App. 2008).

We could then further define the rule for the reader by looking to Michigan cases where the court has applied this statute to the facts of a case and reached a conclusion as to whether the provocation element was met. These fact-specific applications of the rule can be called fact-specific holdings.

A fact-specific holding is the court's holding stated in one or two sentences that incorporates the rule and the facts that the court relied upon. The fact-specific holding states how a court applied the rule under a given set of facts. It is a specific application of the rule and thus, a specific statement of the rule. Fact-specific holdings can be viewed as part of the rule section of an IRAC, as a transition between the rule section and the application section of an IRAC, or as part of the application section of the IRAC. Your legal writing professor will likely have specific views on this placement issue. So, follow that advice. For this example, we are placing the fact-specific holdings in the rule section.

There are two Michigan cases where the courts applied the provocation element to the facts of the case and reached a conclusion. The writer could choose to discuss the cases together to explain the rule or discuss them separately. We have chosen to discuss them together, and the concluding part of the rule section could be written as follows:

> Under this definition, the court in *Brans* held that the owner was not liable because the plaintiff provoked the dog when she inadvertently stepped on the dog's tail. 701 N.W.2d at 166–167. The court in *Koivisto* agreed with the rule set forth in *Brans*, but determined that the plaintiff had not provoked the dogs that were viciously attacking her cats, because the dogs were already in a provoked state. *Koivisto*, 745 N.W.2d at 829.

These fact-specific holdings would end the rule section analysis. They are the most specific statement of the rule. The writer would then move to an application of the rule and the precedent cases to the instant facts, which will be discussed in the next section concerning the application section of an IRAC. But first, a few more points regarding the rule section analysis.

There are a number of settings where the relevant legal rule is the focus of challenge. One common example arises when a legal rule is ambiguous and is susceptible to multiple competing interpretations. In such a scenario, the rule section in the IRAC template will often be fairly elaborate. It would be necessary to discuss cases where the courts have interpreted that rule in different ways. The courts' reasoning supporting their interpretation of the rule would be the focus of that discussion.

Another common example arises when a court must adopt a particular rule among competing rules. This situation most typically arises in the context of issues of first impression. In this setting, it is helpful to have an expansive rule section that focuses on the courts' reasons for adopting a specific rule and the policy considerations supporting that rule. Examples of more elaborate rule sections are provided in Chapter 10 and 11.

Rule sections often require multi-layered explanations, incorporating deductive reasoning and analogical reasoning to complete the rule explanation. A common problem for novice legal writers is incomplete rule sections. An incomplete rule section will result in an incomplete application section. The rule section is the foundation for the application section. To avoid this problem, determine how much more information you must supply for the reader to understand the rule. As you work through your legal writing problems, you will become proficient at determining the depth of treatment of the rule required in various contexts. Here is a list of questions to help you get started.

Does the rule come from enacted law?

➢ Is there more than one rule that must be discussed?

➢ Do any of the relevant rules have multiple elements? Does each element need to be discussed separately?

➢ Are there any rules or elements of the rules that are "not at issue" and can be satisfied using deductive reasoning?

➢ Do any of the rules or elements of the rules need to be explained by demonstrating how other courts have applied them in similar factual contexts? If so, what are the fact-specific holdings from those courts?

➢ Are any of the terms ambiguous? How have the courts interpreted those ambiguous terms and why?

➢ Are there competing rules that may govern? Which rule or rules are more likely to govern and why?

➢ Do any of the rules or elements of the rule need to be explained by introducing policy considerations—either by the legislative or administrative body that enacted the rule or the judicial body that interpreted and applied it?

Does the rule come from the common law?

➢ Are any cases controlling, i.e., mandatory authority? How will you demonstrate that those cases are binding? How will you set forth that binding rule?

➢ If there are not any binding cases in your jurisdiction, how will you demonstrate that the cases used are persuasive to the issue? How will you set forth that persuasive rule?

- ➢ If the rule has evolved from a series of cases, how will you synthesize the cases to formulate a statement of the rule?

- ➢ Are there policy implications that need to be discussed?

Is this an issue of first impression for the court?

- ➢ How has the court decided similar issues?

- ➢ How have courts in other jurisdictions decided the issue?

- ➢ Is there a "majority" and "minority" rule or interpretation?

- ➢ What was the reasoning of the courts in adopting one rule or interpretation over another?

- ➢ How does this reasoning help in determining which rule or interpretation your jurisdiction will adopt (in predictive writing) or ought to adopt (in persuasive writing)?

3. Application

The legal writer must apply the rule to the facts of the problem. Again, this sounds simple enough in the abstract, but, like the rule section, it can be highly nuanced. Some legal writers merely state that if the court applies the rule, then the client will prevail. That is not what we mean by "apply." The application of the rule to the facts is the written expression of the legal reasoning process—be it predictive or persuasive.

a. *Simple Application: Deductive Reasoning*

In general, when the rule is not at issue and the relevant facts are undisputed, the legal writer will quote and cite the rule in the rule section and then in the application section provide a short statement of the facts to demonstrate that the requirements of the rule are met. An example of this type of straightforward deductive reasoning can be seen for the dog-bite hypothetical if instead of suing Mr. Smith, the Johnsons contemplated suing Mr. Smith's tenant, Mr. Leonard. Assume that the additional undisputed facts were that Mr. Leonard rents a room in Mr. Smith's home and often cares for the dog when Mr. Smith is not home. Mr. Smith purchased the dog, pays for its expenses, and is the registered owner of the dog.

Given the undisputed facts and rule, the analysis would be straight forward. It would start with a thesis statement stating that Mr. Leonard would not be liable because he was not the owner of the dog. In the rule section, the Michigan dog-bite statute would be quoted and cited, its elements stated, and then the writer would move to the application section. The analysis in the application section could proceed as follows:

> Under this Michigan statute, a person cannot be liable for a dog bite unless that person owns the dog. Mr. Leonard rents a room in Mr. Smith's home, and often watches Mr. Smith's dog when Mr. Smith is out of town. Mr. Smith, however, is the registered owner of the dog. He purchased the dog and pays for its food and medical expenses. Mr. Smith, not Mr. Leonard, is the dog's owner. Consequently, Mr. Leonard cannot be held liable under the statute.

This deductive reasoning analysis would be in the application section because the ownership element of the rule is not at issue. No further explanation of the Michigan dog-bite statute and the ownership element is necessary. The deductive reasoning is the analysis that resolves the issue, and it would appear in the application section.

b. Complex Application: Analogical Reasoning

Such a straight-forward analysis is rarely the only analysis needed. Instead, even where the legal rule is not at issue, there is often a question as to whether the facts are sufficient to meet the legal standard, as is the case in the dog-bite hypothetical concerning Mr. Smith's liability. In such a situation, the legal writer will need to compare and contrast the facts and reasoning from the precedent cases to the facts from the current case. As mentioned above, this type of analysis is called analogical reasoning.

Return now to the original hypothetical in which the Johnsons are contemplating suing dog-owner Smith. We had just finished the rule section for this hypothetical by providing fact specific holdings from precedent cases. The application section would then begin with analogical reasoning to support the conclusion that Ms. Johnson provoked the dog and could be written as follows:

> Based on Michigan case law, a court would likely conclude that Ms. Johnson provoked the dog when she incited the dog to violence by stepping on its tail. Ms. Johnson's actions are similar to those that the *Brans* court determined constituted provocation. In *Brans*, the plaintiff was helping her brother remove chicken wire from a dog kennel. He was walking forward holding one end of the chicken wire, and she was walking backwards. In this process, the plaintiff accidently stepped on her brother's elderly dog. The dog yelped and bit the plaintiff's leg. 701 N.W.2d at 164. The court set forth several definitions of provocation and determined that those definitions do "not take into account the intent of the actor; rather, the definition[s] focus[ ] on the nature of the act itself and the relationship between that act and an outcome." *Id.* The court then reasoned that "unintentional acts could constitute provocation" under the statute. *Id.* Similarly, although Ms. Johnson did not intend to provoke the dog, she did step on the sleeping dog while playing tag. Under the court's reasoning in *Brans*, this unintentional action of stepping on the dog constitutes provocation under the Michigan statute because it incited the dog to bite.

Notice that the application section generally starts with a topic sentence. It is helpful to the reader if this topic sentence also acts as a transition between the rule section and the application section. Here the reference to the Michigan case law mentioned previously in the rule section would act as a transition. Next the writer provides what can be called the story of the case or the case explanation. The reader wants to know the facts of the precedent case and wants to know how the court applied those facts to the rule—the court's reasoning. The example above gives both for *Brans*. The facts of the *Brans* case are very similar to the facts of the Jones/Smith hypothetical. Recognize, however, that analogical reasoning most often involves not only comparing the similar facts, but also distinguishing facts. If there are relevant facts in the precedent case that are different, it is necessary to explain why those facts do not lead to a different conclusion. But for the *Brans* case, there are not any distinguishing facts that need to be discussed. For example, the fact that in *Brans* the plaintiff was carrying chicken wire, whereas Ms. Johnson was playing tag, is not a meaningful difference.

There is another Michigan Court of Appeals opinion regarding provocation that could be addressed. We discuss it here to demonstrate how to distinguish authority. Below is a possible example:

> Ms. Johnson's situation is distinguishable from *Koivisto* where the court determined that the plaintiff did not provoke a dog. 745 N.W.2d at 828. In *Koivisto*, the court considered whether the plaintiff provoked a dog when she stuck her fingers in a dog's eyes and kicked two dogs to protect her cats. The dogs had escaped from a kennel and were attacking her cats. The court reasoned that the dogs were already in a provoked state when they unexpectedly appeared on plaintiff's property and "immediately exhibited vicious and aggressive behaviors." *Id.* Under those circumstances, although plaintiff's actions were intentional and aggressive, the court determined that "[d]ogs that are already in a provoked state cannot, by definition, become provoked." *Id.*
>
> The dogs' pre-existing aggressive condition in *Koivisto* led that court to determine that the plaintiff did not provoke the dogs; by contrast, the dog's condition in Ms. Johnson's situation was quite different. In *Koivisto,* the dogs were attacking the plaintiff's cats at the time that the plaintiff fought the dogs. *Id.* Mr. Smith's dog was not exhibiting any aggressive behavior when Ms. Johnson stepped on it—it was asleep on the ground. Mr. Smith's dog was therefore not in an aggressive state at the time of the provocation. The *Koivisto* case is distinguishable, and unlike the dogs' owner in *Koivisto*, Mr. Smith will not likely be held liable.

As with the discussion of the *Brans* case, we first provide the case explanation, discussing the relevant facts and court reasoning. We mention that the plaintiff in *Koivisto* had also hurt the dogs. There is no need to state that these facts are similar because it is obvious. In the application section, when using analogical reasoning, it is necessary to the extent possible to *compare* and *contrast* each case. In the example analysis of the *Brans* case, there were not any meaningful differences. But in discussing the *Koivisto* case, even though we knew that we would distinguish the case, we first state the similarities to establish the precedential value of the case. Here we are establishing that the *Koivisto* case is precedential because the court was ruling on the provocation element of the Michigan dog-bite statute where the plaintiff had also hurt the dog.

With the analysis of both cases, we are implicitly stating that a court would interpret the *Brans* case broadly and the *Koivisto* case narrowly. What that means is that a court would reach the same result as in *Brans* (that the dog owner is not liable) by interpreting its holding broadly as being able to also apply to the facts of the Johnson situation. Further, we are stating that a court would interpret the *Koivisto* case narrowly. A court would not reach the same result in *Koivisto* (that the owner is liable) but instead would interpret the holding narrowly as not applying to the Johnson situation.[7] Having compared and contrasted the facts in the Johnson hypothetical with the facts in *Brans* and *Koivisto*, the application section could be complete, unless a counter argument should be addressed. A counter argument is discussed next.

c.   Counter Arguments

There is often a possibility of a different result than the result you predict (in predictive writing) or argue for (in persuasive writing). Indeed, in persuasive writing there will be an opposing lawyer who will likely argue for a different result than you. We call arguments for a different result than the result you support "counter arguments."

Sometimes, this different result might occur under the same rule due to a different application of the facts. Sometimes, it is not a different factual application, but instead there is a possibility that a different interpretation of the same rule should govern or maybe even that a different rule should govern. Under these circumstances, it may be necessary before

---

[7]   See KARL N. LLEWELLYN, THE BRAMBLE BUSH: THE CLASSIC LECTURES ON THE LAW AND LAW SCHOOL 55–71 (Oxford Univ. Press Inc. 2008) for an in-depth discussion on the use of precedent.

concluding to present and address any counter arguments. Predictive writing, as well as persuasive writing, should address potential counter arguments. Depending upon the context, the counter arguments may be addressed within the same IRAC or it may be necessary to develop a separate IRAC.

If possible, address the counter arguments in the original IRAC. If the counter argument involves a different factual application of the same rule, address it in the application section. If the counter argument involves a different rule or a different interpretation of the same rule, then it would be addressed in the rule section. If, however, the original IRAC becomes unwieldy, it may be necessary to address these points in a separate IRAC.

For the Smith/Johnson dog-bite hypothetical, there is a possibility that unintentional acts do not constitute provocation because the Michigan Supreme Court has not directly addressed this issue. It would be best, given that this argument is not a strong one and would convolute an otherwise straightforward analysis, to address it in a separate IRAC. You can review this counter argument at the end of this chapter.

Overall, and importantly, a common problem for students is a disembodied application section: The writer discusses the facts of her problem and never makes reference to the rules, cases, reasoning, or policies discussed in the rule section. Do not make the reader do the work. It is the writer's job to connect the threads between the rules and the facts—to weave the analysis. Err on the side of giving more information in your analysis. Here are some considerations to keep in mind when crafting application sections.

Is there a question as to whether the relevant facts satisfy the rule?

➢　Can deductive reasoning be used because the relevant facts and rule, or part of the rule, are undisputed?

➢　Is it necessary to compare and contrast the facts and reasoning of other cases with the relevant facts?

➢　When comparing the cases, are there logical links for the reader so that she can easily understand how the factual similarities between and among the cases justify a similar result in the instant case? As to any relevant differences in these cases, was it explained why the similarities outweigh the differences and lead to a similar result?

➢　Conversely, if it is necessary to contrast cases, are the factual differences between and among the cases fully developed so as to justify why despite some similarities, there should be a dissimilar result in the instant case?

Is there a question as to which rule or interpretation of a rule the court should apply?

➢　Is the discussion in the rule section regarding which rule or which rule interpretation should apply logically linked and applied to the instant situation?

➢　Are there policy considerations that should be expanded upon?

Is a counter argument necessary?

➢　Is a discussion of cases necessary so as to properly counter the competing rule or interpretation?

➢   If it is necessary to contrast cases supporting the counter argument, are the factual differences between and among the cases fully developed so as to justify why despite some similarities, there should be a dissimilar result in the instant case?

4.   Conclusion

Just as in the syllogism, the conclusion should follow from the application of the rule to the facts. The conclusion may be brief, as in the case of a single issue and single governing statutory provision or common law rule, or the conclusion may have to bring together competing rules and applications. There are, of course, other possibilities. Writing the conclusion, just like writing the introduction, rule, and application sections, requires looking at the context of the problem and analysis. For example, a separate conclusion to a discrete analysis and argument is not always necessary. On the other hand, a lengthy analysis or argument may need summation. A short conclusion can be used for the Smith/Johnson hypothetical.

> Under current Michigan law, Ms. Johnson's unintentional act of stepping on the dog constitutes provocation, relieving Mr. Smith of liability for her dog-bite injuries.

B.   LINKING DISCRETE IRACs

There may be multiple IRACs in the analysis section of the memorandum, the body of the client letter, and the argument sections of trial and appellate briefs. When an entire issue or argument can be discussed in one IRAC, then there is often no need to link to other IRACs, even where there are other issues and arguments. However, even a single issue may need several IRACs to flesh out the complete analysis because there may be discrete rules or separate elements that have to be applied or there are counter arguments that need to be fully addressed.

The following outline illustrates a macro IRAC formula composed of discrete micro IRACs for an issue involving a statutory rule with two elements at issue. Recognize that all possible listed items may not be available for each category.

ANALYSIS SECTION	CONTENT
I: *Overall Introduction*	• Thesis statement including the resolution. • Brief context facts. • Roadmap listing the order of the issues and possibly an overview of the analysis.
R: *Overall Rule*	• Quote the rule • If possible, give definition to the overall rule using statutory definitions or case law further interpreting the rule. • If possible, use deductive reasoning to move the rule section forward to the part or element of the rule at issue.

A: *Overall Application*	(Each micro IRAC could be set off with a separate mini heading.) **I:** Thesis statement regarding first element at issue and a transition from the previous discussion of the rule. **R:** Statutory requirement (it would not be necessary to repeat the statutory language); statute or court's definition; deductive reasoning if possible for any element; a fact-specific holding or holdings. **A:** Apply language to instant facts; analogize and distinguish cases as necessary. **Counter argument:** Discussion of why alternative application is not convincing. **C:** Briefly conclude analysis for this element.
	I: Thesis statement regarding second element at issue and transition from the previous micro IRAC. **R:** Statutory requirement; statute or court's definition; deductive reasoning if possible; fact-specific holding or holdings. **Counter argument:** Discussion of why alternative interpretation of the rule is not convincing. **A:** Apply to instant facts; analogize and distinguish cases as necessary. **C:** Briefly conclude analysis for this element.
C: *Conclusion*	A brief conclusion would state the overall conclusion and briefly re-state the conclusion for each statutory element. A longer conclusion could be used if needed to sum up the analysis for the reader.

In memoranda, there is the option of including headings before each micro-IRAC to aid the reader.[8] The introduction section of the micro IRAC could then start with a more specific thesis statement, which should also serve as a transition from the previous section.

When linking discrete IRACs, be careful not to adhere too technically to the IRAC formula because you could lose sight of the bigger picture—communicating with your audience. IRAC after IRAC after IRAC can become tedious to the reader. Modify the introduction and conclusion sections as needed to provide a flow to your prose, without sacrificing the analysis.

Furthermore, when communicating your analysis, do not describe your analytical process. Instead, provide your analysis—the resolution to the legal problem. Sometimes, legal writers make the mistake of describing what they are doing, erroneously thinking that a description of their process serves as a transition. Statements such as "now I will discuss the relevant rules" or "now it is important to analogize the instant facts to the facts of three cases" are examples of describing the analytical process. Instead, provide transitions that

---

[8] Rarely is it appropriate to use "Rule" and "Application" as mini-headings in the analysis section of a memorandum, the body of a client letter, or the argument sections of trial and appellate briefs.

substantively move the analysis forward: "The Michigan statute also requires that the plaintiff prove that she did not provoke the dog. The Michigan Court of Appeals has defined provocation as . . . ."

An example of linked IRACs can be seen by adding a counter analysis to the analysis we have provided so far for the Smith/Johnson dog-bite hypothetical. Where there is a possible argument that a different rule applies, it may be necessary to use another, micro IRAC to set forth that information. In this dog-bite example, there is a possible argument that unintentional acts do not constitute provocation. A separate but linked micro IRAC with that analysis could be presented as follows:

> The Michigan Supreme Court has indirectly addressed whether an unintentional act can constitute provocation under Michigan Compiled Laws Annotated § 287.351 (West 2003). Since then, two Michigan Court of Appeals decisions have reached different conclusions on what the Michigan Supreme Court's position is. But the latest, better-reasoned, and more authoritative decision concluded that an unintentional act can constitute provocation. Thus, a Michigan court is likely to conclude that Mr. Smith is not liable for Ms. Johnson's dog-bite injuries.
>
> The competing positions stated in the Michigan Court of Appeals are based initially on the Michigan Supreme Court order in *Palloni v. Smith*, 429 N.W.2d 593 (Mich. 1988). In *Palloni*, a child attempted to hug a dog, and the dog bit the child. The jury determined that the child provoked the dog and ruled in favor of the dog's owner. *Palloni v. Smith*, 421 N.W.2d 699, 700 (Mich. Ct. App. 1988). The trial court ruled that this verdict was against the great weight of the evidence and ordered a new trial. *Id*. On appeal, the Michigan Court of Appeals held that an unintentional act could constitute provocation. It then ruled that the trial court had abused its discretion in ordering a new trial and reinstated the jury verdict. *Id*. at 702. The Michigan Supreme Court stated that there was no abuse of discretion and reinstated the order for a new trial. 429 N.W.2d at 593.
>
> Subsequently, the Michigan Court of Appeals in *Bradacs v. Jiacobone* stated, in dictum, that the Michigan Supreme Court's order in *Palloni* indicated that the Court would conclude that only intentional acts can constitute provocation. 625 N.W.2d 108, 112–113 (Mich. Ct. App. 2001).
>
> In 2006, the *Brans* court rejected the *Bradacs* court's argument, determining instead that the Michigan Supreme Court's reason for allowing a new trial could have been based on its determination that an unintentional act could constitute provocation, but that the child hugging the dog was not sufficient provocation. 701 N.W.2d at 166. The *Brans* court also discussed the Michigan Supreme Court's decision in *Nicholes v. Lorenz*, 237 N.W.2d 468 (Mich. 1976), where a child was pushed and accidently stepped on a dog's tail, and the dog bit the child. The issue before the court was whether the dog's prior behavior was relevant to liability under the dog-bite statute. *Id*. at 469. The *Brans* court stated, however, that *Nicholes* implied that provocation under the Michigan dog-bite statute is based on whether the action could cause the dog to bite and not whether the actor intended to act. 701 N.W.2d at 166. Lastly, the *Brans* court noted that several states with similar dog-bite statutes have determined that unintentional acts can constitute provocation. *Id*. at 167.
>
> Based on its analysis of the Michigan Supreme Court order and opinion and a review other jurisdictions, the *Brans* court determined that an unintentional act can constitute provocation under the Michigan dog-bite statute. *Id*. at 166–67. Absent a contrary Michigan Supreme Court decision directly on point, the current state of the law for a trial court in Michigan is that an unintentional act can constitute provocation. There is a possible argument under the *Bradacs* court's decision that the Michigan Supreme

Court could reach the opposite conclusion. But the *Bradacs* court's point was made in dictum. Further, later Michigan Court of Appeals decisions have reached a different conclusion. Thus, it is likely that an unintentional act can constitute provocation under the Michigan dog-bite statute.

Although Ms. Johnson accidently stepped on Mr. Smith's dog, her unintentional action will constitute provocation under the Michigan dog-bite statute, preventing her from recovering for her injuries from Mr. Smith.

Let's walk through the IRAC. The first paragraph is a thesis paragraph. The first sentence is a transition from the previous IRAC because it references the unintentional provocation issue. The remaining sentences in the paragraph state the conclusion to the counter argument.

The rule section in this IRAC is complex because it discusses the evolution of the law on this issue. A rule explanation discussing how a rule has evolved over time is sometimes necessary if the law is not settled. The focus of this IRAC is the proper interpretation of the element of provocation under the Michigan dog-bite statute. Often when the focus is on the proper interpretation of the rule, the application section is a short paragraph, as it is here. If unintentional acts can constitute provocation, then application of the provocation rule can be straight forward. Notice how this straightforward application section is different from the application section in the previous micro IRAC that required analogical reasoning and the compare/contrast analysis of *Brans* and *Koiviso*.

As to the conclusion, you should include one unless it would be repetitive of the analysis in the application section. A separate overall conclusion section for the macro IRAC may not be needed if it is repetitive. It could be included if it referenced both micro IRACs.

What would be needed is notice to the reader in the macro IRAC introduction section that this micro IRAC regarding the Michigan Supreme Court's position is included in the analysis. The dog-bite example in Chapter 10 includes the needed information to incorporate this micro IRAC and includes an overall conclusion section.

C. ETHICAL CONSIDERATIONS

This chapter has provided tools to help you organize and draft a legal analysis. Working through the legal analysis by reviewing the facts of the client's case, determining and analyzing the relevant law, and communicating your analysis of how the law applies to the facts is hard work that you do for your client. Having gathered and reviewed all of this relevant information, it is important to know that there are serious consequences if you reveal this hard work, which often contains confidential client information, to individuals outside of the law firm.

Thus, when you are employed by a legal department in any capacity, including as a summer associate or law clerk, you have a duty of confidentiality.[9] Generally, you cannot divulge information that you learn while working there. Two common situations can arise that are worth noting. You may have an acquaintance who asks you about a matter at your law firm, or you may know someone who is involved in a matter that your law firm is handling. In either situation, you cannot discuss client information with people outside of

---

[9] MODEL RULES OF PROF'L CONDUCT R. 5.3 (2016).

your law firm.[10] Although there are some exceptions, such as to prevent a death, the exceptions are limited.[11]

The law firm is responsible for educating its employees on the governing ethical rules.[12] As a summer associate, your supervisory attorney should discuss ethical matters with you, especially those concerning confidentiality.[13] The supervisory attorney is required to take reasonable efforts to ensure ethical compliance by subordinate attorneys and nonlawyer assistants.[14] If a subordinate attorney or a nonlawyer employee breaches a governing ethics rule, the supervisory attorney could face consequences.[15]

So assume you are meeting some law school friends on a Friday night. One of your friends, employed at a different firm, wants to talk about the interesting matters you are working on at the law firm. You can generally discuss the type of work you are doing, but you must be careful that during the conversation, you do not mention the client or give any information that might allow your friend to determine the client's identity.[16]

Another situation can occur when you know the opposing party. For example, if your firm is representing Mr. Smith, it might be that the Johnsons are your close family friends. What if Ms. Johnson calls you to discuss Selena's options, stating that she cannot afford to hire an attorney and needs your help? You must inform her that you cannot discuss the case. A lawyer cannot give legal advice to a person, not represented by an attorney, who the lawyer believes has interest adverse to a client, other than to advise the individual to speak with an attorney.[17] Even if she is represented by an attorney, you cannot discuss the matter with her. A lawyer cannot talk to a person about the representation when that person is represented by other counsel.[18] What a lawyer cannot ethically do, the summer associate cannot ethically do.[19]

Further, if you have not yet passed the bar, you should not be giving legal advice in the first place.[20] This latter situation will likely be the one you run into the most. The sweet lady in the neighboring apartment needs just a little advice about her estate. Don't engage in the unauthorized practice of law. Advise her to hire an attorney.

You will study these rules in detail in a professional responsibility course in law school. But prior to that time, having some information about ethical situations that could arise when you are a summer associate might prevent a problem before it occurs.

---

[10]   MODEL RULES OF PROF'L CONDUCT R. 1.6, 1.6 cmt. 5 (2016) (generally members of the law firm can discuss client matters with each other).

[11]   *Id.* at 1.6(b) (listing exceptions).

[12]   MODEL RULES OF PROF'L CONDUCT R. 5.1, 5.3 (2016).

[13]   *Id.* at 5.3, 5.3 cmt. 2 (emphasizing the need for education and assistance especially as it relates to confidentiality).

[14]   *Id.* at 5.1, 5.3.

[15]   *Id.* at 5.1(c), 5.3(c). Subordinate lawyers are held responsible for ethical breaches unless there is "an arguable question of professional duty." *Id.* at 5.2. Under those circumstances, the subordinate attorney can defer to the supervisory attorney's resolution of the question. *Id.*

[16]   MODEL RULES OF PROF'L CONDUCT R. 1.6 cmt. 4.

[17]   MODEL RULES OF PROF'L CONDUCT R. 4.3 (2016).

[18]   MODEL RULES OF PROF'L CONDUCT R. 4.2 (2016). There are limited exceptions, including consent by representing counsel. *Id.*

[19]   MODEL RULES OF PROF'L CONDUCT R. 8.4(a). (A lawyer is guilty of misconduct if the lawyer attempts to engage in unethical conduct through another person.)

[20]   MODEL RULES OF PROF'L CONDUCT R. 5.5(a) (2016).

D. CONCLUSION

Learn to work with the IRAC formula—or, more aptly, learn to make it work for you. The IRAC formula can be useful in organizing a complex analysis, as long as you do not simply apply it rotely.

CHAPTER 8

Basic Writing Principles

LEARNING OBJECTIVES

1. Students will learn how to effectively communicate in writing: directly, with organization, focus, purpose, and clarity.

2. Students will learn to tailor communication to applicable format restrictions and how to avoid common grammar mistakes.

There are many books on the market that discuss writing style. We have referred our students over the years to the following texts:

➤ Anne Enquist & Laurel Currie Oates, *Just Writing: Grammar, Punctuation, and Style for the Legal Writer* (4th ed., Wolters Kluwer 2013).

➤ Bryan A. Garner, *The Redbook: A Manual on Legal Style* (3d ed. 2013).

➤ Bryan A. Garner, *The Winning Brief* (3d ed. 2014).

➤ C. Edward Good, *Mightier than the Sword: Powerful Writing in the Legal Profession* (1989).

➤ Terri LeClercq & Karin Mika, *Guide to Legal Writing Style* (5th ed., Wolters Kluwer 2011).

➤ William Strunk Jr. & E.B. White, *The Elements of Style* (4th ed., Longman 2000).

➤ Joseph M. Williams, *Style: Ten Lessons in Clarity and Grace* (6th ed., Pearson 2000).

➤ Richard C. Wydick, *Plain English for Lawyers* (5th ed., Carolina Academic Press 2005).

➤ Ross Guberman, *Point Made: How to Write like the Nation's Top Advocates* (2d ed. 2014).

➤ Noah Messing, *The Art of Advocacy* (2013).

➤ Morton S. Freeman, *The Grammatical Lawyer* (1979).

➤ Deborah Cupples & Margaret Temple-Smith, *Grammar, Punctuation & Style* (2013).

Any readers who wish detailed advice on stylistic matters can profit from reviewing one or more of these books. In various ways, they contain the advice in this chapter. We make no claim of great original insight into the thoughts below. But there are certain basic principles that legal writers must absorb, which we list below.

A. PREFER SIMPLICITY

Principle No. 1: Keep your writing simple. Great communicators take complex topics and reduce them to simple components that are easily understood.

Your audience members are likely to be busy people, with too much to do in too little time. If you give them unnecessary complexity, they will ignore you, or worse. They want answers to problems, and they want the answers in a form that will be easy for all of the necessary actors to understand and adopt.

Be aware also that making complex topics simple is a difficult business. A writer cannot do that unless and until he thoroughly understands the relevant problem, the applicable legal principles, the material facts, and his proposed solution. In our experience, it is often *harder* to be simple than to be complex.

B. PREFER THE FAMILIAR

Principle No. 2: Help the reader through the use of familiar words, concepts, and analogies. This is a corollary to the first rule. Audiences like to see terms, ideas, and comparisons about which they already know something. So, if you have a choice between a big word that the audience will have to look up and a familiar word that the audience already knows, pick the latter, all other things being equal. Similarly, try to lead with information and ideas that the audience already knows before introducing new information. Finally, if you can explain a complicated new idea by drawing an analogy to something the reader already understands, do so; it will help the communication process.

C. PREFER CONCISION

Principle No. 3: Express your thoughts in the fewest words that are adequate to cover the subject matter. Prefer short words. Prefer short sentences (no more than twenty to twenty-five words). Prefer short paragraphs (no more than eight to ten sentences). Prefer short documents. Your audience members are busy. Get to the solution to the relevant legal problem as quickly as possible, and then stop (and conclude).

Recall, however, that your audience members want your writing to be interesting. Not *every* word in the document you are writing should be short. Not *every* sentence should be twenty words. Not *every* paragraph should be eight sentences. Variety is important.

D. PREFER ACTION

Principle No. 4: Emphasize action to keep your audience's attention. This means emphasize verbs, particularly active verbs.

Example:

- The court decided that . . . .

Instead of:

- The court's decision was that . . . .

Prefer active voice.

Example:

- Robert sued William.

Instead of:

- William was sued by Robert.

Short, simple, active sentences will keep your audience focused upon the unfolding scene.

Example:

- Jane hit the ball. The ball smashed through Robert's window. Robert stormed out of the house.

Note, however, that there are times when you want variation. For example, the use of passive voice ("William was sued by Robert") may be ideal when you want the attention of the reader focused upon the recipient of the action, rather than upon the actor. Indeed, you may have reasons for not wanting to name the actor at all ("William was sued"). So we are not suggesting *only* use active verbs and active voice. We are stating a preference, albeit an important one, but not an absolutely infallible rule.

E.   AVOID OVERUSE OF ADJECTIVES AND ADVERBS

Principle No. 5: Let nouns and verbs do most of the work, not adjectives and adverbs. Try to avoid conclusory modifiers such as "clearly," "plainly," "very," "obviously," "outrageous," "unconscionable," and the like. Lawyers must get used to living with uncertainty much of the time. Reasonable people can disagree about the scope of the problem that needs to be resolved, what the law says or should say about the problem, what the facts are, and what the solution should be. As a result, it is often hard to say credibly that an answer is "plain," or that particular conduct is "outrageous," or that facts are "very clear."

F.   PAY ATTENTION TO FLOW

Principle No. 6: Pay attention to the flow of your sentences. Modifying clauses are least disruptive to the flow of your thoughts if they come at the beginning or the end of a sentence, rather than in the middle.

Example:

- Even if it is a remote one, we must consider the possibility.

- The possibility, even if it is a remote one, we must consider.

- We must consider the possibility, even if it is a remote one.

The middle example is generally less effective than the other two. Why? Because the middle example appears choppy. Lead or conclude with the language that you want your reader to think about the most—in this example, that the possibility must be considered.

Note, however, that there may be times when you want the reader to pause on the interrupting clause. (In fact, you will see examples in this text.)

G. BE METICULOUS

Principle No. 7: Pay attention to detail. The credibility of a legal writing piece and of the writer suffers when the writer is sloppy.

➢   Be precise in your wording of, and citations to, facts and rules.

➢   Use correct grammar.

➢   Use correct punctuation.

➢   Proofread your writing carefully.

➢   If there are court rules, office rules, client rules, or the like that apply to the document, make sure you follow them.

➢   If there is a deadline for turning in the work product, meet it.

In other words, be careful in small things because if you are not careful in small things, your audience will not trust you on the large ones.

H. COMMON MISTAKES TO AVOID

The following are the corrections that editors have to make most often.

➢   "**It's**" is the abbreviation for "it is." "**It's**" is NOT the possessive form of the word "it." If you want the possessive of the word "it," then you use the word "**Its**."

Example:

•   The car's motor is not running properly.

•   Its motor is not running properly.

•   It's not running properly.

➢   A corporation or other entity is an "**it**," NOT a "they."

Example:

•   Acme announced its year-end stock dividend.

•   It announced its year-end stock dividend.

Better yet, refer to the corporation by name to avoid any ambiguity.

➢   Do not mix verb tenses. If you are using the past tense to describe action in a paragraph, do NOT suddenly switch over to present tense to describe the same action.

Example:

•   The court announced a rule of lenity. The court resolved the doubt over the meaning of the law in favor of the defendant.

NOT:

- The court announced a rule of lenity. The court resolves the doubt over the meaning of the law in favor of the defendant.

➤ More important, discuss a case in the past tense because the case has been decided. But discuss a current statute in the present tense because it applies to present behavior.

➤ Watch out for ambiguous pronouns. A pronoun ordinarily refers to the preceding noun. In sentences that use multiple nouns, the pronouns can be confusing.

Example:

- Maria was with Sofia when she bought a gift at the department store. She mailed it to Roberto.

- Does the first "she" refer to Sofia or Maria? How about the second "she"? Does the "it" refer to the department store or the gift? In context, the reader may be able to determine that one meaning of an ambiguous pronoun is nonsensical. For example, Sofia is not likely to be mailing a department store to Roberto. But deciphering the correct reference is not always that easy, and, in any event, why make the reader go through the work?

➤ Do not mix singular nouns with plural verbs, and vice versa.

Example:

- The controlling decisions are *Baxter* and *Connolly*.

NOT:

- The controlling decision are *Baxter* and *Connolly*.

In our experience, this particular error is most likely to result from incomplete editing by the writer when the writer suddenly discovers a new case to include in the paragraph. The writer decides to insert a reference to *Connolly*, remembers to change the verb, and then forgets to add an "s" to the word decision.

I. PROFESSIONAL CONSIDERATIONS

Your written product is a reflection of your legal analysis, your attention to detail, and your credibility. But, as discussed above, writing effective legal analysis does not mean using big words and complex sentences. Quite the opposite. In the legal community, a writer garners respect when he is able to take complex and convoluted issues and present them to the reader concisely and in a way that is easy for the reader to follow and understand. It is much more difficult to write a brief in ten pages, then it is to write it in twenty. Thus, editing documents to eliminate not only grammar errors, but also to eliminate ambiguity and verbosity is a necessary task.

Further, when you draft written documents on behalf of your clients, a poorly written one with grammar errors not only reflects negatively on you, but it can negatively impact your client's interests. Courts care about grammar. Judges are not afraid to express, in their court opinions, their frustration with attorneys who submit poorly written documents.[1] One judge offered the following piece of advice before referring to a party's briefs as "inadequate and disappointing."[2]

> Underinclusive and inadequate presentations shift the responsibility to the court to do the lawyer's work. That's a risky business, for it requires the judge to be clairvoyant or intuitively to know the contours of the unmade argument. And, it rests on the hope that the judge will explicate the arguments that the briefs have left undeveloped, rather than resorting to the rule that superficial, skeletal, and unsupported arguments will be deemed waived or forfeited. . . . The hope is, more often than not, vain, for judges are not like pigs hunting for truffles buried in the briefs.[3]

As stated succinctly by another judge, "By submitting a poorly written brief, the attorney fails the Court as well as the client."[4] Recognize that although the substance of your written product is vitally important, how that information is presented matters.

---

[1] *See e.g.,* Alexander v. City of South Bend, 433 F.3d 550, 552 (7th Cir. 2000) (Judge referred to attorney's appellate briefs as "poorly written, convoluted and confusing."). Sometimes, the judge will chastise the attorney only in a footnote, but then provide a much harsher statement. *See e.g.,* In re Jacoby Airplane Crash Litigation, No. 99–6073(HAA), 2007 WL 5037683, at n. 28 (D.N.J. Aug. 27, 2007) (judge detailed numerous grammatical and typographical errors found in the attorney's brief, stating that some mistakes might be inevitable, but concluding that the volume of mistakes in the attorney's submissions were a "byproduct of carelessness" and a lack of professionalism); Pierce v. Visteon Corp., 791 F.3d 782, 788 (7th Cir. 2015) ("The brief's writing is careless to boot; it conveys the impression of 'dictated but not read.' Here are two sentences: 'This Court should be entered a high daily statutory penalty in this matter. Respectfully, the award of the District Court to the contrary law and an abuse of discretion.' There's more, equally ungrammatical").

[2] Donnelly v. Chicago Park District, 417 F. Supp. 2d 992, 994 (N.D. Ill. 2006).

[3] *Id.*

[4] See Kuzmin v. Thermaflo, No. 2:07–CV–00554–TJW, 2009 WL 1421173, at n. 6 (E.D. Tex. May 20, 2009).

CHAPTER 9

Citation and Quotation Basics

Solving legal problems requires applying authority to the facts of the client's case and stating predictive or persuasive propositions. The source of the authority that supports the propositions is expressed through legal citations. A citation communicates several things to the reader. First, the citation gives the location of the source—where the reader can find the exact source.[1] Second, the citation demonstrates the value of the authority—whether it is primary or secondary, mandatory or persuasive, and whether it supports or contradicts a specific proposition. Third, the citation demonstrates that the propositions in the document are supported by authority, which enhances the author's credibility. Finally, the citation provides proper attribution to the words and ideas of others.[2]

LEARNING OBJECTIVES

1. Students will understand the purposes of legal citation and will know that they must provide legal citations for the authority used in their legal writing.

2. Students will learn the correct possible placements for legal citations and the basic format requirements for cases and statutes.

3. Students will learn basic rules regarding how to quote information and cite to quotations in legal documents.

A. ETHICAL AND PROFESSIONALISM CONSIDERATIONS

Providing proper attribution to the words and ideas of others is necessary to prevent plagiarism. In law school, plagiarism can be described as "[t]aking the literary property of another, passing it off as one's own without appropriate attribution, and reaping from its use any benefit from an academic institution."[3] When creating documents that you will submit in law school, it is required that you cite to all of your sources. Failure to do so could be a violation of the school's honor code and have serious repercussions.[4] This chapter provides basic citation information to help you learn how to give proper attribution and avoid plagiarism.

In practice, lawyers often incorporate others' work product into their own. For example, several lawyers may work on one brief with only one lawyer signing the brief.

---

[1] Statutes are located in "code" volumes, which are organized by subject and separated by "title" or "chapter." Cases are published in multi-volume "reporters," which are organized by date. A citation to a statute is to a code volume, and a citation to a case is to a reporter volume.

[2] For an expanded discussion of these purposes, see ALWD & COLEEN BARGER, ALWD GUIDE TO LEGAL CITATION 2 (5th ed. Wolters Kluwer 2014) [hereinafter ALWD GUIDE].

[3] Legal Writing Institute, *Law School Plagiarism v. Proper Attribution* 2 (2003), available at www.lwionline.org/publications/plagiarism/policy.pdf.

[4] A finding of plagiarism on your law school record may also create concerns when you apply to become a member of the state bar. *See e.g.,* In re Worthy, 991 N.E.2d 1131 (Ohio 2013); In re White, 656 S.E.2d 527 (Ga. 2008).

Additionally, a lawyer might draft a contract based on a sample form from a published form book without citing the form book or the lawyer might review other lawyers' briefs on an issue and adapt the arguments for her brief without attribution to the authors of the original briefs. Further, a judge might use part of an attorney's brief or a law clerk's memorandum in her opinion without attribution to the authors. Although these scenarios occur routinely, in the extreme situations mentioned below, lawyers have been disciplined for plagiarism under Model Rule of Professional Conduct 8.4(c), which prohibits "engaging in conduct involving dishonesty, fraud, deceit or misrepresentation."[5]

Plagiarism is sometimes viewed as a competency concern.[6] Even though lawyers routinely incorporate others' work, the lawyer drafting a document must verify that he is using current law in the governing jurisdiction and has applied it correctly to his client's facts. In extreme situations, such as where a lawyer adapts seventeen pages from a law review article in his brief[7] or copies large portions of a treatise into his brief,[8] then it is not clear that the lawyer has competently drafted a document on behalf of his client. Competency requires that attorneys draft documents relying on the current governing law applied to the client's specific facts. Although as a lawyer you may rely on others' work product, wholesale cutting and pasting without tailoring the product to your client's situation may lead to ethical problems. If it makes sense to rely heavily on another source outside of your law firm, proper attribution would alleviate most concerns and highlights the importance of learning proper citations.

B. CITATION BASICS FOR LAW STUDENTS

Citations are a shorthand language, containing words, abbreviations, symbols, and numbers. How well the lawyer "speaks" this language through her citations can affect the reader's perception of the lawyer. A lawyer's brief, filled with grammatical and punctuation errors, reflects negatively on the lawyer's credibility and ability—which may ultimately affect the client. The same is true when a lawyer submits a poorly supported brief, filled with incorrect citations or a lack of citations, or both.

First-year law students are typically taught legal citation through a uniform system, even though practicing lawyers often use citation systems mandated by court rules or state statutes. Most legal writing professors choose to teach legal citation through a uniform system because once students have mastered the basics of citation, they can easily adapt to a jurisdiction's citation rules. The two most common uniform systems are the *ALWD Guide* and *The Bluebook*.[9] The *ALWD Guide* was developed as a "restatement" of citation by the Association of Legal Writing Directors (ALWD) and Dean Darby Dickerson.[10] It is currently published by ALWD and Coleen Barger.[11] *The Bluebook* is currently published by the law review students at Harvard University, Yale University, Columbia University, and University of Pennsylvania.

---

[5] MODEL RULES OF PROF'L CONDUCT R. 8.4(c) (2016).

[6] Peter A. Joy & Kevin C. McMunigal, *The Problems of Plagiarism as an Ethics Offense*, CRIMINAL JUSTICE, Volume 26, No. 2, at 2 (Summer 2011). Model Rule of Professional Conduct 1.1 concerns competency.

[7] *Id.* at 1 (citing Iowa Sup. Ct. Att'y Disciplinary Bd. v. Cannon, 789 NW.2d 756 (Iowa 2010)).

[8] *Id.* (citing Iowa Sup. Ct. Bd. of Prof'l Ethics and Conduct v. Lane, 642 N.W.2d 296 (Iowa 2002)).

[9] THE BLUEBOOK: A UNIFORM SYSTEM OF CITATION (The Columbia Law Review et al. eds., 20th ed. 2015) [hereinafter THE BLUEBOOK].

[10] For an in-depth discussion of the first edition of the ALWD Guide and The Bluebook, including their virtues and shortcomings, see Christine Hurt, *Network Effects and Legal Citation: How Antitrust Theory Predicts Who Will Build a Better Bluebook Mousetrap in the Age of Electronic Mice*, 87 IOWA L. REV. 1257 (2002).

[11] ALWD GUIDE, *supra*, note 1.

The remainder of this chapter provides general citation rules and basic citation formats for commonly cited sources and some rules relating to quotations.[12] This chapter is not a substitute for learning how to use the citation manual that your legal writing professor has assigned. In fact, you will need your citation manual to look up abbreviations, to understand the more nuanced applications of the basic citation rules discussed below, and to cite sources not covered in this chapter. Do not use these uniform citation formats or follow the examples below if your professor requires that you conform your citations to the local citation rules of a particular jurisdiction.

This chapter starts with basic citation information to serve as a foundation for learning legal citation.[13] It also addresses areas where we have found students have the most trouble.

C. GENERAL CITATION PRINCIPLES

1. Full and Short Citations

Full citations have a variety of components that provide all the information necessary to locate the source and to determine its relative value. Full citations must be used the first time the source is cited in the document. Short citations have fewer components but still contain sufficient information to locate the source.

Full citation example (see page 91 below for an explanation of the components):

Mendenhall v. Barber-Green Co., 531 F. Supp. 951, 954 (N.D. Ill. 1982).

Short citation example:

Mendenhall, 531 F. Supp. at 954.

---

2. *Id.* as a Short Citation

One short citation format, *id.*, can be used as a short cite with almost any source. When *id.* is used, it tells the reader that the source is identical to the immediately preceding source. If there is an intervening authority cited, then *id.* cannot be used.

3. Pinpoint References

A specific reference to the precise page on which the cited source appears is known as a "pinpoint cite" or "jump cite." Some legal writers make the mistake of omitting the pinpoint cites to the precise page. This omission irritates legal readers, who want to know exactly what portion of the particular source you are citing. In the example above, both the full and short citation examples contain a pinpoint cite—page 954.

4. Citation Placement and Use

There are three placement options for legal citations in the text of a document. First, the citation can be placed in a citation sentence. Just like a regular sentence, the citation sentence comes after a textual sentence, it stands alone, and it ends with a period. Second, the citation can be placed in a citation clause. A citation clause is part of the textual sentence, and is separated by commas. If the clause ends the textual sentence, then it requires a period

---

[12] An ALWD Guide citation and a Bluebook citation are usually the same. If there is a discrepancy, we have followed the ALWD Guide.

[13] This chapter covers legal citation format for citations that are in the body of the document, as opposed to citations in footnotes. Footnotes are not routinely used in the legal documents discussed in this book. Instead, footnotes are used in scholarly writing, and a different format is required.

at the end. The third placement option is an embedded citation, which is a citation incorporated into the sentence as part of the text. Use a citation sentence when the cited source relates to the full textual sentence. Use a citation clause when the cited source relates to part of the sentence. Use an embedded citation when the authority is referenced within the textual sentence.

Citation sentence:

The court rejected the charitable subscription standard in the *Restatement (Second) of Contracts*, stating that to adopt a " 'theory which affords charities a different legal rationale than other entities, is to approve fiction.' " *Mount Sinai Hosp. of Greater Miami, Inc. v. Jordan*, 290 So. 2d 484, 487 (Fla. 1974) (quoting *Jordan v. Mount Sinai Hosp. of Greater Miami, Inc.*, 276 So. 2d 102, 108 (Fla. Dist. Ct. App. 1973)).

Citation clause:

The Sixth Circuit certified the question to the Michigan Supreme Court, *Frey Dairy v. A. O. Smith Harvestore Prods., Inc.*, 886 F.2d 128, 131 (6th Cir. 1989), but the Michigan Supreme Court declined to address the issue. *Frey Dairy v. A. O. Smith Corp.*, 443 N.W.2d 782, 782 (Mich. 1989).

Embedded citation:

In *Davis v. Findley*, 422 S.E.2d 859, 861 (Ga. 1992), the court held that "a violation of the Code of Professional Responsibility alone could not establish a basis for a negligence action."

Be cognizant of where you place citations. Try to avoid too many citation clauses or embedded citations because they interrupt the flow of the text. Consider editing the passage and placing the citation in a citation sentence. For the same reason, avoid beginning sentences with a citation. Note, however, an embedded citation sometimes serves as a transition that moves the analysis forward.

5. Abbreviations

Citations contain abbreviations. For example, case reporters are always abbreviated. In the above example labeled "Embedded citation," "S.E.2d" is the abbreviation for *South Eastern Reporter, Second Series*. Certain words in a case name will also be abbreviated. In the above example labeled "Citation clause," several words in the case names are abbreviated. One is "Products," which was abbreviated as "Prods." Abbreviations must be used in all sources cited, not just cases. Uniform citation manuals have a general rule that discusses using abbreviations for various sources. You will also need to consult the rules for each source, relevant appendices, and various charts for the required abbreviations.

A principle that tends to surprise students involves abbreviation rules based on citation placement and source. Different abbreviation rules apply depending on whether the citation is in a citation sentence, citation clause, or embedded citation, and based on the type of source cited. So knowing when to abbreviate words is just as important as knowing the proper abbreviation.

6. Capitalization

Another rule that seems to pose difficulties for students is when to capitalize the word "court." Capitalize "court" when (1) naming any court in full; (2) referring to the United States Supreme Court, but only after the court has been identified by its full name; (3) referring to a state's court of last resort, but only after the court has been identified by its full name; and (4) referring to the instant court to which the document is being submitted.

Further, capitalize the words, "plaintiff" and "defendant" when referring to the instant litigants—the parties to the litigation that is the subject of the document—and only when submitting that document to a court. Do not capitalize the words when referring to the plaintiff or defendant in a precedent case.

7. Citing Statutes and Cases

a. *Statutes Currently in Force*

When citing a statute, cite the official code if available. Otherwise, cite an unofficial code. For federal statutes, an official version of the United States Code is available electronically in PDF from the Government Publishing Office Federal Digital System (GPO FDsys) website. The *ALWD Guide* and *The Bluebook* allow the United States Code to be cited from this website as if it were the official print code. The citation is the same as if the print source was accessed. There are five components to a full cite to a federal statute published in an official code:

Title number

Code abbreviation

Section symbol

Section number

(Date of publication of volume).

There are six in a full cite to a statute in an unofficial code:

Title number

Code abbreviation

Section symbol

Section number

(Publisher

Date of publication of volume [Date of supplement if statute appears therein]).

Full cite to official federal code:

20 U.S.C. § 1001 (2012).

Full cite to unofficial federal code:

20 U.S.C.A. § 1001 (West 2010 & Supp. 2016).

20 U.S.C.S. § 1001 (LexisNexis 2009 & Supp. 2016).

For short citations, use *id.* if appropriate. *Id.* can be used even when referring to a different statutory section. If you had cited to 20 U.S.C. § 1001 (2012) and wanted to cite to § 1002 in the next citation sentence, the citation would be: *Id.* § 1002. If *id.* cannot be used, then follow one of the formats listed below:

Short cite to official federal code:

20 U.S.C. § 1001.

or § 1001.

Short cite to unofficial federal code:

20 U.S.C.A. § 1001.

or § 1001.

20 U.S.C.S. § 1001

or § 1001.

To cite state statutes currently in force, you can consult the appendix in the *ALWD Guide* or in *The Bluebook* that lists information for each state and locate the name of the official (and unofficial, if necessary) statutory codes. The basic components for full and short citations to state codes are similar to those for the federal code. Similar to GPO FDsys, some state legislatures designate the statutory code on their websites as official. If so designated, the *ALWD Guide* and *The Bluebook* allow the statutes to be cited as if they were accessed from the print source. Many jurisdictions, however, publish the state's code electronically but have a disclaimer on the website that it is an unofficial version. Careful reading of website disclaimers and information regarding the currency of the sources on the website is always required.

Full citations are often constructed in the following order, although there are variations.

Name of statutory compilation

Section symbol

Section number

([Publisher if applicable] Date of publication of volume).

Examples of full citations to state statutes:

Utah Code § 46–4–201 (2000).

Me. Rev. Stat. Ann. tit. 10, § 9407 (2009).

For short citations, use *id.* if appropriate. As stated above, *id.* can be used even if you are referring to a different statutory section. If *id.* cannot be used, then follow one of the following formats:

Examples of short citations to state statutes:

Utah Code § 46–4–201.

or

§ 46–4–201.

Me. Rev. Stat. Ann. tit. 10, § 9407.

or

tit. 10, § 9407.

or

§ 9407.

If you are citing multiple consecutive or non-consecutive sections or subsections, you will need to consult additional rules.

b.   Cases

A full citation to a case that has no subsequent history has seven components. If the case has a subsequent history—for example the case has been affirmed or reversed—then there are nine components:

Case name,

Reporter volume

Reporter abbreviation

Initial page,

[Pinpoint page if needed]

(Court

Date),

[Subsequent history abbreviation if needed],

[Subsequent history citation if needed].

Full citation without subsequent history:

Georgetown Manor, Inc. v. Ethan Allen, Inc., 753 F. Supp. 936, 939 (S.D. Fla. 1991).

Full citation with subsequent history:

Jordan v. Mount Sinai Hosp. of Greater Miami, Inc., 276 So. 2d 102, 105 (Fla. Dist. Ct. App. 1973), *aff'd*, 290 So. 2d 484 (Fla. 1974).

There are three ways to provide a short citation to a case. First, use *id.* if appropriate. You can use *id.* even when citing to a different page. In that situation, you use *id.* at {pinpoint page number}. For example: *Id.* at 940. Second, if the case name is not included in the textual sentence (of the memorandum, client letter, or brief), then include the following components:

Name of one party,

Volume number

Reporter abbreviation

at

Pinpoint page.

Third, if the case name is part of the textual sentence, then include the following components:

Volume number

Reporter abbreviation

at

Pinpoint page.

Short citation where case name is not included in textual sentence:

MCI Commc'ns. Corp., 708 F.2d at 1084

Short citation where case name is included in textual sentence:

708 F.2d at 1084.

When citing to a plurality, concurring, or dissenting opinion, you must provide a parenthetical that identifies the source as a non-majority opinion. If you are citing a plurality opinion, then merely note "plurality" in the parenthetical. If you are citing a concurring or dissenting opinion, then provide the last name of each judge who participated in the concurring or dissenting opinion and his or her official designation (usually J. for judge or justice; JJ. for judges or justices), followed by the type of minority opinion. This rule applies to full and short citations.

Full citation denoting dissenting opinion:

Howard v. Babcock, 863 P.2d 150, 161 (Cal. 1993) (Kennard, J., dissenting).

Short citation:

Howard, 863 P.2d at 161 (Kennard, J., dissenting).

In some situations, you may have to provide a parallel citation, which is a citation to another source or sources that have published the exact same authority. For example, it is not uncommon for a state appellate court decision to be published in an official reporter, published by the state government, and an unofficial reporter, published by a commercial publisher. Some local court rules require citations to all the sources. In a parallel citation, the court abbreviation is not provided in the parenthetical because the official reporter identifies the court.

> **Parallel citations:**
>
> *In re Estate of Timko v. Oral Roberts Evangelistic Assn.*, 51 Mich. App. 662, 215 N.W.2d 750 (1974).
>
> *Waters v. Union Trust Co.*, 129 Mich. 640, 89 N.W. 687 (1902).

There are different rules regarding how to cite cases not yet reported, cases that are unreported, and cases published on websites.

8.   Working with Signals

Signals are used as part of a citation to authority to explain the type and degree of support (or contradiction) that the source cited provides. For example, if "See" appears before a citation, it "signals" to the reader that the cited authority: a) implicitly supports or b) contains dicta that supports the stated textual proposition. Signals are common in law review articles. When using a signal, explanatory parentheticals are highly encouraged. Do not use a signal if the authority directly supports the stated proposition. In writing office memoranda, client letters, and briefs, use signals sparingly.

> **Signal example:**
>
> *See Congregation B'Nai Sholom v. Martin*, 173 N.W.2d 504 (Mich. 1969) (holding mutual promise between pledge subscribers for a lawful purpose are enforceable).

D.   GENERAL RULES ON QUOTING AUTHORITY

Legal writers often quote sources in documents that they submit to members of their firm and to the court. For example, your legal writing professor might state that you should always quote the rule because the exact language of the rule is important to the legal analysis. Consequently, we next discuss some fundamental mechanics of proper quotation formats.

1.   Block Quotations

A direct quotation of fifty or more words should be set off from the rest of the text by indenting the right and left margins and using single space. Students seem to struggle with the following block quotation rules.

First, once the quote is blocked, there is no need to further set it off with quotation marks. Only use quotation marks internally to denote a quote within a quote. Second, provide the citation at the left margin, one double space below the end of the block quote. The citation is *not* part of the block quote. Third, limit your use of block quotations. We suggest using them to quote long rules or an especially important passage from a case only.

Example of a block quotation:

Michigan's enactment of the Uniform Electronic Transactions Act states,

> (1) An electronic record or electronic signature is attributable to a person if it is the act of the person. The act of the person may be shown in any manner, including a showing of the efficacy of any security procedure applied to determine the person to which the electronic record or electronic signature was attributable.

Mich. Comp. Laws Ann. § 450.839(1) (West 2014).

2. Shorter Quotations

Quotations of fewer than fifty words should be enclosed in quotation marks and integrated within the body of the text of the document. A quote within a quote, i.e. the cited authority quotes another source, is set off by single quotation marks. Further, recognize that in legal writing, commas and periods always appear inside the quotation marks. Other punctuation marks appear in quotation marks only if they are part of the original text. In court documents and legal memoranda, place the citation to the quote immediately after the quoted passage. Do not wait until the end of the paragraph to provide the citation.

Example of a shorter quotation:

The Michigan Supreme Court reaffirmed its previous holdings that the mutual promises between subscribers of pledges for a lawful purpose are enforceable. *Congregation B'Nai Sholom v. Martin,* 173 N.W.2d 504, 510 (Mich. 1969). The Court reasoned that the doctrine reflects the sound public policy that one who has " 'voluntarily made a valid and binding subscription to a charity of his choice should not be permitted to evade it.' " *Id.* (quoting *More Game Birds in Am. v. Boettinger,* 14 A.2d 778, 780 (N.J. 1940)).

---

3. Alterations and Omissions

When you use quotation marks or a block quote, you are signaling to the reader that you are quoting the text *exactly* as it appears in the original. If you want to alter the original, so that the quoted material fits better into the text of your document, you *must* indicate the changes made. Brackets are used to demonstrate alterations, such as when a letter is changed from upper to lower case, or vice versa. Similarly, brackets are used to denote inserted material and substituted words or letters.

Original:

We disagree with the Collection's contention that the words expressed on the pledge form are sufficient to make promises of donations legally binding. {Insert citation}

Alteration:

The court "disagree[d] with the [charity's] contention that the words ['I welcome the privilege of subscribing'] expressed on the pledge form [were] sufficient to make [the] promise[ ] of [a] donation[ ] legally binding." {Insert citation}

This is an extreme example of altering the text. As you can see, the symbols to denote the alterations interfere with ease of reading. In this example, changing the plural forms to singular is not necessary. The verb changes were necessary; and the substituted and inserted words help to clarify the meaning. However, in making any alteration, ask if it is even necessary to use a quotation. (Constitutional provisions, statutes, and administrative and court rules must be quoted.) Consider the following revision based on the above example.

Revision:

The charity claimed that the words "I welcome the privilege of subscribing" were sufficient to make the pledge enforceable. {Insert citation} The court disagreed. {Insert citation}

Ellipses are used to indicate omissions in the original text. An ellipsis is three periods, each separated by a space (. . .). Do not use an ellipsis in the following situations: when quoting a phrase or a clause, when beginning a quotation, and when omitting footnotes or citations. Do use ellipses to indicate the omission of words or sentences from the middle of the quoted material. There are two examples provided below. The first is based on an edited version of the Uniform Electronic Transactions Act quoted above. The second is based on original text from a case.

Original:

(1) An electronic record or electronic signature is attributable to a person if it is the act of the person. The act of the person may be shown in any manner, including a showing of the efficacy of any security procedure applied to determine the person to which the electronic record or electronic signature was attributable.

Mich. Comp. Laws Ann. § 450.839(1) (West 2014).

Quote with omissions:

Under Michigan's enactment of the Uniform Electronic Transactions Act, "[a]n . . . electronic signature is attributable to a person if it is the act of the person. The act of the person may be shown in any manner . . . ." Mich. Comp. Laws Ann. § 450.839(1) (West 2014).

Original:

(Excerpt from *Thomas v. Bethea*, 718 A.2d 1187, 1194–95 (Md. 1998))[14]

    The principle that a lawyer may be held liable for negligence in the handling of a case that was ultimately settled by the client, whether based on deficiencies in preparation that prejudiced the case and more or less required a settlement or on a negligent evaluation of the client's case, has been accepted by nearly every court that has faced the issue. In addition to the cases cited above, *see Edmondson v. Dressman*, 469 So. 2d 571 (Ala. 1985); *Callahan v. Clark*, 321 Ark. 376, 901 S.W.2d 842 (1995); *Bill Branch Chev. v. Philip L. Burnett*, 555 So.2d 455 (Fla.Dist.Ct. App. 1990); *McCarthy v. Pedersen & Houpt*, 250 Ill.App.3d 166, 190 Ill. Dec. 228, 621 N.E.2d 97 (1993); *Braud v. New England Ins. Co.*, 534 So.2d 13 (La.Ct.App. 1988); *Fishman v. Brooks, supra*, 396 Mass. 643, 487 N.E.2d 1377 (1986); *Lowman v. Karp, supra*, 190 Mich.App. 448, 476 N.W.2d 428; *Cook v. Connolly*, 366 N.W.2d 287 (Minn. 1985); *Bruning v. Law Offices of Palagi, P.C.*, 250 Neb. 677, 551 N.W.2d 266 (1996); *Malfabon v. Garcia, supra*, 111 Nev. 793, 898 P.2d 107; *Rodriguez v. Horton*, 95 N.M. 356, 622 P.2d 261 (App. 1980); *Becker v. Julien, Blitz & Schlesinger*, 95 Misc.2d 64, 406 N.Y.S.2d 412 (Sup. 1977); [FN5] *DePugh v. Sladoje*, 111 Ohio App.3d 675, 676 N.E.2d 1231, 1239 (1996); *Crowley v. Harvey & Battey*, 327 S.C. 68, 488 S.E.2d 334 (1997); *Helmbrecht v. St. Paul Ins. Co.*, 122 Wis.2d 94, 362 N.W.2d 118 (1985); *Hipwell By and Through Jensen v. Sharp*, 858 P.2d 987 (Utah 1993).

Quote with omissions, using a short citation form:

The *Thomas* court, citing numerous cases, explained that "[t]he principle that a lawyer may be held liable for negligence in the handling of a case that was ultimately settled by the client, whether based on [poor] preparation . . . or on a negligent evaluation . . . , has been accepted by nearly every court that has faced the issue." 718 A.2d at 1194–95 (citations omitted).

---

[14] Note in the text quoted from the case, the citation spacing does not conform to either the ALWD Guide or The Bluebook. One should not copy citation formats from any source. Instead use the format required by the governing jurisdictions' citation rules or the format required by your professor. Other sources often are using different citation rules or an outdated citation format.

Alterations and omissions can be useful when incorporating quotations; but quotes should be used sparingly. Novice and sometimes experienced legal writers tend to include too many quotations in their legal memoranda and briefs. Be judicious in using quotes and saintly in editing them: Never distort the original meaning.

E. COMMON QUESTIONS ABOUT WHEN AND WHAT TO CITE

The bulk of this chapter has been devoted to *how* to cite, but there are five related questions that frequently surface about *when* and *what* to cite. We will cover them because they commonly plague legal writers.

Question: When do I have to cite authority?

Answer: Remember that citing authority provides support for your predictions and arguments. Our advice is to follow the rules provided in the materials created by the Legal Writing Institute. Provide a citation when:

> ➢ Directly using another's words;

> ➢ Paraphrasing another's words;

> ➢ Directly using another's idea; and

> ➢ Building upon the analysis or sources of another.[15]

Question: What do I do when I find a recent case that in turn cites an older case as support for a legal principle? Do I cite the recent case? Do I cite the older case? Do I cite both?

Answer: It depends. All other things being equal, you rely on recent cases rather than older ones. But everything is not always equal. Sometimes the older case is from a higher court than the recent case. Sometimes the older case is a landmark case. Sometimes you want your audience to understand that the legal principle is venerable. Sometimes one of the cases is binding authority in your jurisdiction, while the other is from a court whose opinions are only persuasive authority. Here are our suggestions:

> ➢ If (a) you are only going to cite one case and (b) the two opinions are from the same court, then cite the most recent opinion.

> ➢ If (a) you are only going to cite one case, (b) the two opinions are from different courts, and (c) the opinions of both courts are binding in your jurisdiction (e.g., one of the opinions is from your state's supreme court and the other opinion is from your state's intermediate court of appeals), then cite the higher court.

> ➢ If (a) you are only going to cite one case, (b) the two opinions are from different courts, and (c) one opinion is binding authority in your jurisdiction while the other is from a court whose opinions are merely persuasive authority, then cite the binding authority.

---

[15] For a more in-depth explanation of attribution, including examples, see the Plagiarism Brochure on the Legal Writing Institute's website, located at www.lwionline.org. Once on the website, select "Member Resources," then "Plagiarism Resources."

➢   If (a) you are only going to cite one case, (b) the two opinions are from different courts, and (c) neither opinion is binding in your jurisdiction, then cite the higher court first. If they are courts of equal rank (e.g., both are state supreme courts,) then cite the most recent opinion.

➢   When in doubt, cite both cases. If you are going to cite both, then follow the above suggestions in deciding which case to list first, and put in a descriptor for the second case: *Doe v. Roe*, XX F. Supp. 2d 25, 29 (D. Minn. 2014) (citing *Jones v. Wombat*, XX F. Supp. 2d 45, 49 (D. Minn. 2012)). If the *Roe* case quoted from the *Wombat* case, then you would say "quoting" in place of "citing."

Question: What do I do when I find two cases, and the more recent one refers to the older one, but they do not stand for exactly the same legal principle?

Answer: In that setting, our suggestion is to cite the case that most directly fits your own legal problem. Then, if you wish, you may refer to the other case, with an appropriate parenthetical descriptor: *Doe v. Roe*, XX F. Supp. 2d 25, 29 (D. Minn. 2014) (extending *Jones v. Wombat*, XX F. Supp. 2d 45, 49 (D. Minn. 2012)). Other descriptors might include "distinguishing," "relying upon," "expanding upon," and the like.

Question: How do I know when I have cited enough authority to support a legal principle?

Answer: It depends. One great statute or case directly on point and binding in your jurisdiction may be sufficient. You discuss that statute or case in detail, explain why it is controlling, and move on.

But there may not be a great statute or case directly on point. If there is not, then you have to cite enough authority to be able to *synthesize a pattern* in the case law, sometimes from another jurisdiction, that resolves the problem you are addressing.

Question: What if I have cited an authority once in a particular discussion paragraph. Do I have to keep citing the same authority all the time in the same discussion?

Answer: It depends. A simple example will illustrate the point: One of the authors once had a discussion with a student teaching assistant over whether every sentence in an office memorandum she was reviewing should contain a citation to underlying source material. The TA thought it should. The author thought not. The logic of the TA, a law review editor, was that the reader should have a cite for every proposition to enable the reader to look up the sources and take comfort in the accuracy of the propositions. The logic of the author was that the piece was an office memo for a hypothetical colleague and client. Neither of those hypothetical audience members was likely to conduct independent follow-up research. Both audience members likely assumed accuracy. Both mostly wanted an easily readable piece with a quick bottom-line conclusion. Thus, in context, occasional cites were important to establish a basis for the opinion, but cites to every thought just interrupted the flow of the document. The author and the TA explained the difference of opinion to the class and told the students they could make their own decision.

CHAPTER 10

Communicating a Predictive Analysis

Up until now, we have provided the fundamental building blocks for legal analysis and communication. In the next two chapters, we will discuss how to put everything together in the context of preparing four types of legal documents: two predictive forms, office memoranda and client advice letters; and two persuasive forms, trial court briefs and appellate briefs.[1] In other words, the focus is now on the actual presentation of your problem-solving efforts. This chapter provides common features of office memoranda and client advice letters and samples of each. By providing these samples, however, we do not intend to suggest that these are the only ways to present a predictive analysis.

LEARNING OBJECTIVES

1. Students will learn the features of, and how to draft, various forms of objective memoranda to solve legal problems.

2. Students will learn the features of, and how to draft, various forms of client advice letters to solve legal problems.

A. COMMON FEATURES OF GOOD PREDICTIVE WRITING

1.   **In either an office memorandum for a colleague or client, or an advice letter for a client, use some version of the IRAC template.** Most, if not all, office memoranda and client advice letters do the following: identify the problem to be addressed, present the legal rule that will govern the problem, explain the rule, apply the rule to the specific facts of the problem, and formulate a conclusion that predicts how the law will resolve the problem. Client advice letters may additionally provide options and recommendations.

2.   **Offer a solution to a problem.** Lawyers are in the problem-solving business. Colleagues and clients do not want mere interesting discussions. They want to know how the law will likely apply to a specific problem. Give them an answer. If you need to qualify it with "likely," "maybe," "unlikely," or some other descriptor that is needed because the answer is not certain, then do so. But you still have to give an answer. "Gee, this is a hard one," is not acceptable. If the questions were easy, you would not be needed.

3.   **Try to find a favorable solution to the problem, and if you have to deliver bad news, then look for ways to soften the blow.** Colleagues and clients do not really want to hear why the law *will not let them* do something they want to do, or alternatively, why the law *will let an adversary* do something they do not want the adversary to do. They want you

---

[1]   There are, of course, many other types of legal documents. We only address those that are most frequently the subject of first-year legal writing courses. The principles described in this book, however, often will be relevant to other types of legal documents.

to give them favorable solutions. Try to do that. Be creative. Do not give them unfavorable answers without first digging hard, really hard, for favorable ones.

Recognize, however, that sometimes your answer will be bad news. Sometimes the law simply prohibits your client from doing something. Sometimes ethical constraints prevent you from recommending a particular course of action. And then there are those circumstances covered by a famous quote from a former United States Secretary of State, Elihu Root, who is reported to have said that " '[a]bout half of the practice of a decent lawyer is telling would-be clients that they are damned fools and should stop.' "[2]

This does not mean that you should relish saying no or giving bad news. The client, however, must be given honest, straightforward advice, even if this news will be unwanted or distressing.[3] So assuming that for legal, ethical, and/or common-sense reasons you decide you must tell a client or colleague something he or she does not want to hear, look for ways to soften the news. For example, suggest options: "No, you cannot do X, but you can accomplish much of your objective by doing Y, which is lawful." Or invite further fact exploration: "Given the currently known facts, you should not do X. However, there might be some additional relevant facts. Is it the case that . . . ?"

4. Remain objective. Office memoranda and client advice letters are intended to be predictive: How *will* the law likely resolve a particular problem, not how *should* the law resolve the problem.[4] (The *should* question is for persuasive writing pieces like briefs.)

To remain objective, identify and consider both favorable and unfavorable facts, and favorable and unfavorable law, in your memorandum or letter. Do not ignore facts, law, and policies that cut against your proposed solution because they are somehow unfavorable. When you explain your conclusions and recommendations based on your objective analysis, make sure to explain the implications to the client if a court were to adopt a view of the law or facts that is unfavorable.

5. Consider your audience. In a memorandum, you may not need to define legal terms of art and legal phrases because the reader is legally trained. In a client advice letter, however, you will often need to provide an explanation, rather than rely on the term itself. For example, another lawyer would immediately understand the term "consideration," as it relates to forming a contract. You may still have to provide a definition of the term as it applies to your analysis. Conversely, the term "consideration" coupled with a definition probably will not suffice for a non-legally trained audience. Instead, you will have to explain the doctrine and how it relates to your client's problem.

Recognize that even in a memorandum where the reader is an attorney, you cannot assume that the attorney will understand your analysis if it is incomplete. Novice legal writers often assume erroneously that an experienced attorney does not need to see the full analysis. Your analysis must explain the governing rules, how these rules have been interpreted, how the rules apply to the facts of the client's case, and the conclusion of that application. You must be thorough. For client letters often even more is required. You must tailor your explanation of the law and its application so that the client can understand and consequently make an informed decision.[5] Make sure that the tone of the letter is polite, professional, and not condescending.

---

[2] McCandless v. Great A. & P. Tea Co., 697 F.2d 198, 201–02 (7th Cir. 1983) (quoting A. Kaufman, Problems in Professional Responsibility (1976)).

[3] Model Rules of Prof'l Conduct R. 2.1 cmt. 1 (2016).

[4] For a good discussion about the difference, see Mary Dunnewold, *A Tale of Two Issues: "Applying Law to Facts" Versus "Deciding What the Rule Should Be,"* 11 Persp. 12 (2002).

[5] Model Rules of Prof'l Conduct 1.4(b) (2016).

What is less obvious is how to treat legal authority, especially in a client advice letter. Citations, as you now know, communicate a great deal about the level and value of the authority used. Consequently, a legally trained reader would consider an analysis without proper citations to authority to be incomplete and potentially incompetent. But a non-lawyer often would not be able to "de-code" the citations. Thus, a question arises as to whether citations should be used in client advice letters. Our advice is to use citations if the reader is legally trained or accustomed to working with lawyers or legal documents.

But even in these situations, use citations sparingly in client advice letters; do not let the citations take the place of providing the necessary detailed analysis the client needs to make an informed decision. If the client has no legal training, then it may not be necessary to provide citations.[6]

A related question is the placement of the citations. Indeed, there is a debate about placement of citations in general.[7] Do they belong in the body of the analysis, in footnotes, or in endnotes? In our view, citations should be placed within the body of a legal memorandum or brief because they are part of the analysis. While this is also true of the analysis in a client advice letter, we think that placement of citations is more of a personal choice in this situation. We tend to use footnotes or endnotes in client letters so as to conform to typical letter-writing conventions.

Presentation is also important. Make your written communications reader-friendly. Certainly use correct grammar and punctuation. But also avoid overly dense documents. Make liberal use of white space, provide headings and sub-headings, and use lists and charts where appropriate. *Help your reader see your analysis*.

6. **Plan ahead and budget your time wisely.** In law practice, as in law school, many things compete for your limited time. You must control your time so that you can handle each client matter competently.[8] It is not always practical to assume that you will be able to ignore everything else to work on one client's case. Other clients and your practice in general will need your time, your family and friends will need your time, and you might need time to take care of personal matters. You must assume life events will need tending to when you budget the time needed to move a client's case forward. A client's case and your reputation can be negatively affected when deadlines are not met or procrastination leads to submission of a poor work product on behalf of the client. Budget your time realistically, plan for inevitable interferences, and try to work on your clients' projects early and often.

7. **If your problem will be resolved through application of enacted law, then begin with that analysis.** Recall that legal rules generally find their genesis in enacted law or common law cases. If the rule governing your problem comes from enacted law, start with that language. If the language is clear, you will apply that language. If possible, use deductive reasoning to predict how the statute resolves the problem.

If, as is often the case, the language is ambiguous, then you will try to ascertain the intent of the drafters in crafting the law from the purpose of the law, the type of rule it is, canons of statutory interpretation, the legislative history, court opinions, and, if applicable, agency interpretations.[9] A common mistake among beginning legal writers is to start the

---

[6] Some legal writers use citations in letters to non-legally trained clients because it is always possible that another lawyer will review the letter. For example, the client may seek a second opinion and show the letter to another attorney. In that situation, the legal writer would probably choose to provide the citations in endnotes or footnotes.

[7] For an overview of the debate, see Bradley G. Clary, *To Note or Not to Note*, 10 PERSP. 84 (2002).

[8] MODEL RULES OF PROF'L CONDUCT R. 1.3 cmt. 2 (2016).

[9] *See e.g.* BRADLEY G. CLARY, PRIMER ON THE ANALYSIS AND PRESENTATION OF LEGAL ARGUMENT 32–41 (West 1992); CLARY ET AL., *supra* chapter 1, note 1, at 21–27.

presentation of any legal analysis by explaining relevant court decisions. This is a natural result of reading first-year law school texts that are primarily casebooks. Begin an enacted law analysis with the enacted law itself. Your presentation of case analysis comes later.

8.   **If your problem will be resolved through application of case decisions, then use analogical reasoning.** Recall that the common law develops one case at a time. A court hears a dispute between two or more parties, decides on a rule to apply and a fair result, and issues a decision. Then a court hears a different dispute between two or more parties, decides whether this latest dispute is similar enough to the first one to apply the same rule (and, if not, decides on a different rule to apply), decides on a fair result, and issues a decision. Over many years, the collection of decisions gives rise to a body of legal principles. The lawyer's job is to predict the legal principle that will govern and how it will apply to the current case. To do so, the lawyer engages in analogical reasoning by comparing and contrasting the current circumstances with those of prior relevant decisions to determine how a court would likely resolve the current case.

There is a similar evolution in courts' applications of certain statutory provisions, and a problem solver may need to use analogical reasoning to determine how a statutory term applies to the current case. For example, a statute may require a buyer to establish that "a seller at the time of contracting had reason to know" of the consequential damages that the buyer is seeking to recover as a result of the seller's breach. If the statute does not define what constitutes "reason to know," then the problem solver will have to present courts' applications of that statutory term and compare and contrast the facts from these decisions with the facts of the current circumstance. Based on this analogical reasoning, the problem solver will predict how the statutory term applies to the current case.

How should you present that analysis of cases? There are four basic presentation levels. The fourth level is the most informative and sophisticated.

Level 1: The level one presenter selects a rule from one of several precedent cases, states the rule, cites the case for the rule, and then applies the rule to the current facts to reach a conclusion. The emphasis is on the "black letter" law. The presentation is quick and concise, but it involves no analysis of the rule and no use of the precedent case to help determine how a court would apply the rule to the current case. Whole pieces of the IRAC template are effectively missing, and the presentation without discussion or mention of the other precedent cases is not fully satisfactory.

> **Example:**
>
> In case 1, the court held that the governing rule was [quote rule]. [citation].
>
> When this rule is applied to the current case, it is likely that [insert conclusion].

Level 2: The level two presenter also finds multiple precedent cases. For each case, the level two presenter states the rule and cites the case for the rule. The presenter then discusses some facts from the case and the court's reasoning, including the court's application of the rule to the facts. The presenter then does the same for all of the relevant cases. After discussing all of the cases, the level two presenter applies the rule to the current facts to reach a conclusion. The emphasis is still on the "black letter" law, although the writer engages in an explanation of the rule by referring to the facts and court reasoning from the cited cases. A level two presentation is more satisfactory than a level one presentation, but again, it is not fully satisfactory because it is a march through a discussion of the relevant cases. It does not synthesize the language of the rule from the cases to formulate the current governing rule. Further, it does not compare or contrast those cases with the current case to explain how the presenter reached the conclusion. The reader must put together the pieces of the analysis.

Example:

In case 1, the court held that the governing rule was [quote rule]. [citation].

In case 1, [state relevant facts]. The court explained that [insert some of court's reasoning]. [citation].

In case 2, the court followed a similar rule and stated it as follows [quote rule]. [citation].

In case 2, [state relevant facts]. The court explained that [insert some of court's reasoning]. [citation].

In case 3, the court also followed a similar rule, stating it as [quote rule]. [citation].

In case 3, [state relevant facts]. The court explained that [insert some of court's reasoning]. [citation].

When this rule is applied to the current case, it is likely that [insert conclusion].

Level 3: Working with the same precedent cases, the level three presenter formulates a rule from the cases and states the rule. The presenter then discusses the facts and the court's reasoning, including its application, for each case one-by-one. At the end of this sequence, the level three presenter applies the rule to the facts of the current problem. This is a more sophisticated approach than the previous two. It does embody a complete Rule segment of the IRAC template. And it may be a useful approach in helping a reader to understand the development of a particular rule of law. It can result in a competent treatment of a problem because it states the current governing rule as synthesized from the relevant cases, along with explaining how the cases have determined that rule and applied that rule. But it does not set forth factual patterns that can be found in the cases. It is still a forced march through cases individually. Thus, as with a level 2 analysis, the presenter has not set forth the analogical reasoning. Instead, the reader must put together the pieces of the analysis.

Example:

In cases 1 and 2, the courts held that the governing rule was [quote rule]. [citation]. The court in case 3 clarified that [state clarified rule]. [citation].

In case 1, [state relevant facts]. The court in case 1 explained that [insert some of court's reasoning]. [citation].

In case 2, [state relevant facts]. The court in case 2 explained that [insert some of court's reasoning]. [citation].

In case 3, [state relevant facts]. The court in case 3 explained that [insert some of court's reasoning]. [citation].

When the rule is applied to the current case, it is likely that [insert conclusion].

Level 4: Working with the same precedent cases, the level four presenter formulates a rule from the cases, states the rule, *synthesizes the patterns* from the cases, identifies the facts and logic common to the patterns, and then applies the rule consistently with the most appropriate pattern to the presenter's current problem.

Example:

In cases 1 and 2, the courts held that the governing rule was [quote rule]. [citation]. The court in case 3 clarified that [state clarified rule]. [citation].

In case 1, [state relevant facts]. The court in case 1 explained that [insert some of court's reasoning].[citation]. In case 3, [state relevant facts]. The court in case 3 explained that [insert some of court's reasoning]. [citation]. In both of these cases, [synthesize pattern].

In case 2, [state relevant facts]. The court in case 2 explained that [insert some of court's reasoning]. [citation]. The opposite result was reached under the rule in case 2 because . . . [explain why facts do not fit pattern].

The pattern in the current case is more like the pattern found in cases 1 and 3 because . . . [compare and explain why any distinguishing facts do not change the result].

The current case is different from case 2 because . . . [mention similarities but explain why distinguishable].

Therefore, a court is likely to determine that [same result as in cases 1 and 3] because [state pattern] . . . .

Alternatively, the level four presenter may find it helpful to bifurcate the analysis. In this model of presentation, she would first synthesize the pattern in the cases to which she is analogizing. She would immediately apply the reasoning of those cases, demonstrating why a similar result is justified. Then she would then identify the pattern in the cases she is distinguishing and apply the reasoning of those cases, demonstrating that a different result is justified.

Example:

In cases 1 and 2, the courts stated that the governing rule was [quote rule]. [citation]. The court in case 3 clarified that [state clarification of the rule]. [citation].

In case 1, [state relevant facts]. The court in case 1 explained that [insert some of court's reasoning]. [citation]. In case 3, [state relevant facts]. The court in case 3 explained that [insert some of court's reasoning]. [citation]. In both of these cases, [synthesize pattern].

The facts in this case are like the pattern found in cases 1 and 3 because . . . [compare and explain why distinguishing facts do not change the result].

Conversely, in case 2, the court applied the rule and reached the opposite result. In case 2, [state relevant facts]. The court in case 2 explained [state court's reasoning]. [citation]. Case 2 does not fit in the pattern because . . . [explain].

Case 2 is distinguishable from the current case, [acknowledge similarities but explain why distinguishable based on pattern].

Therefore, a court likely will reach the same result as the courts in cases 1 and 3 because [state pattern] . . . .

We encourage you to adopt the level four approach as often as you can when presenting an analysis to your reader.[10] Good legal writing synthesizes information and explains the analysis to the reader.

---

[10] There are, however, situations where the analysis will be condensed, such as in a client letter sent by email. These situations are discussed later in this chapter.

B. THE OFFICE MEMORANDUM TEMPLATE

Office memoranda are typically intra-office communications between legal clerks or junior associates and senior associates or partners that may also be sent to clients. Office memoranda are predictive, not persuasive. There are certain identifiable components to formal office memoranda, each serving a particular function to aid the reader. These components are discussed below. Note, however, that while we discuss the components in a linear fashion, many experienced legal writers do not necessarily write memoranda in this precise sequence. For example, they may start with a draft of the question and answer, move to the analysis section, and then write the facts. Conversely, they may begin with the facts, develop the analysis, and then draft the question and answer. But there is one constant to writing a memorandum, or any legal document: revise and edit in the context of the entire document.

1. Title

Many legal documents, including office memoranda, have formal titles, which appear at the top of the first page. The title informs the reader about the nature of the document and signifies its relative importance. A title to a memorandum normally appears at the top of the page in the center. It often resembles the following:

M E M O R A N D U M

2. Heading

The heading of an office memorandum provides basic information: To, From, Date, and Re:, which is short for "Regarding." A good Re: section provides enough information to inform the reader as to the parties and issue. It is usually no more than a line or two. It can list information, meaning it does not have to provide the information in a complete sentence. This section aids in retrieving the document in the future. Many law firms have "Memo Banks" in which memoranda are kept as resources to be used in the future. For example, as a law clerk, you may be asked to update an older memo on an issue that has recently arisen in a different context.

The date section is required because it signifies when the memorandum was completed, and consequently, when the authority in the memorandum was last updated.

3. Question Presented

The question presented provides the focus of the issue or issues. If there is more than one issue, there may be more than one question presented. Each question presented may be designated with a roman numeral. There are several ways to construct a question presented, but all good questions provide the relevant rule, core legal question, and legally significant facts. They also are framed to suggest the answer to the question. We provide three formats below, all based on a single-sentence model. A fourth format, which is a three-sentence model, is considered in Chapter 11 because it is particularly suited to persuasive writing.

The first format is to ask an indirect question, beginning with "Whether." Here is an example:

> Whether Ms. Selena Johnson provoked Mr. Smith's dog when she accidentally stepped on it, so that Mr. Smith would not be liable under Michigan Compiled Law § 287.351, which states that an owner will not be liable for dog-bite injuries when the dog is provoked?

The second format is the "under-verb-when" method, which is useful for legal writers because it forces them to include all the key components of a good question presented.[11] The "under" clause provides the relevant rule. The verb clause, which is usually "did," "can," "is," or "do," focuses on the core legal issue. The "when" clause conveys the most legally significant facts. Here is an example:

> Under Michigan Compiled Law § 287.351, which states that the owner of a dog will not be liable for dog bites if the dog is provoked, did Ms. Selena Johnson provoke Mr. Smith's dog when she accidently stepped on it while playing in Mr. Smith's yard?

The third format is a modification of the second. Here, the writer begins with the verb clause.

> Does accidently stepping on a dog constitute "provocation" under Michigan Compiled Law § 287.351, which states that the owner of the dog will not be liable if the dog is provoked, so that Mr. Smith will not be liable when his dog bit Ms. Selena Johnson after she accidentally stepped on it?

Whichever format you use, aim for clarity and precision. Recognize, however, that a question presented can be longer than a normal sentence. Also, if a memorandum has more than one question presented, use the same format for each one.

4. Short Answer

This section answers the question presented. If there is more than one question, then there will be more than one short answer. For example, if there are three questions, there will be three short answers. A short answer immediately follows a question presented.

A good short answer does more than merely state "Yes," "No," or "Maybe," although the specific answer is the best place to begin. A good answer homes in on the legally significant facts and their significance. Here is an example that answers the question posed above.

> Yes. Although Ms. Johnson stepped on the dog by accident, unintentional acts can constitute provocation under the Michigan dog-bite statute. Thus, Ms. Johnson provoked the dog and cannot recover from Mr. Smith for her dog-bite injuries.

Note how the question presented and short answer, when viewed together, function as an overall introduction. The reader is thus introduced to the key issue, the overall conclusion, the relevant law, and the most legally significant facts. Some legal writers draft these sections after they have completed the analysis section. Others prefer to draft them early to help focus their own writing. Whenever they are drafted, it is always wise to revise and edit these sections after the analysis is complete.[12]

5. Facts

This section tells the reader the factual story. It must be complete in that no facts used in the question presented, short answer, or analysis sections are left out. If a fact not

---

[11]   To the best of the authors' knowledge, this format was developed by Professors Laurel Currie Oates and J. Christopher Rideout of Seattle University School of Law.

[12]   An acceptable alternative to a Question Presented and Short Answer is an Introduction section. The purpose of the Introduction section is to provide the reader with a brief introduction to the issue or issues. For an example of a memorandum with an introduction, see the third sample memorandum below.

included in the fact section is used in another section, the reader can become distracted, wondering about the source of that fact and its relevance.

It is often helpful to think of facts in categories: *Legally significant facts* drive the legal problem. They shape the scope of the problem and its resolution. These are the facts that are used in the analysis—through deductive reasoning, analogical reasoning, or both.

Background facts provide context for the reader. They are not legally significant, but they help tell the story. *Procedural facts* may be either legally significant or included as background facts. Do not include facts unless they fall into one of these three categories and are needed to tell the client's story.

Facts are most often told chronologically, which is easiest for readers to follow. When there are multiple issues, complicated factual scenarios, or both, then it often makes sense to organize the facts by issue or topic. However you choose to organize the facts, do not distort them. Think, instead, of keeping the reader's interest by telling a story.

6. Analysis

The analysis section is the soul of the office memorandum. It is where the issues, the rules, the applications, and conclusions are discussed. Organization is critical in helping the reader "see" the analysis. We have already covered some organizational principles earlier in this chapter, such as introducing the relevant law and then applying it—either through deductive reasoning or analogical reasoning or both. It may also be helpful to review Chapter 7 on IRAC.

There are additional organizational cues that help move the analysis forward. First, begin with a point heading. This heading introduces the reader to the analysis. There are many ways to write these, but a good point heading is directly related to the information that follows.

Sometimes there are sub-issues within an issue. For example, there may be multiple elements of a legal rule that must be discussed. In those situations, create and add sub-headings. There are examples of sub-headings in the sample memoranda below.

The analysis section will be the most difficult to write and certainly the most time consuming. This is because you will need first to think through the analysis so that you understand the law and its application to the problem. Then you will need to write the analysis so that you can concretize it in sentences and paragraphs that make sense to you. Then you will need to revise and edit so that the analysis makes sense to the reader. Recall that topic sentences and substantive transitions are important in moving the analysis forward. Do not simply describe your process ("Now I will discuss X and explain why it is important to the analysis.") Instead, provide substantive transitions for the reader. For example, "The Michigan dog-bite statute also requires . . . ."

7. Conclusion

The conclusion section should be both concise and precise. It should not be a mere reiteration of your short answer but instead can include more detail. In those situations where there are multiple questions presented, the conclusion will necessarily be more detailed, summarizing the analysis for the reader.

C. SAMPLE MEMORANDA

Following are three sample memoranda incorporating the components discussed above, as well as our editorial annotations in the right margins. These samples employ versions of the IRAC structure. The first sample, based on the Michigan dog-bite problem discussed in Chapter 7, is a formal memorandum, using both deductive and analogical reasoning to resolve a statutory problem. The second sample uses the same problem but is an example of an office memorandum sent by email to the supervisory attorney. The annotations in the margins explain the difference between this format and the formal office memorandum format. The third sample returns to a full memorandum format, but it is based on a more complex common law problem using the cases from Chapter 6. The citations generally conform to the *ALWD Guide*.

1.   Formal Memoranda

For the first sample, assume the following facts:

Mr. Wade Smith, who lives in Brighton, Michigan, owns a mixed breed dog named Sam. The dog has a mild disposition and has not previously bitten anyone. A month ago, Mr. Smith invited the Johnson family over for a barbeque. The Johnsons have two children; Selena who is six years old and Stephen who is seven years old. Mr. Smith also has two young children. The four children were playing tag in the yard while the adults watched them and prepared the meal. One of the Johnson children, Selena, accidently stepped on the dog while it was sleeping. Selena was running from her brother who was trying to catch and tag her. The dog jumped up and bit Selena on the calf. The bite was quite deep, so the Johnsons took Selena to the hospital. Selena was properly treated at the hospital, but now has a scar on her calf. The Johnsons believe that Selena will need further medical treatment to reduce the visibility of the scar on her calf and have asked Mr. Smith to pay for any expenses that are not covered by insurance.

Assume that all parties live in Michigan, and that a senior partner has asked a summer associate to draft a formal memorandum as to whether Mr. Smith will be liable to Selena Johnson for the damages resulting from the dog bite injury.

MEMORANDUM	The title of the document is in all caps and either bolded or underlined.
To: Senior Partner	
From: Summer Associate	This heading provides sufficient information to let the reader know the general subject and the parties involved.
Date: July 26, 20XX	
Re: Wade Smith's potential liability under Michigan law for Selena Johnson's dog bite injuries	
Question Presented	The section headings should be set off, typically centered and bolded, for ease of reading.
Under Michigan Compiled Laws § 287.351, which states that the owner of a dog will not be liable for dog bites if the dog is provoked, did Ms. Selena Johnson provoke Mr. Smith's dog when she accidently stepped on it while playing in Mr. Smith's yard?	This question contains all the relevant information: applicable law, core legal question, and legally significant facts.
Short Answer	
Yes. Although Ms. Johnson accidently stepped on the dog, unintentional acts can constitute provocation under the Michigan dog-bite statute. Thus, Ms. Johnson provoked the dog and cannot recover from Mr. Smith for her dog-bite injuries.	This short answer provides a concise conclusion, which

Facts

Mr. Wade Smith owns a mixed breed dog, named Sam. Sam has a mild disposition. Last month, Mr. Smith invited the Johnson family to his home in Brighton, Michigan for a barbeque. Mr. Smith's two children and the Johnson's two children were playing tag in Mr. Smith's yard, as the adults watched and prepared the meal. Sam was sleeping in the yard. Selena Johnson, a six-year old girl, accidently stepped on the dog as she was running from her brother who was trying to catch and tag her. The dog was startled. It jumped up and bit Selena on the calf. Sam had never bitten anyone before.

The bite was quite deep, requiring that the Johnson's take Selena to the hospital. Selena was properly treated, but the bite has resulted in a scar on her calf. The Johnsons believe that Selena will need further medical treatment to reduce the visibility of the scar. The Johnsons have asked Mr. Smith to pay all medical expenses that they incur for Selena's treatment that are not covered by insurance. Mr. Smith has asked the firm whether he is liable for these expenses.

Analysis

Mr. Wade Smith will not be liable to Ms. Selena Johnson for her dog-bite injuries under Michigan Compiled Laws § 287.351.

Mr. Wade Smith, the dog owner, is not liable to Selena Johnson for her dog-bite injuries because Ms. Johnson provoked the dog. Ms. Johnson inadvertently stepped on the sleeping dog when she was playing tag. Under current Michigan law, unintentional acts can constitute provocation which relieves a dog owner of liability. This memo also addresses the potential argument that the Michigan Supreme Court has impliedly stated that unintentional acts cannot constitute provocation and concludes that it is not likely to succeed. As a result, Ms. Johnson's act provoking the dog relieves Mr. Smith of liability for her injuries.

Michigan Compiled Laws Annotated § 287.351(1) (West 2003) governs when a dog owner will be liable for injuries caused by his or her dog. This statute states, in part, "If a dog bites a person, without provocation while the person is . . . lawfully on private property, including the property of the owner of the dog, the owner of the dog shall be liable for any damages suffered by the person bitten. . . ." *Id.*

To recover from a defendant for dog-bite injuries under this statute, a plaintiff must establish that the defendant owned the dog, that the dog bite occurred while the injured party was lawfully on the property, and that the dog was not provoked. The first element is met because Mr. Smith admits that he is the owner of the dog.

The second element of the statute requires that the dog-bite occurred while the injured person was lawfully on the property. Michigan Compiled Laws Annotated § 287.351(2)

Side annotations:

signals the analysis that will follow.

These facts are complete in that they provide all of the legally significant and background facts necessary to understand the issue and the analysis that follows in the next section.

It is often helpful to end with the procedural facts—here the client is seeking advice.

See page 117 for an alternative way to begin the analysis section.

This point heading states the outcome and the applicable law.

The first sentence provides the conclusion and a brief reason supporting it. Although not required, the second sentence can provide some context facts.

This paragraph also includes a roadmap by stating that it will address another potential argument.

The governing rule is provided next. It is best to quote the relevant section of the rule.

This paragraph breaks down the elements of the statute for the reader and then proceeds to use deductive reasoning to explain which elements have been met.

Sometimes, deductive reasoning requires using other defining rules. Such rules can only be

defines when a person is lawfully on the property. It states, in part, "A person is lawfully on the private property of the owner of the dog within the meaning of this act . . . if the person is on the owner's property as an invitee or licensee of the person lawfully in possession of the property . . . ." Under Michigan law, a licensee "is a person who is privileged to enter the land of another by virtue of the possessor's consent." *Stitt v. Holland Abundant Life Fellowship*, 614 N.W.2d 88, 91 (Mich. 2000). It is undisputed that Mr. Smith gave the Johnsons permission to be on the property when he invited the Johnson family to his home for a barbeque. Consequently, Ms. Johnson was a licensee and was lawfully on Mr. Smith's property. Further, it is undisputed that Mr. Smith's dog bit Selena while she was on the property. Thus, the second element has also been met. The remaining element concerning provocation is the element that is at issue.

| used in deductive reasoning where the other side will not contest that they are binding. |

1. Unintentional acts can constitute provocation under current Michigan law.

The Michigan Court of Appeals has defined the term "provocation" in this statute as " '[t]he act of inciting another to do a particular deed. That which arouses, moves, calls forth, causes, or occasions.' " *Brans v. Extrom*, 701 N.W.2d 163, 165–66 (Mich. Ct. App. 2005) (quoting Black's Law Dictionary (4th ed.)). Using this definition, the court determined that intentional as well as unintentional acts could constitute provocation. *Brans*, 701 N.W.2d at 165. A subsequent Michigan Court of Appeals decision agreed with this definition of provocation. *Koivisto v. Davis*, 745 N.W.2d 824, 827 (Mich. Ct. App. 2008).

Under this definition, the court in *Brans* held that the owner was not liable because the plaintiff provoked the dog when she inadvertently stepped on the dog. 701 N.W.2d at 166–167. The court in *Koivisto* agreed with the rule set forth in *Brans*, but determined that the plaintiff had not provoked the dogs that were viciously attacking her cats, because the dogs were already in a provoked state. *Koivisto*, 745 N.W.2d at 829.

Based on Michigan case law, a court would likely conclude that Ms. Johnson provoked the dog. Ms. Johnson's actions are similar to those that the *Brans* court determined constituted provocation. In *Brans*, the plaintiff was helping her brother remove chicken wire from a dog kennel. He was walking forward holding one end of the chicken wire, and she was walking backwards. In this process, the plaintiff accidently stepped on her brother's elderly dog. The dog yelped and bit the plaintiff's leg. 701 N.W.2d at 164. The court set forth several definitions of provocation and determined that these definitions do "not take into account the intent of the actor; rather, the definition focuses on the nature of the act itself and the relationship between that act and an outcome." *Id.* The court then reasoned that "unintentional acts could constitute provocation" under the statute. *Id.* Similarly, although Ms. Johnson did not intend to provoke the dog, she did step on the sleeping dog while playing tag. Under the court's reasoning in

| Subheadings can be helpful guideposts in the Analysis section for the reader. |
| This paragraph continues the rule section, focusing on the element of the statute that is at issue. It further defines the rule for the reader. |
| This paragraph also further defines the rule. It states how higher level courts in the jurisdiction have interpreted the rule under the specific facts before them. |
| This paragraph starts the application section of the IRAC. Notice that it starts with a topic sentence. |
| The paragraph gives a case explanation. It starts with the case that supports the writer's conclusion that unintentional acts can meet the provocation element. It tells the factual story of the precedent case, and it provides the court's reasoning on the issue. It |

Brans, this unintentional act of stepping on the dog constitutes provocation under the Michigan statute.

Ms. Johnson's situation is distinguishable from *Koivisto* where the court determined that the plaintiff did not provoke the dog. 745 N.W.2d at 828. In *Koivisto*, the court considered whether the plaintiff provoked the dog when she stuck her fingers in the dog's eyes and kicked the dogs to protect her cats. The dogs had escaped from a kennel and were attacking her cats. The court reasoned that the dogs were already in a provoked state when they unexpectedly appeared on plaintiff's property and "immediately exhibited vicious and aggressive behaviors." *Id.* Under those circumstances, although plaintiff's actions were intentional and aggressive, the court determined that "[d]ogs that are already in a provoked state cannot, by definition, become provoked." *Id.*

The dogs' pre-existing aggressive condition in *Koivisto* led the court to determine that the plaintiff did not provoke the dogs; by contrast, the dog's condition in Ms. Johnson's situation was quite different. In *Koivisto*, the dogs were attacking the plaintiff's cats at the time that the plaintiff fought the dogs. *Id.* Mr. Smith's dog was not exhibiting any aggressive behavior when Ms. Johnson stepped on it—it was asleep on the ground. Mr. Smith's dog was therefore not in an aggressive state at the time of the provocation. The *Koivisto* case is distinguishable, and unlike the dogs' owner in *Koivisto*, Mr. Smith will likely not be held liable.

Under current Michigan law, Ms. Johnson's unintentional act of stepping on the dog constitutes provocation, relieving Mr. Smith of liability for her dog-bite injuries.

2. The Michigan Supreme Court would likely conclude that unintentional acts can constitute provocation.

The Michigan Supreme Court has indirectly addressed whether an unintentional act can constitute provocation under Michigan Compiled Laws Annotated § 287.351 (2003). Since then, two Michigan Court of Appeals decisions have reached different conclusions on what the Michigan Supreme Court's position is. But the latest, better-reasoned, and more authoritative decision concluded that an unintentional act can constitute provocation. Thus, a Michigan court is likely to conclude that Mr. Smith is not liable for Ms. Johnson's dog-bite injuries.

The competing positions stated in the Michigan Court of Appeals decisions are based initially on the Michigan Supreme Court order in *Palloni v. Smith*, 429 N.W.2d 593 (Mich. 1988). In *Palloni*, a child attempted to hug a dog, and the dog bit the child. The jury determined that the child provoked the dog and ruled in favor of the dog's owner. *Palloni v. Smith*, 421 N.W.2d 699, 700 (Mich. Ct. App. 1988). The trial court ruled that this verdict was against the great weight of the evidence and ordered a new trial. *Id*. On appeal, the Michigan Court of Appeals held that an unintentional act could constitute provocation. It then ruled that the trial court had abused its discretion in ordering a new trial and reinstated the jury verdict. *Id*. at 702. The Michigan Supreme Court stated that there was no abuse of discretion and reinstated the order for a new trial. 429 N.W.2d at 593.

Subsequently, the Michigan Court of Appeals in *Bradacs v. Jiacobone*, stated, in dictum, that the Michigan Supreme Court's order in *Palloni* indicated that the Court would conclude that only intentional acts can constitute provocation. 625 N.W.2d 108, 112–113 (Mich. Ct. App. 2001).

In 2006, the *Brans* court rejected the *Bradacs* court's argument, determining instead that the Michigan Supreme Court's reason for allowing a new trial could have been based on its determination that an unintentional act could constitute provocation, but that the child hugging the dog was not sufficient provocation. 701 N.W.2d at 166. The *Brans* court also discussed the Michigan Supreme Court's decision in *Nicholes v. Lorenz*, 237 N.W.2d 468 (Mich. 1976), where a child was pushed and accidently stepped on a dog's tail, and the dog bit the child. The issue before the Court was whether the dog's prior behavior was relevant to liability under the dog-bite statute. *Id*. at 469. The *Brans* court stated, however, that *Nicholes* implied that provocation under the Michigan dog-bite statute is based on whether the action could cause the dog to bite and not whether the actor intended to act. 701 N.W.2d at 166. Lastly, the *Brans* court noted that several states with similar dog-bite statutes have determined that unintentional acts can constitute provocation. *Id*. at 167.

Based on its analysis of the Michigan Supreme Court order and opinion and a review of other jurisdictions, the *Brans* court determined that an unintentional act can constitute provocation under the Michigan dog-bite statute. *Id*. at 166–67. Absent a contrary Michigan Supreme Court decision directly on point, the current state of the law for a trial court in Michigan is that an unintentional act can constitute provocation. There is a possible argument under the *Bradacs* court's decision that the Michigan Supreme Court could reach the opposite conclusion. But the *Bradacs* court's point was made in dictum. Further, later Michigan Court of Appeals decisions have reached a different conclusion. Thus, it is likely that an unintentional act can constitute provocation under the Michigan dog-bite statute.

This paragraph begins the application section. It sums up the previous rule explanation and provides a topic sentence.

There are often counter-arguments that must be addressed, even when there is little likelihood that they would be successful.

Conclusion

Although Ms. Johnson accidently stepped on Mr. Smith's dog, her unintentional action will constitute provocation under the Michigan dog-bite statute, preventing her from recovering for her injuries from Mr. Smith.

This conclusion is concise and precise and is a summary of both IRACs.

2. Email Memo to the Partner

A supervisory attorney may need an answer to a legal question quickly and may not want a full formal office memorandum. The attorney may instead request the information in a different format, such as an oral explanation in a meeting, an informal memorandum, or an explanation in an email. There are a couple of reasons why it is important to learn how to draft a formal memorandum. Initially, your employer may ask that you draft such a memo as it is how intra-office communication has traditionally occurred. Second, other methods are derivative of the full memorandum. In other words, other methods are often less extensive versions of the formal office memorandum, retaining just some of the components. Thus, regardless of the delivery method, the attorney will still want to know the conclusion to the issue, the governing or relevant law, and how that law applies to the facts.

If you are providing a memorandum to an attorney who states that she does not need a formal memorandum but is not otherwise clear as to the format, you must ask. Informal memoranda can take different forms. Attempt to determine the specific form that the law firm or the requesting attorney anticipates. For example, the attorney may just want a conclusion, as opposed to a question presented and a brief answer, and may want that conclusion followed by a detailed analysis that incorporates the facts, as opposed to having a separate fact and analysis section. Where the required format is not clear, do not guess. Instead, either ask for clarification or, better yet, suggest a format based on the situation and obtain consent.

If the memorandum is to be conveyed through email, there is more of an accepted structured simply because the space limitation dictates the structure. There are several key components to an effective email memorandum. First, use the subject line for the email wisely. State concisely and precisely the conclusion to the issue you were asked.

Second, in the body of the email aim for brevity. A one screen rule is likely too limiting, but try to provide the information in three or four paragraphs. This raises an ancillary point. If you cannot adequately convey the analysis in three or four paragraphs, you should let the attorney know. Complex issues are not necessarily appropriate for short email memoranda. If you do not believe you can adequately explain the analysis in three or four paragraphs, ask the supervisory attorney if you should submit a longer informal memorandum either in the body of an email, or as an attachment, or both. You can take this opportunity to suggest an informal memorandum structure if the required structure is not clear. Also a quick word about attachments. If you are attaching a document or documents, select names for each attachment that describe the document. Further, state in the body of the email the document or documents that you have attached. Attorneys can become frustrated by attachments that are not effectively labeled or identified.

Third, in an email memorandum state the question you were asked and the answer in the first paragraph. Stating the question ensures a mutual understanding of the issue addressed. Fourth, format the information to make it easy to read on a screen. For example, use headings to introduce information. Fifth, you may need a confidentiality statement at the end of your email. Determine the firm's practice on this statement.

Most importantly, submit a polished and professional piece of work. Even if the structure seems less formal, your written communication remains a reflection of your intellect. Emails submitted for work are different than personal emails. Do not hastily send off a written product that you have not taken the time to think through, write concisely, structure effectively, and edit. This point is especially true for email communications because they are so easily transmitted to others. You should assume that your email communications at work will be read by other colleagues or by the client.

Below we provide a sample of an email memorandum for the Smith/Johnson dog bite hypothetical, based on the following additional facts.

Assume bright and early Friday morning the supervisory attorney emailed the summer associate and explained that he is meeting his good friend, Wade Smith, for dinner. Mr. Smith is seeking advice regarding his liability for a dog bite injury. In the email, the attorney sets forth Mr. Smith's story regarding how his dog, Sam, bit Selena Johnson at a barbeque a month ago. The attorney asks the summer associate to research the problem and respond via email by 5:00 p.m.

Under such circumstances, the summer associate might craft the following email.

From: summerassociate@lawfirm.com To: seniorpartner@lawfirm.com Cc:	This information is filled in as part of the email system.
Subject: Mr. Wade Smith is not liable for the dog-bite injuries	You should use the subject line to answer the question
Dear Senior Partner, You asked whether Mr. Wade Smith will be liable for injuries his guest, Selena Johnson, received when his dog bit Ms. Johnson after she accidentally stepped on the dog. Under Michigan law, Mr. Smith will not be liable for those injuries because Ms. Johnson provoked the dog.	Although email formats can be flexible, it is best to restate the question asked and then immediately provide an answer.
Michigan Compiled Laws Annotated § 287.351(1) (West 2003) governs a dog owner's liability for dog bites and states that "[i]f a dog bites a person, without provocation while the person is . . . lawfully on private property, . . . the owner of the dog shall be liable . . . ." This statute states that a person is lawfully on the owner's property "if the person is . . . an invitee or licensee . . . ." *Id.* § 287.351(2). A licensee is defined as "a person who . . . enters land [with] the possessor's consent." *Stitt v. Holland Abundant Life Fellowship*, 614 N.W.2d 88, 91 (Mich. 2000). You explained to me that Mr. Smith had invited the Johnson family over for a barbeque. Under those circumstances, Ms. Johnson would be a licensee.	Your email is to another attorney who understands citations and can digest dense statements of the law. Do not be afraid to set forth the law as concisely as possible. It is best to quote statutory language if the statutory provision is short. If the relevant statutory provision was long, you might consider attaching it. If you attach it, state that you are attaching it and label it clearly.
Because Ms. Johnson was bitten by Mr. Smith's dog while she was lawfully on the premises, the only remaining issue is whether she provoked the dog when she accidently stepped on it. Recent Michigan Court of Appeals decisions have held that unintentional acts can constitute provocation. *Brans v. Extrom*, 701 N.W.2d 163, 165–66 (Mich. Ct. App. 2005); *Koivisto v. Davis*, 745 N.W.2d 824, 827 (Mich. Ct. App. 2008). In *Brans*, the owner was not liable when his dog bit his sister who accidently stepped on the dog while walking backwards and carrying a heavy object. 701 N.W.2d at 164. Under the Michigan dog-bite statute, because Ms. Johnson provoked the dog by accidently stepping on it, Mr. Smith would not likely be held liable for her dog-bite injuries.	Some writers might leave this case illustration out. But it might serve to reassure the attorney that your position is correct.

There is a potential argument against this position because the Michigan Supreme Court has not directly ruled on this issue. In 1991, the Michigan Court of Appeals opined in dicta that the Michigan Supreme Court would conclude that inadvertent acts could not constitute provocation based on the Michigan Supreme Court's order in *Palloni v. Smith*, 429 N.W.2d 593 (Mich. 1988). *Bradacs v. Jiacobone*, 625 N.W.2d 108, 112–113 (Mich. Ct. App. 2001). Subsequently, the Michigan Court of Appeals in *Brans*, discussed above, rejected this reasoning. 701 N.W.2d 163. It reviewed *Palloni*, along with the earlier Michigan Supreme Court case, *Nicholes v. Lorenz*, 237 N.W.2d 468 (Mich. 1976)(issue was relevance of dog's prior behavior); and other state court decisions under similar statutes. Based on this review, the *Brans* court determined that unintentional acts could constitute provocation, reinforcing the above conclusion that Mr. Smith is not likely liable for Ms. Johnson's dog bite injuries.	This counter argument is included last. It makes the email a little long. But it is informative and the attorney might appreciate the extra information.
I would be happy to answer any follow-up questions. The best way to contact me is by email, at summerassociate@lawfirm.com.	
Best Regards,	
Summer Associate	
[Confidentiality Statement]	

3.   More Complex Memorandum

Having reviewed two different memoranda formats involving a straight-forward statutory analysis, the next sample memorandum is in the full format involving a more complex common law problem. Notice that this memorandum uses an Introduction instead of the Question Presented/Short Answer format. For purposes of this sample memorandum, assume that the lawyer writing it has been presented with the following problem:

The lawyer's best client is Acme Company, a civil engineering firm. For some time, Acme has had a written contract to obtain customized computer software from ABC Corporation. Acme and ABC each have the right to terminate the contract at will, upon giving thirty days advance notice to the other party. ABC designs and makes the software from proprietary specifications provided by Acme under a confidentiality agreement that survives any termination of the contract. Acme's specifications are considered an Acme trade secret and are zealously guarded.

Raider Company is in the same engineering business as Acme, but it is not a direct competitor in the sense that, although it serves a lot of the same customers, it offers different services to them than Acme does. Raider has approached ABC to purchase customized software. Raider is aware of Acme's contract with ABC. Acme's business people have reason to believe that Raider has offered ABC incentives to enter into a lucrative software supply agreement, if ABC terminates its existing software supply deal with Acme, and also if ABC allows Raider to see Acme's confidential software specifications before ABC surrenders those back to Acme as part of the termination process.

Acme has now come to the lawyer and asked the following question: If ABC terminates its software supply agreement with Acme, and the incentives prove to be true, does Acme have any recourse against Raider?

Assume for purposes of this sample memorandum that the only relevant cases are the *RJM Sales & Marketing*, *Hough Transit*, *Oak Park Development*, and *J.N.R. Enterprises* decisions discussed in Chapter 6 of this text.

MEMORANDUM

To: Senior Partner

From: Associate

Date: November 1, 20XX

Re: Tortious Interference with a Terminable-at-Will Contract between Acme and ABC.

Introduction

Acme Company ("Acme") has a terminable-at-will contract with ABC Corporation ("ABC") for customized computer software based on Acme's proprietary specifications. Acme questions whether it can sue Raider Company ("Raider") under the doctrine of tortious interference with contract if Raider procures termination of Acme's existing software contract with ABC Corporation ("ABC") and, in the process, obtains access to Acme's propriety software specifications without Acme's consent.

Under those circumstances, Acme will have a cause of action against Raider for tortious interference with the Acme/ABC contract. Acme's contract with ABC is terminable at will. Such contracts are generally not subject to tortious interference claims, but tortious interference does exist when a party commits an independently wrongful act in connection with contract termination. Raider will have wrongfully obtained Acme's proprietary trade secrets in connection with the termination of the contract. Raider's misappropriation of Acme's trade secrets will likely constitute an independently wrongful act that will allow Acme to pursue a claim against Raider for tortious interference.

Facts

For some time, Acme has had a written contract to obtain customized computer software from ABC Corporation. Acme and ABC each has the right to terminate the contract at will upon giving thirty days advance notice to the other party. ABC designs the software from proprietary specifications provided by Acme under a confidentiality agreement that survives any termination of the contract. Acme's specifications are considered an Acme trade secret and are zealously guarded.

Raider Company is in the same engineering business as Acme, but Raider is not a direct competitor in the sense that, although it serves many of the same customers, it offers different services to them than Acme does. Raider has approached ABC to purchase customized software. Raider is aware of Acme's contract with ABC. Acme's business people have reason to believe that Raider has offered ABC incentives to enter into a lucrative software supply agreement, provided

An Introduction section sets forth the issue, the conclusion, along with information to help the reader understand both.

Tell the relevant fact story. Be concise, especially if you are writing the memo to an internal audience who is already generally familiar with the facts.

But do not neglect to identify the key facts—they drive the legal analysis. Further, if someone is reviewing your memo at some future time, the fact section will be critical to understanding why you

that (1) ABC terminates its existing software supply deal with Acme, and (2) ABC allows Raider to see Acme's confidential software specifications before ABC surrenders those back to Acme as part of the termination process.

Analysis

Tortious Interference With A Terminable-At-Will Contract Requires A Wrongful Act That Procures A Breach Of The Relevant Contract Or That Is Accompanied By Other Independently Wrongful, Actionable Conduct.

> *This point heading is framed in generic terms and introduces the analysis.*

A cause of action for tortious interference with a contract requires "(1) the existence of a contract, (2) the alleged tortfeasor's knowledge of that contract, (3) the intentional interference with the contract, (4) without justification, and (5) damages resulting from the interference." *Oak Park Dev. Co. v. Snyder Bro. of Minn., Inc.*, 499 N.W.2d 500, 505 (Minn. Ct. App. 1993).

> *Note that in this sample, the first paragraph sets forth the relevant rule, including the elements, which provide an organizational structure for the analysis that follows.*

In this present circumstance, two of these elements are uncontested. There is a contract between Acme and ABC, and Raider is aware of that contract. The balance of this Memorandum focuses on the three remaining elements.

> *Here, the writer expressly identifies undisputed elements and takes them as given.*

1. If Raider Commits an Independent Tort then Acme can Establish Intentional Interference.

Intentional interference means that a defendant has "induced [another] party to breach [the relevant] contract or that the defendant intentionally interfered with the plaintiff's contractual rights by committing an independent tort." *J.N.R. Enter., Inc. v. Frigidaire Co.*, No. C5–98–2281, 1999 WL 377747, at *3 (Minn. Ct. App. June 1, 1999).

Historically, Minnesota courts did not recognize a claim for tortious interference with a terminable-at-will contract. *Hough Transit, Ltd. v. Nat'l Farmers Org.*, 472 N.W.2d 358, 361 (Minn. Ct. App. 1991); *RJM Sales & Mktg., Inc. v. Banfi Prod. Corp.*, 546 F. Supp. 1368, 1378 (D. Minn. 1982). Recently, however, the Minnesota Court of Appeals has abandoned that view. *J.N.R. Enter.*, 1999 WL 377747 at *3; *Oak Park Dev.*, 499 N.W.2d at 505.

> *When providing an analysis based on elements, it's important to include a statement of the element itself, including a definition or explanation if possible. (Note that the writer cites to an unpublished opinion. Recall that in Minnesota, unpublished opinions may be cited and subsequent courts may adopt the reasoning.)*

Currently, "intentionally interfering" with a terminable-at-will contract requires that the company commit an independent tort that actually interferes with the contract. *J.N.R. Enter.*, 1999 WL 377747 at *3. This is because interference with a terminable-at-will contract does not necessarily rise to the level of tortious conduct when either party was free lawfully to terminate the contract upon giving proper notice. Consequently, to maintain a suit against Raider for tortious interference with the present terminable-at-will contract, Acme will have to establish that Raider committed an independently wrongful act in connection with the termination of the contract.

> *Note how in this expanded rule section, the writer synthesizes the pattern from the cases, looking at the courts' language and the results.*

There is only one case among the four applicable to Acme's situation where the court permitted a plaintiff to continue with a claim that a defendant had tortiously interfered

> *After the rule explanation, note that*

> *gave the legal advice you did.*

with a terminable-at-will contract between the plaintiff and another party. In *J.N.R. Enterprises*, the court determined that defendant's alleged defamation of plaintiff could serve as a basis for plaintiff's tortious interference action. 1999 WL 377747 at *3. Although this opinion is unpublished, it represents the court's clearest statement of the emerging rule with respect to intentional interference with terminable-at-will contracts.

the writer starts with the case that is most similar to the Acme situation.

J.N.R. Enterprises had a terminable-at-will contract with Frigidaire to distribute Frigidaire products. Subsequently, Frigidaire gave J.N.R. notice that it would terminate the distribution contract in sixty days. Prior to the termination, J.N.R. sued Frigidaire and ALL, Inc. to enjoin the contract's termination. J.N.R. alleged that ALL had tortiously interfered with the distribution contract between J.N.R. and Frigidaire and that ALL had defamed J.N.R. because ALL personnel had made statements to Frigidaire that J.N.R. was not fulfilling its contract with Frigidaire. *Id.* at *3. The court refused to grant ALL summary judgment on the defamation claim and then ruled that "the defamation claim may properly serve as a basis" for the tortious interference claim." *Id.* at *4. Acme's situation is similar to J.N.R. Enterprises' in that Raider is seeking access to Acme's proprietary design information—which may be a tortious act—in connection with urging ABC to terminate the Acme-ABC contract.

The facts are given so that they can be compared and contrasted with the facts of the Acme situation.

By contrast, the courts have refused to permit a plaintiff to proceed when there was no independent tortious conduct. In *Oak Park Development*, the court refused to allow a mall owner to proceed with a tortious interference action against a current tenant where there was no evidence of intentional interference. 499 N.W.2d at 506. In *Oak Park*, the owner of a mall alleged that a current tenant delayed providing a needed subordination agreement that would allow the mall owner to obtain a mortgage for the mall's expansion to host a new anchor tenant. *Id.* at 502. The court determined that the owner's actions and a more lucrative offer to the anchor tenant had caused the anchor tenant to breach its contract with the mall owner and that there was no evidence that the current tenant intentionally interfered with the contract between the anchor tenant and the mall owner. *Id.* at 506.

One cannot avoid unfavorable authority. It's best to provide it, address it, and then attempt to do something with it.

Similarly, in *Hough Transit*, the court refused to allow Hough Transit, a hauler of milk, to proceed with a tortious interference claim against a farm co-op, National Farmers Organization, where there was no independently wrongful conduct. 472 N.W.2d at 361. The co-op had asked one of Hough Transit's employees to start his own milk hauling business when the co-op became dissatisfied with Hough Transit's business practices. The employee did, and the co-op stopped using Hough Transit. *Id.* at 359. The court noted that even if Minnesota permitted a claim for tortious interference with a terminable-at-will contract (which it did not at that time), Hough Transit could not show that any of the co-op's actions were independently wrongful. *Id.* at 361.

And in *RJM Sales & Marketing*, the court refused to allow RJM Sales to proceed with a tortious interference claim against Banfi Products Corp. because Banfi's hiring of an RJM Sales employee was not "unconscionable." 546 F. Supp. at 1378. RJM had a terminable-at-will contract with an employee who resigned and began working for Banfi. The court stated that jurisdictions recognizing a claim for tortious interference with a terminable-at-will contract require a plaintiff to prove " 'concomitant unconscionable conduct' . . . such as misappropriation of trade secrets . . . ." *Id.* (internal citation omitted). It concluded that Banfi's conduct of hiring an experienced employee did not rise to that level. *Id.*

> While the synthesis of the pattern from the cases was stated earlier, here the writer has demonstrated the pattern through the case explanations.

Thus, the pattern that emerges in these cases is that a plaintiff must be able to establish that a defendant committed an independently wrongful act in connection with urging a party to breach the relevant terminable-at-will contract.

> The writer then, at the conclusion of the case explanations, can restate the pattern that has emerged.

The above cases are distinguishable and reinforce Acme's position. In those cases, the plaintiffs could not show that the defendants engaged in an independently wrongful action. For example, a defendant hiring an employee from another company without some additional wrongful behavior could not support a tortious interference with contract claim. *RJM Sales*, 546 F. Supp. 1368; *Hough Transit*, 472 N.W.2d 358. If Raider is successful in convincing ABC to terminate its contract with Acme and, in connection with the termination, ABC gives Raider access to Acme's proprietary design information, then Raider has committed an independently wrongful action. Under these circumstances, unlike the above cases, Raider wrongfully acquiring Acme's proprietary information could support Acme's tortious interference with contract claim.

> In this application section, the cases are distinguished.
>
> But they actually buttress the client's position.

Acme's position is consistent with the policy behind "tortious interference" law. In the commercial arena, all kinds of activities may "interfere" with contracts. If all of those interferences were "tortious," the courts would be deluged with lawsuits, and businesses (including Acme) would be reluctant to act. Yet, at the same time, commercial activity must be reasonable and fair. Concluding that Raider's conduct is actionable is consistent with the balance struck by the current rule.

> Note how the writer demonstrates that his conclusion is consistent with the policies behind the rule. Whenever possible, include a policy argument to support your analysis.

2. *Raider Does Not Have a Competitor's Privilege.*

The court in *J.N.R. Enterprises* noted that there is a "competitor's privilege" that might justify a defendant's interference with a terminable-at-will contract. 1999 WL 377747 at *4. The court set forth a four-prong test. "[O]ne who causes a third party 'not to continue an existing contract terminable at will does not interfere improperly with the other's relation if:' (1) the matter involves competition between the actor and the plaintiff; (2) the actor does not employee wrongful means, (3) the action does not constitute an unlawful restraint of trade and (4) the action is taken to advance a competitive interest." *Id.* (internal citation omitted). The court stated that a defendant's promise to another party to double its business is simply good

> When there is more than one element in dispute, or there is a multi-level analysis, provide sub-headings to divide the analysis into manageable parts—both for the writer and the reader.

competition, is protected by the competitor's privilege, and would not be considered defamation. *Id.* The court then determined that because the promise could not be considered to be defamatory, it could not be a basis for a tortious interference claim. *Id.*

Acme has two strong arguments if Raider were to claim a competitor's privilege. First, in *J.N.R. Enterprises*, where the court recognized the privilege, J.N.R. and ALL were direct competitors. *Id.* at *1. Raider is not truly a competitor with Acme. Raider offers different services than does Acme. Thus, Raider should not be able to rely on a competition privilege because it cannot meet the first requirement.

Second, and alternatively, even if Raider is a competitor, Raider is employing wrongful means to compete with Acme. It is unlawful to misappropriate trade secrets, as the *RJM Sales & Marketing* court made clear. 546 F. Supp. at 1378. Thus, unlike a competitive remark that is not defamatory, *J.N.R. Enterprises*, 1999 WL 377747 at *4, Raider's actions of wrongfully obtaining Acme's proprietary information would not be protected by the competitor's privilege.

3. *Acme Will Suffer Damages From Raider's Conduct.*

This part of the equation is less clear on the facts known to date. Acme would likely suffer injury from Raider's unauthorized access to Acme proprietary design specifications.

It would be important to ask for calculations as to the value of the specifications, any additional cost to Acme from having to procure production of the software from another company, and similar information.

> Note that there may be times when you need more facts to perform a sound analysis. Do not be afraid to talk with your client or colleagues and acquire this information.

Conclusion

Acme likely has a viable cause of action against Raider if Raider procures a termination of the ABC agreement with Acme and, in the process, obtains unauthorized access to Acme proprietary design information in exchange for offering a lucrative deal to ABC. All of the elements of tortious interference are present. First, there is a contract between ABC and Acme. Second, Raider knows about that agreement. Third, if Raider improperly obtains confidential information, then Raider has committed an independently wrongful act in procuring a termination of the agreement. In such a situation, intentional interference with a contract exists even if the termination is technically not a breach of the agreement because it is terminable at will on thirty days notice. Fourth, Raider may not rely on a competitor's privilege as justification for its actions because Raider is not a direct competitor and in any event must not engage in wrongful conduct, such as misappropriation of trade secrets, when it tries to claim a competition privilege. Fifth, damages likely will result, although calculations should be completed to verify the amount of potential damages.

> Note that this conclusion is a bit lengthier than the conclusion in the first sample memorandum. Here, the analysis was more complex, with multiple disputed elements, which required summarizing the analysis on those disputed elements in the conclusion.

D. ETHICAL CONSIDERATIONS

Lawyers, like many others, use email to communicate. Email can present some ethical challenges for lawyers. Recall from Chapter 7 that a lawyer owes his client a duty of confidentiality as to all client information that the lawyer learns during the representation.[13] Inadvertent disclosure of information through a misdirected email to a person outside of the firm can violate client confidentiality. A lawyer must take reasonable efforts to prevent inadvertent or unauthorized disclosure of client confidences.[14] Further, lawyers must understand the "benefits and risks associated with relevant technology."[15] Thus, although lawyers can use email, they must be familiar with the email system. In general, it is a good idea to avoid forwarding any email to individuals outside of the firm unless you are absolutely sure that a previous email in the chain does not contain confidential information. Additionally, it is probably best to turn off the "auto complete" function that finishes an email address once typing begins and also check that the email system does not default to "Reply all." These are just a couple of suggestions that might help you avoid sending confidential information in an email to an unintended recipient.

Relatedly, you might receive an inadvertently sent email. Model Rule of Professional Conduct 4.4(b) requires notification to the sender so that the sender can take precautionary steps.[16] The comment to this rule states that the person who receives the inadvertently sent email can delete it or send it back without reading it but does not mandate these actions.[17] What you decide to do with the inadvertently sent email should be based on how you would like opposing counsel to treat an email inadvertently sent from you.

E. THE CLIENT ADVICE LETTER TEMPLATE

Lawyers routinely write various types of letters. Some examples include client letters, which provide legal opinions and advice; demand letters, which are often sent in furtherance of adversarial matters; and general correspondence letters, which serve a variety of functions.[18] Our focus is on client advice letters, but the principles discussed below are applicable to most letter writing.

<u>All letters should be written with three things in mind: purpose, audience, and</u> <u>credibility.</u> The primary *purpose* of a client advice letter is to inform the client so that she understands what the law requires. More specifically, the client advice letter assists the client in making an informed decision about a specific matter. As the primary purpose of the client letter is to inform the client, she must be able to understand what is being stated.[19] For example, highly nuanced discussions of complex statutes and complicated judicial opinions that may be suitable for a trial or an appellate brief will have to be made more accessible to the client. More fundamentally, always ensure that the question posed by the client is clearly answered.

Although the primary *audience* is the client, do not assume that others will not see the letter. For example, the client may show the letter to another lawyer or to other colleagues.

---

[13] MODEL RULES OF PROF'L CONDUCT R. 1.6 (2016). This duty extends even after the representation is complete. MODEL RULES OF PROF'L CONDUCT R. 1.9(c)(2) (2016).

[14] MODEL RULES OF PROF'L CONDUCT R. 1.6(c).

[15] MODEL RULES OF PROF'L CONDUCT R. 1.1 cmt. 8 (2016).

[16] MODEL RULES OF PROF'L CONDUCT R. 4.4(b) (2016).

[17] *Id*. at 4.4(b) cmt 3.

[18] For a more in-depth discussion of these types of letters, see MARY BARNARD RAY & BARBARA J. COX, BEYOND THE BASICS 312–370 (2d ed. West 2003). *See also* THOMAS E. KANE, LETTERS FOR LAWYERS: ESSENTIAL COMMUNICATIONS FOR CLIENTS, PROSPECTS, AND OTHERS (2d ed. 2004).

[19] MODEL RULES OF PROF'L CONDUCT R. 1.4 (b).

The information in the letter, therefore, should be conveyed in a personable yet professional manner.

Finally, any legal document a lawyer signs, including a client letter, reflects on the lawyer's *credibility*, and can affect his professional reputation. Consequently, the lawyer's analysis and recommendations must have a sound basis in law, as well as in the facts provided by the client. The letter must also be edited to ensure it is free of grammatical and punctuation errors.

All letters include certain basic components: the introduction, the body, and the conclusion. Beyond those basic components, however, the lawyer has flexibility in formatting the letter to suit the situation.

The *introduction* in a client letter, which will consist of one or more paragraphs, connects with the client and provides the issue and a brief conclusion. It is our opinion that a personal connection is a good way to start a letter to a client. For example, a letter could start by stating: "Since our meeting last week, I have reviewed . . . ."

The issue and brief conclusion come next. Unlike the office memorandum, these are not formally titled. In particular, the issue, or question posed by the client, is not labeled as in the office memorandum.[20] If the conclusion reached is unfavorable, suggest, if possible, that there are options, and then delve into those options in the body of the letter. Additionally, lawyers often provide a caveat, explaining that their conclusions are predictions, not absolute guaranties, of a particular outcome.

The *body* of the letter often accomplishes three things: First, it states the facts as provided by the client. Second, it provides the analysis or explanation. Both of these sections are similar to the facts and analysis sections of an office memorandum. If the letter is relatively lengthy, then it may be prudent to provide section headings, point headings, and sub-headings, just as in the office memorandum. Third, the body of the letter includes options, recommendations, and advice, where appropriate.

The *conclusion* offers a summary and a closing, and should suggest next steps for the client. A sample of a formal client advice letter with these sections is provided in the next section.

Sometimes, a client does not want a formal client letter but instead wants a short summary of how the law applies to the client's situation. This short summary is often submitted by email. The format then is similar to an email memorandum and many of the suggestions stated previously regarding the email memorandum apply to a client advice letter sent by email. There is, however, an important difference between an email memorandum and an email client letter. The substantive content of the client letter sent by email must be tailored so that the client can understand the information.

Another possible scenario is that a supervisory attorney may want to send a summary client letter as a cover letter introducing an attached full memorandum. When a client letter is a cover letter or when the client only wants a short summary, the client letter is less detailed, although it still contains the same components. Examples of how this summary client letter format might look if it were being sent by email are provided after the formal client letter example in the next section.

---

[20] For example, compare the Question Presented and Short Answer in the first sample memorandum with the introductory paragraphs in the first sample client letter.

1. Ethical Considerations

Regardless of the format, an attorney is required to give information to a client so that the client can make informed decisions.[21] Thus, as stated above, an attorney's recommendations to clients must be based on a correct interpretation of the governing law and the existing facts and must be stated in a manner in which the clients can understand. Further, the attorney must be candid, even when he knows that he is delivering bad news to the client.[22] The goal is for the client to be able to intelligently make decisions about the representation.[23]

2. Sample Client Letters

Three sample client letters follow. The first sample is a formal client letter based on the Acme Company memorandum above. The second sample is based on the same Acme memorandum but assumes that the client letter is being sent by email to an in-house attorney for Acme. The third sample, based on the Smith/Johnson dog-bite hypothetical, assumes a client letter sent by email, but assumes that it is being sent to an individual who does not regularly encounter legal documents.

We want to emphasize that there are various formats for letter writing. If your legal writing professor prefers another format, then you should adapt the following samples to conform to his or her template. As with the office memorandum samples, the citations generally conform to the *ALWD Guide*.

As a reminder for this first sample client letter, you are also assuming that the only relevant cases are the *RJM Sales & Marketing, Hough Transit, Oak Park Development*, and *J.N.R. Enterprises* decisions discussed in Chapter 6 of this text, and that the question Acme asked the lawyer was: If ABC terminates its software supply agreement with Acme, and the incentives prove to be true, does Acme have any recourse against Raider?

Solock & Pherwood, P. C. **Attorneys and Counselors at Law** **333 Not Real Street** **No Place, Minnesota 1234X** **555.555.5555**	Letterhead of firm
November 15, 20XX	Date
Mr. Jonathon Drake Vice President of Risk Management Acme Company 111 Any Street Any Town, Minnesota 1255X	Recipient's address
Re: Contract Interference by Raider Company	Reference
Dear Mr. Drake: We have reviewed whether Acme has any recourse against Raider Company if Raider successfully causes ABC Corporation to terminate its contract with Acme and, in the process, Raider improperly obtains access to Acme's	In these introductory paragraphs, the writer connects with the client, states the issue in terms the client can

---

[21]   MODEL RULES OF PROF'L CONDUCT R. 1.4(b).

[22]   MODEL RULES OF PROF'L CONDUCT R. 2.1

[23]   MODEL RULES OF PROF'L CONDUCT R. 1.4 cmt 5.

proprietary software specifications. In brief, we conclude that under these circumstances, Acme would have a cause of action against Raider because Raider's intentional conduct is accompanied by Raider's theft of a trade secret.

Our conclusion, while not a guaranty of how a court would ultimately rule, is based on relevant cases from the Minnesota courts as applied to the facts you presented to us, as well as the Acme-ABC contract we reviewed.

Facts

Acme has a written contract with ABC to obtain customized computer software. Each party has the right to terminate the contract at will upon giving thirty days advance notice to the other party. ABC designs the software from proprietary specifications that Acme provides to ABC under a confidentiality agreement that survives any termination of the contract. Acme's specifications are considered an Acme trade secret and are zealously guarded.

Raider is in the same business as Acme. They are not, however, direct competitors. Although they serve many of the same customers, Raider offers different services to these clients than does Acme. Raider is aware of Acme's contract with ABC.

Acme executives have learned that Raider recently approached ABC to purchase customized software. Moreover, Acme executives have reason to believe that Raider has offered incentives to ABC to enter into a lucrative software supply agreement with Raider, provided that (1) ABC terminates its existing software supply deal with Acme, and (2) ABC allows Raider to see Acme's confidential software specifications before ABC surrenders them to Acme as part of the ABC/Acme contract termination.

If these facts have changed since we met last week, or if there are additional facts not known to us, please contact the law firm because our analysis could change.

Explanation

Acme's recourse against Raider would be to file suit for tortious interference with a contract. To prevail, Acme will have to establish the following five elements: (1) there is a contract between Acme and ABC; (2) Raider has knowledge of that contract; (3) Raider has intentionally interfered with that contract; (4) Raider has no justification to interfere with that contract; and (5) Acme has incurred damages as a result of Raider's intentional interference.[1]

---

[1] The Minnesota Court of Appeals set forth the elements of a tortious interference with a contract claim in *Oak Park Dev. Co. v. Snyder Bro. of Minn., Inc.*, 499 N.W.2d 500, 505 (Minn. Ct. App. 1993).

---

understand, and gives a brief answer to the client's question.

Note the statement that the writer's conclusion is not a guaranty of how a court will rule, but that it is a prediction of how a court would likely rule in light of the current law as applied to the facts.

The body of this letter includes the facts provided by the client. In general, it's wise to state the source of the facts and to suggest that if the facts are not as stated here, then the analysis could change.

The use of section headings is helpful to the reader, who can then easily distinguish between the facts and the explanation.

The body of this sample client letter includes an introduction to the analysis. It also signals an organizational structure—the elements of the claim that comprise the rule.

In Acme's situation, elements one and two are uncontested: There is a contract between Acme and ABC, and Raider is aware of that contract. The last three elements, however, need further examination and explanation.

1. If Raider Commits an Independent Tort Then Intentional Interference can Exist.

In general, "intentional interference with a contractual relationship" means that a company (such as Raider) induced a party (such as ABC) to breach the relevant contract (such as the Acme-ABC contract) or that the company intentionally interfered with the parties' contractual rights by committing an independent, wrongful act.[2]

Historically, there was no recourse against a company like Raider when the contract interfered with was "terminable at will," which is the type of contract between Acme and ABC.[3] The Minnesota Court of Appeals, however, now recognizes tortious interference with a terminable-at-will contract.[4] But "intentionally interfering" with a terminable-at-will contract requires that the company commit an independent wrong that actually interferes with the contract. This is because interference with a terminable-at-will contract does not necessarily rise to the level of wrongful conduct—tortious conduct—when either party was free lawfully to terminate the contract upon giving proper notice. Consequently, to maintain a suit against Raider for tortious interference with the present terminable-at-will contract, Acme will have to establish that Raider committed an independently wrongful act in connection with the termination of the contract.

There is only one case among the four applicable to Acme's situation where the court permitted a plaintiff to continue with a claim that a defendant had tortiously interfered with a terminable-at-will contract between the plaintiff and another party. In *J.N.R. Enterprises v. Frigidaire Co.*, the court allowed the plaintiff to proceed with a tortious interference action because the defendant had allegedly defamed the plaintiff. This is an "unpublished opinion," which means that while it is not authoritative, it can be cited as an authority and the court's reasoning may be adopted by later courts. Acme's situation is similar to J.N.R. Enterprises' in that Raider is seeking access to Acme's proprietary design information, which may be an independently wrongful act—a tortious act—in connection with urging ABC to terminate the Acme-ABC contract.

The sub-headings help to move the analysis forward while also keeping the reader focused.

Providing a good explanation of the rule is just as important in client letters as it is in office memoranda.

Note how the writer synthesizes the cases for the reader and then applies the pattern to the client's facts.

Here, the writer provides the client with an explanation of the value of an unpublished opinion.

[2] *J.N.R. Enter., Inc. v. Frigidaire Co.*, No. C5–98–2281, 1999 WL 377747, at *3 (Minn. Ct. App. June 1, 1999).

[3] *See Hough Transit, Ltd. v. Nat'l Farmers Org.*, 472 N.W.2d 356, 361 (Minn. Ct. App. 1991); *RJM Sales & Mktg., Inc. v. Banfi Prod. Corp.*, 546 F. Supp. 1368, 1378 (D. Minn. 1982).

[4] *See Oak Park Dev.*, 499 N.W.2d at 506; *J.N.R. Enter.*, 1999 WL 377747 at *3.

By contrast, the courts have refused to permit a plaintiff to proceed when there was no independently tortious conduct. In *Oak Park Development*, the court refused to allow the plaintiff to proceed with a tortious interference action when defendant could not agree with plaintiff on a related contract in time to allow plaintiff to sign a contract with a third party. The delay and negotiation between plaintiff and defendant was not evidence of intentional interference or independent wrongdoing. The *Hough Transit* court also refused to allow the plaintiff to proceed. It noted that even if Minnesota permitted a claim for tortious interference with a terminable-at-will contract (which it did not at that time), the plaintiff could not show that any of the defendant's actions in encouraging one of plaintiff's employees to start his own business to compete with plaintiff's were independently wrongful. Finally, in *RJM Sales & Marketing*, the court refused to allow the plaintiff to proceed and stated that jurisdictions recognizing a claim for tortious interference with a terminable-at-will contract require a plaintiff to prove " 'concomitant, unconscionable conduct' . . . such as misappropriation of trade secrets. . . ."[5] Thus, the pattern that emerges in these cases is that a plaintiff must be able to establish that a defendant committed an independently wrongful act in connection with urging a party to breach the relevant terminable-at-will contract.

These cases are distinguishable and actually reinforce Acme's position. If Raider is successful in convincing ABC to terminate its contract with Acme and, in connection with the termination, ABC gives Raider access to Acme's proprietary design information, then Raider has committed an independently wrongful action. Acme's proprietary design information constitutes a trade secret. Under these circumstances, Acme would be able to satisfy this element.

This conclusion is consistent with the general public policy that appears to be evolving, as evidenced in the most recent, albeit unpublished, opinion by the Minnesota Court of Appeals that balances freedom of action and fair dealing.

If applicable, tell the client that the conclusion is consistent with public policy.

2. *Raider Does Not Have a Competitor's Privilege.*

Raider could claim that it has a "competitor's privilege," which would justify its interference with Acme's terminable-at-will contract with ABC. In the *J.N.R. Enterprises* case, the court noted that a defendant's interference with a terminable-at-will contract may be justified by a "competitor's privilege." More specifically, the court commented that a promise by a defendant to a third party to double its business is simply good competition. But the court also stated that a defendant may not employ wrongful means.[6]

The body of the letter continues to provide a well-organized explanation in terms the client can understand.

---

[5]   546 F. Supp. at 1378 (internal citation omitted).

[6]   *J.N.R. Enter., Inc.*, 1999 WL 377747, at *4.

Acme has two strong arguments if Raider were to claim a competitor's privilege. First, Raider is not truly a competitor. Raider offers different services than does Acme. Thus, Raider should not be able to rely on a competition privilege.

Second, and alternatively, even if Raider is a competitor, Raider is employing wrongful means to compete with Acme. It is unlawful to misappropriate trade secrets, as the *RJM Sales & Marketing* court made clear. Thus, Raider's actions are not protected by the competitor's privilege.

3. *Acme Will Suffer Damages From Raider's Conduct.*

To prevail, Acme must establish that it suffered damages. Although it appears that Acme will suffer injury from Raider's unauthorized access to Acme's proprietary design specifications, it is not clear precisely how, and how much Acme will be damaged.

Therefore, we recommend that Acme calculate the value of the specifications and determine any additional cost to Acme from having to procure production of the software from another company.

Note that the body of this client letter ends with a specific request of the client. Without this information, the lawyer cannot fully answer the client's question.

Summary

If Raider is able to procure a termination of the Acme-ABC contract and, in the process, obtains unauthorized access to Acme proprietary design information in exchange for offering a lucrative deal to ABC, then Acme will be able to sue Raider and establish all of the elements of a tortious-interference-with-contract claim. First, there is an Acme-ABC contract. Second, Raider knows of that contract. Third, Raider will have committed an independent, wrongful act to procure ABC's termination of the agreement. Fourth, Raider may not rely on a competitor's privilege as justification for its actions. Fifth, damages will likely result, although precise calculations should be completed to determine the amount of those damages.

Formally conclude and provide a summary. If specific recommendations are necessary, include them here.

Please do not hesitate to contact us if you have any questions. We would be happy to meet with you.

At the end of the conclusion, reconnect with the client.

Very truly yours,

Christian Solock

Christian Solock

3. Client Letter Email

This second example assumes that the same client advice letter is being sent via email and that it is being sent to Ms. Day, the Associate General Counsel for Acme Company, who is an attorney. When an attorney is working with a sophisticated consumer of legal services, such as Ms. Day, the attorney may send a client letter via email that explains the analysis. This letter could be in addition to, or in place of, a full memorandum. If a full memorandum was completed, the attorney attaches it because the client has paid for it, and because the client might want to see the detailed legal analysis. Note also that the citations are in the text of the client letter email because here the client is familiar with legal documents and because adding footnotes to email is impractical.

From: christian.solock@solockpherwood.com To: emeline.day@acme.com Cc: _____ Subject: Acme may have a claim for tortious interference with contract against Raider. _____ Attachment: Acme.RaiderInterference.Memo.pdf	Note that in an email letter, certain letter components are not necessary: letterhead, date, address, and reference.
	The subject line concisely states the conclusion.
	The attachment is clearly labeled.

Dear Ms. Day,

> Here the associate attorney has not met with the client and does not have a personal connection, but thanking a client for their business is a good starting point.
>
> It is important to describe any attachments.

  Thank you for your inquiry regarding whether Acme Company has any recourse against Raider Company. We understand that Raider may offer ABC Company a lucrative software supply agreement on the condition that: ABC (1) allow Raider to see Acme's confidential software specifications; and then (2) terminate ABC's existing software supply contract with Acme. I have researched Minnesota law on this issue and conclude that under those circumstances, Acme will likely have a claim for tortious interference with contract against Raider. I have attached the legal memorandum fully addressing this issue. Below, I briefly set forth my analysis and conclusions.

Analysis:

  Under Minnesota law, a claim for tortious interference with contract requires "(1) the existence of a contract, (2) the alleged tortfeasor's knowledge of that contract, (3) the intentional interference with the contract, (4) without justification, and (5) damages resulting from the interference." *Oak Park Dev. Co. v. Snyder Bro. of Minn., Inc.*, 499 N.W.2d 500, 505 (Minn. Ct. App. 1993).

  Because Acme has an existing contract with ABC, and Raider is aware of the Acme/ABC contract, Acme can meet the first two requirements.

  We also believe that Acme can meet the remaining three requirements. I address each one separately.

1. Intentional Interference

  To prove the third requirement, intentional interference with a contract, Acme must show that Raider has committed a legal wrong that intentionally interfered with a contract. *J.N.R. Enter., Inc. v. Frigidaire Co.*, No. C5–98–2281, 1999 WL 377747, at *3 (Minn. Ct. App. June 1, 1999). Acme's contract with ABC is terminable at will because either party can terminate the contract at will upon giving thirty days notice. Intentional interference with a terminable-at-will contract without an independent legal wrong is not actionable. *Hough Transit, Ltd. v. Nat'l Farmers Org.*, 472 N.W.2d 358, 361 (Minn. Ct. App.

1991); *RJM Sales & Mktg., Inc. v. Banfi Prod. Corp.*, 546 F. Supp. 1368, 1378 (D. Minn. 1982). However, if Raider convinces ABC to allow Raider to access Acme's proprietary software design information in connection with convincing ABC to terminate its contract with Acme, then Raider has committed an independent legal wrong that interferes with Acme's contract with ABC. Acme's proprietary software design information is a trade secret, and it is unlawful to misappropriate trade secrets. *RJM Sales*, 546 F. Supp. at 1378.

2. Without Justification

Raider would likely argue that it has what is known as a "competitor's privilege" that justifies the intentional interference with the Acme/ABC contract. This privilege, however, is only available if the parties are competitors, the actions are taken to advance a competitive interest, and wrongful means or unlawful restraints of trade are not used. *J.N.R. Enter., Inc.*, 1999 WL 377747, at *4. As an example, a court has stated that a promise to double another party's business is simply good competition. *Id.* Raider's position is weak. First, Raider is not a true competitor. Raider offers different services than Acme. Also, Raider would likely lose the competitor's privilege due to the wrongful conduct of misappropriating trade secrets as a means to compete with Acme.

3. Damages

Lastly, Acme must show that it will suffer damages, such as injury from Raider's unauthorized access to Acme's proprietary design specifications or additional costs in finding another production company. If Raider takes the actions that Acme anticipates, I would ask that Acme calculate its potential damages due to Raider's actions.

Conclusion:

Assuming the exact factual circumstances you describe occur and Acme suffers damages, Acme would have a cause of action against Raider for the tort of interference with contract because all five requirements would be met.

Please do not hesitate to contact me with any questions. I will wait to hear from you as to how Acme would like to proceed if Raider takes these anticipated actions.

Best Regards,

Christian Solock
Solock & Pherwood, P.C.
Attorneys and Counselors at Law
333 Not Real Street
No Place, Minnesota 1234X
555.555.5555

[Confidentiality Statement]

This third example is based on the Smith/Johnson dog-bite memorandum set forth earlier in the chapter. It assumes that the client does not regularly encounter legal documents.

From: supervisory.attorney@lawfirm.com

To: wade.smith@cablecompany.com

Cc:

Subject: Likely No Liability for Ms. Johnson's Dog-bite Injuries.

Dear Mr. Smith,

I enjoyed meeting you for dinner last week. I know you are concerned about your potential liability because your dog, Sam, bit Selena Johnson when she was at your home for a barbeque last month. As you requested, I reviewed Michigan law regarding dog owner liability for dog bites because the Johnsons have asked that you pay any expenses not covered by insurance. It is my conclusion that you will not be liable for Ms. Johnson's injuries. I set forth a brief analysis below, and conclude with my recommendation on how to proceed.

Analysis:

Under Michigan law, if a person is bit by a dog while lawfully on the property, the dog owner will be liable unless the dog was provoked. As you explained to me, you invited Mr. and Mrs. Johnson and their children, Stephen and Selena, over for a barbeque. Therefore, Selena was lawfully on your property when Sam bit her. The remaining question then is whether she provoked Sam when she accidently stepped on Sam while playing tag.

Recent Michigan court decisions have ruled that even accidental or unintentional acts can constitute provocation. In one such case, the dog owner was not held liable when his sister who was walking backwards carrying a heavy objected accidently stepped on the dog. The court stated that she had provoked the dog. Consequently, a Michigan court is likely to conclude that because Selena accidently stepped on the dog, she provoked the dog, and you will not be liable.

Michigan's highest court has not directly ruled on this issue. Thus, my conclusion is not a guarantee. But based on my review of the current state of the law, I believe that you would not be held liable.

Recommendation:

You shared with me that you have been friends with the Johnsons for many years, and that they were kind to you and the kids after your wife passed away. I agree with your idea of offering to pay some of the expenses as a gesture of good

---

Note that in an email letter, certain letter components are not necessary as those are part of the email fields that should be completed.

The subject line concisely states the answer to the issue. Because no attorney can guaranty a result, the language used does not impliedly guarantee a result.

In writing the email to the client, retain the salutation and connect with the client.

Here in the first paragraph state the question asked and the answer.

Headings can be helpful in an email communication.

Notice the difference from the email memorandum on this subject sent to the supervisory attorney. Here the client would not understand citations so they are omitted. Additionally, there is no need to quote the law for the client.

Notice that similar to the email memorandum, there is not a separate fact section, but the facts are introduced when they are needed to complete the analysis.

An attorney is also a counselor. A recommendation that an attorney makes can take social and political factors

will. You might want to inquire as to the amount of out-of-pocket expenses that they anticipate and offer some money accordingly. I would recommend, however, that when you send the money you include a note stating that although you believe you are not legally responsible for these expenses, you would like to help pay for them.	into account, not just economic.
Please do not hesitate to contact me if you have any further questions or if you need any further assistance.	
Best regards,	Most law firms include a statement at the end of all email messages, noting the confidential and privileged nature of the communication.
Supervisory Attorney	
[Signature Block]	
[Confidentiality Statement]	

4. One More Ethical Consideration

Notice the Recommendation section in the above client letter makes a suggestion that seems contrary to the attorney's legal conclusion that Mr. Smith is not liable for Selena's dog bite injuries. In giving advice, lawyers can consider moral, social, political, or economic factors[24] and are not required to recommend only the "winner takes all" solution if the lawyer believes a different solution would benefit the client.

---

[24] MODEL RULES OF PROF'L CONDUCT R. 2.1.

CHAPTER 11

Communicating a Persuasive Analysis

In the previous chapter, we provided fundamental templates for two forms of predictive writing: office memoranda and client letters. Now, in this chapter, we provide fundamental templates for two forms of persuasive writing, trial court and appellate court briefs.[1] First, however, we will provide basic principles that apply to both forms of persuasive writing.

LEARNING OBJECTIVES

1. Students will learn how to provide critical analysis of competing legal positions and options.

2. Students will learn how to advocate for a particular legal position or option, and how to advocate for clients.

3. Students will learn how to tailor communication to applicable format restrictions and comply with procedural requirements.

A.   COMMON FEATURES OF GOOD PERSUASIVE WRITING

1.   In either a trial court brief or an appellate court brief, use some version of the IRAC template. All court briefs do the following: identify the problem to be addressed, present the legal rule that will govern the problem, analyze the rule, apply the rule to the specific facts of the problem, and formulate a conclusion that tells the court how the law should resolve the problem. Notice how this is different from the use of the IRAC template in the predictive setting. Now you are arguing how the law *should* apply, not just exploring how it *will* apply.

2.   Offer a solution to a problem. You are still in the problem-solving business. Your clients and colleagues do not want mere interesting discussions, nor does the court to which you are directing the brief. The court wants to know your client's view as to the proper legal resolution of the dispute that is already in litigation. So assert that view. Do so positively and with conviction.

---

[1]   As was true of the predictive writing examples, our examples of trial court and appellate court briefs are not intended to provide the only way to present a persuasive analysis. If your particular audience prefers or requires a different format, use that one. In the case of court briefs, each jurisdiction has format rules. These rules govern such topics as the sequence of the components, margin sizes, font types and sizes, paper size, length, use of numbered or non-numbered paper, use of covers, colors of covers, and the like. Ignore these rules at your peril. Failure to follow them can result in a court rejecting your brief.

Because the technical rules vary from court to court, we do not claim that our models comply with the requirements in every court. We do intend, however, to provide models that illustrate the basic concepts inherent in good persuasive writing and that illustrate the format that is relatively standard in many trial and appellate courts.

3.   Offer a solution that is favorable to your client. Your job in a brief is to present your client's view of the case as favorably as you can. So try to do that. If the best you can do is, "the other side wins," then you should have settled the matter.

But how do you face bad facts and legal authorities? There are four classic approaches:

➢   Claim that the facts and/or the authorities are not actually bad by using them affirmatively in support of your position. It is not unusual for facts and authorities to be double-edged, good for one party from one standpoint, but good for the other party from another standpoint. ("What this fact really proves is . . . ." "What that case really stands for is . . . .")

➢   Claim that the facts and/or the authorities do not matter. Not every bad fact or authority will be relevant to the case because the case will be resolved on another basis. ("The Court may disregard this fact because it is not material to the application of the relevant threshold rule." "The Court may disregard that case because it does not reflect the law in this jurisdiction on the point at issue.")

➢   Claim that the facts and/or the authorities are distinguishable. ("This fact is only unfavorable when combined with certain other facts that are not present in the instant case." "That case only reached this [unfavorable] result because the court based its decision on a combination of factors that are not all present in the instant case.")

➢   Claim that the facts and/or the authorities are simply wrong. ("Plaintiff in this case assumes the existence of [fact x], and [fact x] is simply not true." "That court adopted the view of only two other courts, while ten courts have rejected that view as incorrect.")

4.   Advocate. Your job now is to convince a court "that society's interest in drawing a line in a particular place, in order to resolve a case or controversy, coincides with the client's interest in winning particular relief."[2] Ask yourself the following questions:

➢   What relief *does* my client want?

➢   What argument will convince a court that the relief my client wants is also in the best interest of a broader constituency—the public, the court system, specific third parties, etc.?

➢   In what sequence do I have to make my points so that they lead to the desired conclusion?

5.   Focus on the factual story to tell. Recall that facts drive legal results. How you tell the story of the case will matter significantly. As you present the facts, try to follow these tips:

➢   Make sure there is a logical beginning, middle, and end to your fact recitation.

➢   Make sure you cover all the material facts that drive the legal result.

➢   Try to start and end with favorable facts.

---

[2]   CLARY, PRIMER ON THE ANALYSIS AND PRESENTATION OF LEGAL ARGUMENT, *supra* chapter 10, note 9, at 7.

> ➤ To the extent you can, make the characters come alive. Give the court a sense of the kind of people with whom it is dealing on one or both sides of the case, if that is to your advantage. (Of course, sometimes it is not to your advantage.) Additionally, once you have identified the parties' legal designations, use their names or a suitably descriptive noun in your argument.

> ➤ Think about what in the story makes it interesting. Even the most technical of legal issues arises from a clash among people and ideas. Draw the court's attention to that clash.[3]

6.   If your problem will be resolved through application of enacted law, begin your analysis with that. Recall that legal rules generally find their genesis in enacted law or common law cases. If the rule governing your problem comes from enacted law, start with that language. If the language is clear, you will apply that language. If possible, use deductive reasoning to predict how the statute resolves the problem.

If, as is often the case, the language is ambiguous, then you will try to ascertain the intent of the drafters in crafting the law from the purpose of the law, the type of rule it is, canons of statutory interpretation, the legislative history, court opinions, and, if applicable, agency interpretations.[4] A common mistake among beginning legal writers is to start the presentation of any legal analysis by explaining relevant court decisions. This is a natural result of reading first-year law school texts that are primarily casebooks. Begin an enacted law analysis with the enacted law itself. Your presentation of case analysis comes later.

7.   If your problem will be resolved through application of case decisions, then use analogical reasoning. Recall that the common law develops one case at a time. A court hears a dispute between two or more parties, decides on a rule to apply and a fair result, and issues a decision. Then a court hears a different dispute between two or more parties, decides whether this latest dispute is similar enough to the first one to apply the same rule (and, if not, decides on a different rule to apply), decides on a fair result, and issues a decision. Over many years, the collection of decisions gives rise to a body of legal principles. The lawyer's job is to write a persuasive analysis of the legal principle that will govern and how it will apply in a client's favor to the client's case. To do so, the lawyer engages in analogical by comparing and contrasting the current circumstances with those of prior relevant decisions to argue how the law *should* apply to resolve the current case.

8.   Start with your "high ground." Consistent with other fundamental principles, try where possible to start with your strongest argument and stay there as long as you can. Lead with strength. You may, of course, adopt an "even if" structure. For example, "My client wins for [reason number 1], but EVEN IF the Court adopts a different view, my client still wins for [reason number 2]."

Note two things about "even if" arguments. First, using too many of them will dilute the strength of your best position. Second, sometimes "even if" arguments work better with

---

[3]   There is an art to storytelling that goes well beyond the scope of this text. If you wish to learn more about that art, you might read such literature as Tom Galbraith, *Storytelling: The Anecdotal Antidote*, 28 Litig. 17–23 (2002). Galbraith reminds us that "[s]uccess in litigation revolves around two questions: What is legally important, and what is emotionally persuasive? The difference is that of the head and the heart. Law school and, increasingly, apprenticeship instruct the head and ignore the heart. As an antidote, I offer this suggestion: Come back to the oldest art form. Storytelling will teach you how to move an audience." *Id.* at 23. *See also* J. Christopher Rideout, *Applied Legal Storytelling: A Bibliography*, 12 Legal Comm. & Rhetoric 247 (2015) (collecting publications on the Applied Legal Storytelling movement); Jonathan K. Van Patten, *Storytelling for Lawyers*, 57 S.D. L. Rev. 239 (2012) (listing twenty-five propositions about storytelling).

[4]   Chapter 5 addresses issues of statutory interpretation. *See also* Clary, Primer on the Analysis and Presentation of Legal Argument, *supra* chapter 10 note 9, at 32–41; Clary et al., Advocacy on Appeal *supra* chapter 1 note 1, at 21–27.

legal points than factual ones. It is hard, for example, to argue, "My client was not at the scene. But even if he was, my client did not shoot the gun." On the other hand, it is not too implausible to argue, "The Court should interpret [legal rule] as meaning [X], but even if the Court interprets the rule to mean [Y], then my client still wins because . . . ."

9.   **Consider your audience.** Notice that you are now writing for a judge or judges (although other relevant audiences will include your client, your colleagues, and your adversaries). What are some of the features of judges as an audience?

> ➢   Judges are legally trained and may already be familiar with your type of legal problem from experience with other disputes. Indeed, judges may be the authors of the very authorities you are discussing. Know what perspective your specific judge (or judges) brings to your case.

> ➢   Judges are busy. They have too much to do, and too little time within which to do it. What does this mean? First, it means be precise. Do not assume that just because a judge is legally trained you can simply skip over parts of the legal analysis. Second, be concise. There is a reason why arguments to the court are called briefs.

> ➢   Judges expect you to give them deference and to treat opposing counsel deferentially. Judges do not like *ad hominem* personal attacks on your adversaries. ("I regret to inform the Court that Mr. X is a lying scumbag." *Do not say this*.) Judges expect civility. Convey the strength of your position using the facts and the law.

> ➢   Judges expect a certain degree of formality, i.e., no use of slang terms or colloquialisms unless those are peculiarly relevant to the specific facts of the dispute.

In addition, as you consider your audience, think about ways to present information that will be helpful. Lists are useful presentation devices in briefs, just as they are in predictive writing. List the elements of relevant legal rules. List helpful facts, and link that list to the legal element to which the facts pertain. Sometimes putting the lists in charts or tables can be visually appealing. *Help the court to see your analysis*.

10.   **Pay attention to the standard of review or burden of proof the court will have to apply in reaching a decision.** Courts do not always get to decide questions in any manner they may wish. For example, you will learn in your federal civil procedure course that a district court reviewing a Rule 12(b)(6) motion to dismiss a complaint on its face must take the facts well-pleaded in the complaint as true for purposes of the motion. A federal district court reviewing a Rule 56 summary judgment motion may not decide disputed issues of material fact. An appellate court reviewing a district court decision on a matter of law will typically review that decision *de novo* and substitute the appellate court's own view of that law, but an appellate court ordinarily must defer to a district court's fact findings unless those findings are clearly erroneous. There are a number of important procedural rules relating to the standards that courts must use to review certain kinds of questions at specific stages of proceedings. Your briefs typically should remind the court of the relevant standards of review.

B.   ETHICAL CONSIDERATIONS

In drafting a document for a court, there are numerous ethical rules that will govern. We have discussed some of these rules in previous chapters, but they are worth mentioning again in the context of persuasive writing.

Initially, as previously discussed, when you submit a document to the court, it cannot contain frivolous arguments,[5] and it should contain all controlling authority—even authority that is adverse.[6] It must also be timely submitted. This diligence requirement[7] takes on added importance because failure to timely submit documents to the court can have enormous negative impact on your client's case, resulting in a forfeiture of arguments, defenses, or the entire case when a statute of limitations has run.[8]

Additionally, and importantly, a document submitted to the court must be truthful: it cannot contain false statements of law or fact.[9] Such requirements are not at odds with presenting your client's case persuasively and favorably.[10] Instead, the rules set the outside limit, preventing omission or a false description of the law or facts that would mislead the court.[11] There is an additional duty not to make false statements of material fact or law to third parties, including opposing counsel.[12] Thus, the lawyer as an advocate for his client should craft a story that favors his client and should describe the governing law in a way that allows for the resolution the client is seeking, limited by his duty to be truthful.

C. THE TRIAL COURT BRIEF TEMPLATE

Putting together everything you know so far, how might you prepare a standard federal district court brief?

As you review the sample trial court papers that follow at page 142, notice some of the following components.

1. The Motion Itself

Requests for a ruling from a trial court are normally made by written notice and motion. The notice tells the court and all of the lawyers in the case that the moving party will be requesting a hearing from the judge at a particular day, time, and place. The motion tells the court and lawyers what order (relief) the moving party wants, and it recites a shorthand version of the grounds. The motion also typically identifies for the court and lawyers the materials upon which the moving party relies to support the motion. Sometimes the notice and the motion are combined into a single document for efficiency. An example of a notice and motion is included with the third sample trial brief on page 155.

2. The Brief Itself

a. Introduction

The purpose of this section is to provide the court with a brief introduction to the issue or issues. As you will recall, judges are busy people, and they want to know up front two things: "What do you want me to do, counsel, and why should I do that?"[13]

---

[5]   MODEL RULES OF PROF'L CONDUCT R. 3.1 (2016).

[6]   MODEL RULES OF PROF'L CONDUCT R. 3.3(a)(2) (2016).

[7]   MODEL RULES OF PROF'L CONDUCT R. 1.3 (2016) ("[a] lawyer shall act with . . . promptness in representing a client.").

[8]   *Id.* at cmt. 3.

[9]   MODEL RULES OF PROF'L CONDUCT R. 3.3.

[10]   *See id.* at 3.3 cmt. 2 (recognizing that a lawyer must present the client's case persuasively).

[11]   *Id.* at 3.3.

[12]   MODEL RULES OF PROF'L CONDUCT R. 4.1(a) (2016).

[13]   One of the authors was in court when a United States Magistrate Judge literally began an oral argument on a motion with those very words to the assembled lawyers.

The Introduction sets the focus for the rest of the brief. It tells the court why, based on precedent and policy, your client should win. Developing a focus is an important part of persuasive writing, especially when writing to a court. The focus often acts as the glue that holds together the various arguments. For example, if your client has been charged with conspiracy to commit first-degree murder, and your research reveals that an agreement—express or implied—is an essential element of finding a conspiracy, then one focus you may select is that your client never agreed to the conspiracy. Your brief would emphasize those facts that would lead the trier of fact to conclude that there is no evidence on that point.

Some judges, and some professors, require a persuasive question presented or statement of the issue in this section. There are several ways to construct a question presented, which are discussed in the section of this book on appellate briefs because that is the context in which the requirement is most likely to arise.

b. Statement of Facts

In working with the facts, it is often useful to categorize facts as either material (directly legally significant), contextual, or procedural. *Material facts* are those facts that are critical to resolving the client's problem—the facts that drive the analysis. *Contextual facts* are not essential to the analysis, but they provide important background for "selling" the story. Contextual facts may lend an emotional edge to the story, for example, and experienced advocates know that judicious use of emotional facts can help to make their clients appear sympathetic. Be cautious, though. Inexperienced advocates sometimes rely too heavily on emotional facts, which may cause the reader to recoil. *Procedural* facts describe how the parties and the case proceeded through the court system to arrive at the current issue before the court.

Sometimes facts will be undisputed. Alternatively, the parties may stipulate that the facts are undisputed for the limited purposes of a specific motion. ("Your Honor, even assuming the facts are exactly as [the adversary] wishes they were, we still win this motion as a matter of law because . . . .") Often, however, the parties will not agree on the facts for any purposes. In any case, it is the advocate's job to put her client's best foot forward while ensuring as an officer of the court that all material facts—favorable and unfavorable—are accounted for.

Those facts that are favorable should be given greater emphasis. Those that are unfavorable should be given less emphasis. The easiest way to emphasize facts is to place them at the beginning or ending of paragraphs. Similarly, to deemphasize facts, place them in the middle of a paragraph. Many readers look predominantly at the first and last sentences of a paragraph and tend to skim over the middle section. Minimizing unfavorable facts by placing them between favorable facts promotes reader attention to the favorable ones.

c. Argument Point Headings

The argument section of your brief will contain the bulk of the analysis. The analysis of each issue addressed in the brief is presented separately. In general, for each issue, there should be a major point heading, a complete sentence set off from the text. This point heading introduces the argument for that issue. Often, however, there is more than one argument for each issue. In those cases, the major point heading is stated in general terms, often in a way that previews your focus. Then the minor point headings introduce each discrete argument. Crafting persuasive point headings is an applied art. They take time, patience, and skill.

Point headings can be written neutrally, so as to only introduce the issue without resolving it. Point headings can also be written persuasively, in a way that both introduces and resolves the issue at once. Generally, writing persuasive point headings promotes your argument and helps preview your reasoning to the reader. Several examples of major and minor point headings can be seen in the sample briefs in this Chapter.

For example, assume that your client has been charged with violating the federal drug analogue statute. Further assume that you have a legitimate argument that the relevant section under which your client was charged is ambiguous because it is not clear from the text whether the definition of an analogue requires a conjunctive reading (subsection i must be satisfied *plus* either subsection ii or iii) or a disjunctive reading (*only one* of subsections i, ii, or iii must be satisfied). Finally, assume that you have authority for the proposition that Congress never intended the statute to reach your client's conduct.

Example of Major and Minor Point Headings:

I.   The Definition of a Controlled Substance Analogue Is Most Properly Read in the Conjunctive.

A.   The statutory definition of "controlled substance" is ambiguous.

B.   The legislative history supports a conjunctive interpretation.

C.   Under the rule of lenity, an ambiguity in a criminal statute should be interpreted in Defendant's favor.[14]

Notice that these headings are full sentences. They are also framed as assertions, not questions.

d.   *The Argument*

The remainder of the argument section of a legal memorandum is composed of the various arguments. Like the analysis section in a memorandum or the explanation section in a client letter, it is the heart and soul of the brief.

In general, there are five types of arguments, each representing a type of authority available to the problem-solver/advocate: text, intent, precedent, tradition, and policy.[15] *Text arguments* are based on the actual language used in the particular document—e.g., a constitution, statute, administrative rule, or contract. These textual arguments primarily rely on the plain meaning of the text and the canons of statutory construction.[16]

Intent arguments focus on what the drafters of the document intended by the words they used. Often, intent arguments are paired with text arguments. Thus, in interpreting a constitutional provision, the advocate looks to the framers' intent; similarly, when interpreting a statute, the advocate looks to the legislature's intent.

Precedent arguments focus on the evolution of the law through judicial opinions. The United States, you will recall, is fundamentally a common law system. In the absence of a controlling statute, courts give great deference to prior courts' opinions. Even when there is a statute, courts will look to how other courts have interpreted and applied that statute.

---

[14]   Statutory interpretation begins with the plain meaning. But there are times, such as in this example, when the advocate's best argument is that the term or statute is ambiguous. In that situation, the advocate may forego the plain meaning argument.

[15]   This discussion of the types of arguments draws heavily from Wilson R. Huhn, *Teaching Legal Analysis Using a Pluralistic Model of Law*, 36 GONZAGA L. REV. 433 (2000–2001).

[16]   A more detailed discussion of plain meaning, canons of construction, and legislative intent is provided in Chapter 5.

Tradition arguments are somewhat elusive because they are not based on enacted law or judicial opinions, but on recognized traditions—or fundamental beliefs—that inform our way of life. In business, for example, these types of arguments are based on the ways and customs in which businesses traditionally conduct their affairs.

Policy arguments look at the potential consequences of a proposed rule, interpretation, or outcome. Those consequences are then balanced against the values or policies the law was designed to protect. It is not uncommon for each side to have a policy argument, and the court must choose between competing policies. Additionally, policy arguments can be emotionally and politically charged.

e. Conclusion

The conclusion is a succinct summary and request for relief. Do not try to summarize all the arguments. Instead, state the relief requested and the primary reasons why the relief should be granted.

3. A Strategy for Getting Started

Beginning a brief can be daunting. These four steps will help you begin the process of writing:

First, become thoroughly familiar with the record facts. Draw a three-column chart, listing favorable facts, neutral facts, and unfavorable facts.[17]

Second, develop working major and minor point headings. These can be drafted while you are researching and developing your strategy. Do not get overly attached to your initial drafts. They are merely starting points. You will revise and refine them as you revise and refine your arguments.

Third, annotate your working drafts of the point headings. Under each point heading, list the relevant authorities and how you intend to use them. Additionally, list the key points that you intend to make. Finally, list the facts or evidence on which you will rely.

Fourth, select one point heading that relates to a discrete argument and its corresponding annotations and start writing a first draft of the argument. Once you have completed a first draft of that argument, select another point heading and repeat the process.

This strategy allows you to divide up your writing into manageable units. It is simply not feasible to write a brief from beginning to end in one sitting unless, perhaps, you have a single issue and a single argument for that issue.

4. Sample District Court Motion Documents

The following samples provide templates that employ a version of the IRAC structure to advocate. The citations in these samples generally conform to *The Bluebook.*

The first two samples involve an issue of statutory construction, similar to the discussion in Chapter 5. These samples are placed in a fictitious jurisdiction—the State of

---

[17] The authors thank University of Detroit Mercy School of Law Professors Cara Cunningham Warren and Michelle Richards for this exercise.

Hosmer. Assume that the U.S. District Court for the District of Hosmer is the only district in the 12th Circuit,[18] and that this case presents an issue of first impression for the Court.[19]

The procedural posture for this case is as follows:

The Defendant, Susan Anderson, was arrested, following an investigation conducted by federal special agents into her activities at the Bank of Hosmer. Anderson was subsequently charged with bank fraud in violation of 18 U.S.C. § 1344 and aggravated identity theft in violation of 18 U.S.C. § 1028A(a)(1). Prior to trial, Anderson moved for dismissal of all charges. First, she argued that the bank fraud statute was not applicable. Second, she argued that even if the bank fraud statute were applicable, she could not be found guilty of aggravated identity theft because the Government did not allege and could not prove that she knew the identification matched a real person. A jury convicted Anderson of both charges. During the trial, the 12th Circuit ruled in a different case that the bank fraud statute applies in situations such as the one presented in this case. So defense counsel dropped that legal argument.

Immediately after the trial, Anderson renewed her objection to the application of the aggravated identity theft statute, and moved for judgment of acquittal on the Section 1028A conviction under Federal Rule of Criminal Procedure 29. The Government opposed the motion. The trial court requested briefs. The parties stipulated to certain factual findings for the purpose of deciding this motion.

---

[18] A fictitious jurisdiction is often employed when a professor wants to control the scope of permissible authority allowed for a particular writing problem or examination. While this contrivance is not fully consistent with what students will encounter in the practice of law, it does allow students to focus on specific analytical and writing skills.

[19] The problem is based on a case that was pending before the United States Supreme Court. For purposes of these samples, assume that the fictitious trial and Rule 29(c) motion pre-date the Supreme Court's grant of certiorari, as well as its ultimate ruling on the merits. To learn how the Court resolved the issue, *see* Flores-Figueroa v. U.S., 556 U.S. 646 (2009).

UNITED STATES DISTRICT COURT
DISTRICT OF HOSMER
CRIMINAL CASE NO. 08–1094

Virtually all court documents contain a caption, setting forth the court, names of the parties, case number, and document title.

UNITED STATES OF AMERICA,
        Plaintiff,

        v.

SUSAN ANDERSON,
        Defendant.

Hon. Andrew Aguecheek
United States District Judge

MEMORANDUM IN SUPPORT OF DEFENDANT'S MOTION FOR JUDGMENT OF ACQUITTAL UNDER FEDERAL RULE OF CRIMINAL PROCEDURE 29(c)

INTRODUCTION

The Defendant, Susan Anderson ("Ms. Anderson"), submits this Memorandum in support of her Motion for Acquittal under Federal Rule of Criminal Procedure 29(c). In this case, the United States of America ("Government") charged Ms. Anderson with bank fraud and aggravated identity theft in violation of 18 U.S.C. Sections 1344 and 1028A, respectively. Ms. Anderson asks the Court to grant her Rule 29 Motion to set aside the jury verdict and enter a judgment of acquittal on the Section 1028A conviction because the Government failed to prove that Ms. Anderson knew that the identification belonged to an actual person, which is an element of Section 1028A. Without this actual knowledge, Ms. Anderson cannot be convicted of aggravated identity theft under Section 1028A.

This introduction provides the issue and the relief sought, as well as the Defendant's theory of the case. Note how the writer chose to personalize her client, referring to the Defendant as "Ms. Anderson."

FACTUAL BACKGROUND

Susan Anderson believed that her sister was in grave danger in her home country and sought a way to help her sister escape the situation. (Def.'s Trial Test. 1.) Her sister had visited the United States previously but was deported in May 2006 after her visa lapsed. (Tr. Summ. ¶ 11.) Seeing no better way to obtain funds for her sister's emigration, Ms. Anderson decided to take money temporarily from her employer, Hosmer Systems United ("HSU"), where she worked in the accounts payable/employee payroll department. (Def.'s Trial Test. 1.) Ms. Anderson had always intended to repay HSU once her sister was safely removed from her dangerous situation and able to work. (Def.'s Trial Test. 2.)

Counsel begins these facts by putting Defendant's best foot forward and painting a sympathetic picture of the Defendant's actions. While this strategy can work, the advocate must use it wisely.

Note that all the facts are supported by references to specific documents.

On four dates in August and September in 2008, Ms. Anderson wrote in the name "Karen Johnson" and the amount of "$3,000" on four pre-signed checks from HSU. (Stipulated Facts ¶ 1.) On those four dates, she cashed these checks under the alias Karen Johnson at the Bank of Hosmer, a federal bank. (*Id.*) She used a fake driver's license as identification. (*Id.* ¶ 5.)

The preparer was likely a professional forger, who is unidentified in these proceedings. *(Id.)*

Unbeknownst to Ms. Anderson at the time of the check cashing, an actual Karen Johnson lives in Farewell, Hosmer, at the same address shown in the fake driver's license, and with similar physical characteristics. *(Id. ¶ 2.)* Ms. Anderson could not have easily known of this coincidence, as a "Karen Johnson" was not listed in the telephone book at that address, and Ms. Johnson and Ms. Anderson are unknown to each other. *(Id. ¶ 4.)* Indeed, Ms. Anderson only gave the forger of the identification the last name of a person named Johnson at an address listed in the telephone book, purposely changing the first name. *(Id. ¶ 3.)* The forger used Ms. Anderson's own physical characteristics on the driver's license. *(Id.)*

Ms. Anderson was convicted as charged by a jury of her peers of bank fraud and aggravated identity theft. The Government is seeking an additional two-year penalty for the aggravated identity theft under 18 U.S.C. Section 1028A. Ms. Anderson has moved for judgment of acquittal under Federal Rule of Criminal Procedure 29(c). The Court requested briefs on whether Section 1028A requires the Government to prove that Ms. Anderson knew that the means of identification used in the false driver's license belonged an actual person. (Ct. Order 1.)

> The facts often conclude with the procedural posture.

ARGUMENT

SECTION 1028A REQUIRES THE GOVERNMENT TO PROVE THAT MS. ANDERSON KNEW THAT THE IDENTITY SHE USED BELONGED TO ANOTHER PERSON.

Aggravated identity theft under 18 U.S.C. § 1028A provides for additional penalties when that theft is in conjunction with an additional felony enumerated under the section, in this case, subsection (c)(5), "any provision contained in chapter 63 (relating to mail, bank, and wire fraud)." The additional penalties sought by the Government for aggravated identity theft are defined under Section 1028A:

(a) Offenses.

(1) In general. Whoever, during and in relation to any felony violation enumerated in subsection (c), knowingly transfers, possesses, or uses, without lawful authority, a means of identification of another person shall, in addition to the punishment provided for such felony, be sentenced to a term of imprisonment of 2 years.

The plain meaning of the statute, supported by the legislative history, demonstrates that the Government must prove that Ms. Anderson knew the identification belonged to a real person. In the alternative, because there are two plausible interpretations of the statute, and the legislative history

> The major point heading introduces the argument for the specific issue before the court. When there are discrete arguments within the argument, as here, the major point heading functions as an "umbrella" section by providing a broadly worded assertion. The discrete arguments in this brief provide the legal and policy reasons why the Government must prove that the Defendant knew the identity belonged to another, real person.
>
> Because the issue involves the meaning of the statute, it is important to provide the text of the statute. The final paragraph in this section provides a roadmap of the arguments.

supports both interpretations, the rule of lenity applies and the statute should be construed in favor of Ms. Anderson.

A. The Plain Meaning of the Statute Requires That Ms. Anderson Must Know That the Identity Belonged to an Actual Person.

This case presents an issue of first impression for the Court, involving the proper interpretation of Section 1028A. When interpreting a statute, the Court will begin by looking at the plain meaning of the statute. *Williams v. Taylor*, 529 U.S. 420, 431 (2000). Congressional intent is presumed to be expressed through the plain meaning of a statute. *Park 'N Fly, Inc. v. Dollar Park & Fly, Inc.*, 469 U.S. 189, 194 (1985). Moreover, the plain meaning cannot be interpreted by taking the words in isolation. *Dolan v. U.S. Postal Service*, 546 U.S. 481, 486 (2006).

> Because this is an issue of statutory interpretation, the writer begins with the plain meaning. Note, however, it may make more sense to begin with an ambiguity argument.

There are two plausible constructions of the statute. The Fourth, Eighth, and Eleventh circuits have relied on rules of grammar to find that the knowledge requirement only modifies the more immediate clauses: the transfer, possession or use of a means of identification. *United States v. Mendoza-Gonzalez*, 520 F.3d 912, 915 (8th Cir. 2008); *United States. v. Hurtado*, 508 F.3d 603, 609 (11th Cir. 2007); *United States. v. Montejo*, 442, F.3d 213, 215 (4th Cir. 2006). Conversely, the First, Ninth, and D.C. Circuits have interpreted Section 1028A(a)(1) as capable of extending the knowledge requirement to the phrase "of another person." See *United States v. Villanueva-Sotelo*, 515 F.3d 1234, 1240 (D.C. Cir. 2008); *United States v. Godin*, 534 F.3d 51, 58 (1st Cir. 2008); *United States v. Miranda-Lopez*, 532 F.3d 1034, 1038 (9th Cir. 2008). These circuits have ruled ultimately that the statute is ambiguous and applied the rule of lenity.

> It is important to acknowledge adverse authority.
>
> While the writer begins with the plain meaning argument, she lays the foundation here for alternative arguments.

Reviewing the competing interpretations, a federal district court in Utah has ruled that the better view was that "knowing" extends to the entire clause, including the phrase "of another person." *United States v. Hairup*, 565 F. Supp. 2d 1309, 1310–12 (D. Utah 2008). The court reasoned that "transfers, possesses, or uses, without lawful authority, a means of identification of another person" is an indivisible predicate and that the term "knowingly" was placed as close as possible to that predicate. *Id.* at 1311. The court criticized the hyper-technical approach advanced by the government in that case, stating that it is inconsistent with the plain meaning of the statute. *Id.* at 1311–12. In other words, read in its ordinary terms, "knowingly" most naturally modifies the entire predicate.

> Here, Defendant counters a plain meaning argument that she expects the Government to make. It is often best simply to make the argument in the affirmative, rather than to specifically identify what the opposing party may argue. Defendant, as the moving party, will have an opportunity to directly address the Government's arguments in a reply brief.

This reading is consistent with the statutory interpretation approach taken by the drafters of the Model Penal Code. As the D.C. Circuit explained, the Model Penal Code "adopts as a general principle of construction a rule under which, absent evidence to the contrary, the mens rea requirement encompasses all material elements of an offense." *Villanueva-Sotelo*, 515 F.3d at 1239 (citing Model Penal Code § 2.02(4) (1985)); see also *United States v. X-Citement Video*, Inc.,

> The plain meaning argument is buttressed by the Model Penal Code approach to interpreting the meaning

513 U.S. 64, 79 (1994) (Stevens, J., concurring) ("In my opinion, the normal, commonsense reading of a subsection of a criminal statute introduced by the word 'knowingly' is to treat that adverb as modifying each of the elements of the offense identified in the remainder of the subsection.").

Thus, under the plain meaning, the Government must prove that Ms. Anderson knew that the identification belonged to an actual person.

B. The Legislative History Also Supports the View That Congress Did Not Intend for Section 1028A to Apply Unless a Defendant Knew That the Identification Belonged to a Real Person.

When a court cannot interpret the statute based solely on the plain meaning, it is necessary to turn to the legislative history. *Fla. Power & Light Co. v. Lorion*, 470 U.S. 729, 737 (1985). Because there are two plausible interpretations of Section 1028A, as evidenced by the split among the circuit courts, a review of the legislative history here is instructive.

The legislative history lists eight specific examples to demonstrate situations in which criminals received relatively insignificant sentences in relation to their crimes. In each of these examples, the defendant knew that the identity belonged to another and had an active hand in procuring the identity, such as through databases available at their place of employment or by personal relationship to the victim. H.R. Rep. No. 108–528, "Background and Need for the Legislation" (2004). When viewed in light of these examples, Congress intended to punish those who purposely steal identities from others. *Villanueva-Sotelo*, 515 F.3d at 1244.

Put another way, and consistent with the term "theft," there must be an intent to deprive an individual of his or her identity. As the court in *Villanueva-Sotelo* stated, "at no point in the legislative record did anyone so much as allude to a situation in which a defendant 'wrongfully obtained' another person's personal information unknowingly, unwittingly, and without intent." 515 F.3d at 1245. The *Villanueva-Sotelo* court went on to differentiate between "theft" and "accidental misappropriation." *Id.* at 1246. The common law definition of "theft" includes an "intent to deprive the rightful owner" of her property. *Id.* at 1243. If a defendant accidentally selects an identification number like a made-up Social Security number that belongs to someone else, "it is odd—and borders on the absurd—to call what [the defendant] did 'theft.'" *Id.* at 1246 (citation omitted). Thus, the legislature's intent was that Section 1028A only apply where the defendant knows the identification belongs to a real person.

Ms. Anderson never intended or knew that the name she used belonged to a person at the address given. On the contrary, she merely looked in a telephone book to find any person at an address, and then changed the first name of that person. By changing the first name, she intended to use, and

of criminal statutes. Note that the writer lays a foundation for the MPC's relevance.

When making a plain meaning argument, support it with a legislative history argument whenever possible.

The writer focuses on what harm Congress intended to protect against—i.e., those instances in which the defendant knew the identity belonged to another.

It is not unusual to refer to the common law definition of a crime when interpreting a criminal statute. An exception to this practice is where the legislature intended to modify or abrogate the common law definition.

Note that the writer uses the facts to demonstrate that the Defendant did not engage in the type of

believed she did use, a fabricated identity, not the identity of someone who was listed in the phone book. Further, even if Karen Johnson's name had been in the telephone book, information in that book is a matter of public record and is not considered to be sensitive or personal-identifying information. It was merely coincidence that the physical characteristics listed on the driver's license, which were intended to match Ms. Anderson, also matched Ms. Johnson. Because Ms. Anderson did not purposely steal Karen Johnson's identity from her, she cannot be convicted of aggravated identity theft. Thus, the Court should grant Ms. Anderson's Rule 29 Motion and enter a judgment of acquittal.

C. In the Alternative, Section 1028A is Ambiguous and the Rule of Lenity Applies.

When there are two plausible readings of what conduct Congress has made a crime, it is appropriate to infer that Congress should have spoken in more clear and definite language. *Jones v. United States*, 529 U.S. 848, 858 (2000). Under the rule of lenity, ambiguous criminal statutes are to be construed in favor of the accused. *Staples v. United States*, 511 U.S. 600, 625 (1994). This rule precludes a court from "interpret[ing] a federal criminal statute so as to increase the penalty that it places on an individual when such an interpretation can be based on no more than a guess as to what Congress intended." *Ladner v. United States*, 358 U.S. 169, 178 (1958). Indeed, the Court has repeatedly rejected "the impulse to speculate regarding dubious congressional intent." *United States v. Santos*, 533 U.S. 507, 515 (2008) (plurality opinion). As Chief Justice Marshall explained, "probability is not a guide which a court, in construing a penal statute, can safely take." *United States v. Wiltberger*, 18 U.S. 76, 105 (1820). Nothing in the text of the statute or its legislative history definitively resolves the ambiguity, thus the Court must decide the statutory question in favor of Ms. Anderson. *See Villanueva-Sotelo*, 515 F.3d at 1239; *Godin*, 534 F.3d at 61; *Miranda-Lopez*, 532 F.3d at 1040. Moreover, application of the rule of lenity is supported by Supreme Court precedent and theories of culpability.

The Supreme Court has construed similar statutory language and has concluded that the "words themselves provide little guidance" as to the reach of the mens rea requirement. *Liparota v. United States*, 471 U.S. 419, 424 (1985). In *Liparota*, the Court analyzed whether, under the federal food stamp fraud statute, which makes it a criminal offense to "knowingly use[ ], transfer[ ], acquire[ ], alter[ ], or possess[ ] coupons or authorization cards in any manner not authorized by [the statute] or the regulations," 7 U.S.C. § 2024(b)(1), the term "knowingly" required the government to prove that the defendant knew the use was not authorized by the food stamp regulations. The Court found that although Congress clearly intended the word "knowingly" to apply to some elements, "the interpretations proffered by both parties . . . would accord with ordinary usage." *Liparota*, 471 U.S. at 424. Thus, as the D.C. Circuit explained in *Villanueva-Sotelo*, the Supreme Court in

conduct that Congress intended to prohibit.

The rule of lenity argument is an alternative argument that defendants in criminal cases often make. To make this argument, it is important to establish that the statute is ambiguous. Here, the writer uses Supreme Court rulings on similarly structured statutes. But once the rule of lenity applies, the application is fairly straightforward, and "the tie must go to the defendant." *Santos*, 553 U.S. at 514. The circuit court cases that ruled on lenity each did so in two short paragraphs, so not much more is required here.

Liparota provided a "clear finding that text alone cannot resolve statutes structured" like § 1028A(a)(1). 515 F.3d at 1241.

Similarly, in *X-Citement Video, Inc.*, the Court analyzed a provision of the child pornography statute found at 18 U.S.C. §§ 2252(a)(1) and (2), which provides that "any person who— knowingly transports or ships . . . any visual depiction [when the depiction involves or depicts a minor engaging in sexually explicit conduct] shall be punished . . . ." In essence, those provisions criminalize "knowingly" shipping or receiving any visual depiction, if the production of the visual depiction involved the use of a minor engaging in sexually explicit conduct. The question before the Supreme Court was whether "knowingly" modified only the verbs and not "the use of a minor." The Court concluded that "as a matter of grammar it is difficult to conclude that the word 'knowingly' modifies one of the elements in [a] subsection . . . , but not the other." 513 U.S. at 77–78. In short, the Supreme Court has recognized that when, as here, criminal culpability rests on multiple statutory elements conducted "knowingly," plain meaning is often not dispositive.

Although one motivating factor in the *Liparota* and *X-Citement Video* decisions was the Court's concern with criminalizing non-culpable conduct, "the Court has never held that avoiding such a result is the only reason to do so." *Villanueva-Sotelo*, 515 F.3d at 1242. Rather, the Court has traditionally interpreted criminal statutes "in light of the background rules of the common law," and one of those rules is the "requirement of some mens rea for a crime." *Staples*, 511 U.S. at 605. Moreover, a harsh penalty imposed under a statute has been a significant consideration historically in determining the reach of the scienter requirements of that statute. *See X-Citement Video*, 513 U.S. at 70–72 (discussing cases). Here, the statute imposes a two-year mandatory sentence to run consecutively to whatever other sentence is imposed. Under the Government's proposed construction, this two-year sentence would apply whenever a number that a defendant made up just happened to match that of a real person, even though the defendant had no knowledge of that coincidence. Such an outcome is inconsistent with well-established principles of culpability, as well as the rule of lenity.

> Here, the writer directly addresses the Government's proposed interpretation, pointing out that such a construction is also inconsistent with fundamental principles of criminal law—the requirement of a guilty mind.

CONCLUSION

The plain meaning, supported by the legislative history, of Section 1028A demonstrates that the Government must prove that Ms. Anderson knew that the identification belonged to Ms. Karen Johnson. This the Government cannot do. In the alternative, if the Court determines that the Section 1028A is ambiguous, then the rule of lenity applies and the Court should construe the statute in favor of Ms. Anderson. Thus, the Court should grant Ms. Anderson's Motion for Acquittal under Federal Rule of Criminal Procedure 29(c).

> This conclusion succinctly summarizes the arguments and sets forth the relief requested.

Dated: January 5, 2009

Respectfully submitted,

/s/ Viola Cesario

Viola Cesario #12Z78
Reifert, Gallo, & Long
651 E. Jefferson
Farewell, Hosmer 1918X
999.555.1212

Attorney for Susan Anderson

UNITED STATES DISTRICT COURT
DISTRICT OF HOSMER
CRIMINAL CASE NO. 08–1094

UNITED STATES OF AMERICA,
    Plaintiff,

v.

SUSAN ANDERSON,
    Defendant.

Hon. Andrew Aguecheek
United States District Judge

MEMORANDUM IN OPPOSITION TO DEFENDANT'S MOTION FOR JUDGMENT OF ACQUITTAL UNDER FEDERAL RULE OF CRIMINAL PROCEDURE 29(c)

INTRODUCTION

After a full and fair trial, a jury of her peers convicted Susan Anderson ("Defendant") of bank fraud and aggravated identity theft. The United States of America ("Government") proved beyond a reasonable doubt that Defendant knowingly obtained money from a financial institution under false pretenses in violation of 18 U.S.C. § 1344. Defendant was similarly convicted under 18 U.S.C. § 1028A for using the identification of another person, without lawful authority, in connection with the bank fraud.

The Government opposes Defendant's Motion for Acquittal under Federal Rule of Criminal Procedure 29(c). This Court should deny Defendant's request and impose additional sentencing based on the plain meaning of 18 U.S.C. § 1028A, which is supported by the legislative history.

FACTS

Defendant cashed four pre-signed checks at the Bank of Hosmer, a federal bank, on August 7, August 21, September 4, and September 18, 2008, each in the amount of $3000. (Stipulated Facts ¶ 1.) Each time, Defendant used a fake driver's license displaying the alias "Karen Johnson," as well as the address and physical characteristics of a real Karen

---

This caption is the same as the caption in the previous sample. The difference is the title of the document. This brief is in opposition to the Defendant's motion.

This introduction provides the issue and the relief sought. Note how the writer focused on the conviction. Additionally, the writer elected to refer to Ms. Anderson as "Defendant." Some court rules require that names, rather than party designations, be used in briefs. This is another reason to always refer to the relevant court rules.

Compare these facts to the Facts section in the Defendant's brief.

Johnson. (*Id.* ¶ 2.) A real Karen Johnson has lived in Farewell, Hosmer, since June 1, 2008. (*Id.* ¶ 6.)

Brian Regalson, the manager of the Bank of Hosmer, testified that Defendant was nervous each time she cashed her checks. (Test. of Brian Regalson ¶ 6 ("Regalson") Dec. 4, 2008.) These financial transactions made Mr. Regalson realize "something was not right." (*Id.* ¶ 8.) He testified that he thought "it was odd Ms. Johnson would routinely cash the checks rather than deposit them." (*Id.*) Also, when Mr. Regalson tried to stop and talk with Defendant, she would not "give [him] the time of day." (*Id.* ¶ 6.) Acting on these suspicions, Mr. Regalson contacted the authorities. (*Id.* ¶ 9.)

FBI Special Agent Alan Strong was assigned to investigate. (*Id.*) Agent Strong testified that he compared the video of Defendant cashing the checks with the photo of Karen Johnson on file and determined they were not the same person. (Test. of Special Agent Alan Strong ¶ 11 ("Strong") Dec. 4, 2008.)

Defendant used a false identification to cash these checks because she did not have check signing authority from her employer. (Regalson ¶ 8.) Defendant selected the name "Johnson" through the telephone book, only changing the first name. (Stipulated Facts ¶ 3.) Defendant admitted that her goal was to "obtain a plausible fake [identification]." (Test. of Susan Anderson ¶ 8 Dec. 4, 2008.) Agent Strong confirmed that Defendant instructed the identification forger to "use the name Karen Johnson and the Privy Lane address." (Strong ¶ 7.)

Defendant has moved under Rule 29(c) for judgment of acquittal on the charge of aggravated identity theft. The Government opposes this motion.

ARGUMENT

THE GOVERNMENT DOES NOT NEED TO PROVE UNDER 18 U.S.C. § 1028A THAT DEFENDANT KNEW THE FAKE IDENTIFICATION REPRESENTED AN ACTUAL PERSON.

This major point heading introduces the issue and the arguments that follow. Because there is only one issue before the court, there is only one major point heading. There are exceptions to this convention, as noted in the third sample brief.

Congress passed § 1028A to increase the penalty for individuals who use a fake identification to commit various enumerated felonies. The relevant provision of 18 U.S.C. § 1028A provides:

> (1) In general. Whoever, during and in relation to any felony violation enumerated in subsection (c), knowingly transfers, possesses, or uses, without lawful authority, a means of identification of another person shall, in addition to the punishment provided for such felony, be sentenced to a term of imprisonment of 2 years.

In this case of first impression, the Court must determine what the term "knowingly" modifies. Three circuit courts have held that the statutory language is clear and does not require the Government to prove that the Defendant knew that the identification belonged to an actual person. *United States v. Mendoza-Gonzalez*, 520 F.3d 912, 915 (8th Cir. 2008); *United States v. Hurtado*, 508 F.3d 603, 609 (11th Cir. 2007) (per curiam), *cert. denied*, 128 S. Ct. 2903 (2008); *United States v. Montejo*, 442 F.3d 213, 215 (4th Cir. 2006), *cert. denied*, 549 U.S. 879 (2006). Three other circuits have held that the language and legislative history are unclear and have relied on the rule of lenity to conclude that the Government is required to provide this proof. *United States v. Godin*, 534 F.3d 51, 56 (1st Cir. 2008); *United States v. Miranda-Lopez*, 532 F.3d 1034 (9th Cir. 2008); *United States v. Villanueva-Sotelo*, 515 F.3d 1234, 1239 (D.C. Cir. 2008).

> These initial paragraphs set forth the text of the statute, the relevant authority, the Government's theory of the case, and a basic roadmap of the arguments that follow.

The plain meaning, which is supported by the legislative history, demonstrates that Defendant only needs knowledge of "transferring, possessing or using" a false identification. The fact that Defendant did not know that the information belonged to a real person is not a requirement of this statute and should not be a bar to conviction under 18 U.S.C. § 1028A.

A. The Plain Language Of § 1028A Indicates That Defendant Merely Needed Knowledge That She Possessed And Used A False Identification Document, Not That The Information Contained In The Document Belonged To An Actual Person.

When interpreting statutes, courts start their analysis by looking at the language of the statute, which "must ordinarily be regarded as conclusive." *Consumer Prod. Safety Comm'n v. GTE Sylvania*, 447 U.S. 102, 108 (1980). The plain meaning canon of statutory construction helps determine the meaning of the statute based on its language. *Am. Tobacco Co. v. Patterson*, 456 U.S. 63, 68 (1982). The plain meaning supports the position that Defendant does not have to know the fake identification belonged to an actual person.

> Even though courts know to begin their analysis of a statute with the plain meaning, the writer must still provide a statement of that rule.

The syntax of § 1028A provides that the word, "knowingly" applies only to "transfers, possesses or uses." It is common in the English language for words that modify other words to be in proximity to the words they are modifying. *The Chicago Manual of Style* ¶ 5.156 (2006). Since "transfers, possesses, or uses" immediately follows the word "knowingly," it should be interpreted that knowingly applies only to those three terms, but not to subsequent terms and phrases in the statute, such as "another person." *Montejo*, 442 F.3d at 215. This interpretation is also consistent with the last antecedent rule, which "holds that qualifying words and phrases usually apply only to the words or phrases immediately preceding or following them, not to others that are more remote." *Mendoza-Gonzalez*, 520 F.3d at 915 (citing 2A Norman J. Singer & J.D. Shambie Singer, *Sutherland Statutory Construction* § 47:33 (7th ed. 2007)).

> Plain meaning arguments are often supported with references to dictionaries. The writer also invokes various rules of grammar to support the plain meaning argument.
>
> The two cases relied on in these paragraphs, *Mendoza-Gonzalez* and *Montejo*, both make similar plain language arguments based on rules of grammar construction. Subsequently, *Hurtado* is used to make an argument for how Congress would have drafted the statute if it

"Knowingly" should not apply to other words or phrases in this statute for two additional reasons. First, "knowingly" is an adverb. *See Random House Webster's Unabridged Dictionary* 1064 (2d ed. 2001). Adverbs only modify verbs, adjectives, or other adverbs, but not nouns. *The Chicago Manual of Style, supra,* at ¶ 5.143. This means that "knowingly" can only modify "transfers, possesses, or uses" because these are the only verbs in this statute. *Hurtado*, 508 F.3d at 609.

Second, adjectives modify nouns. *Chicago Manual of Style, supra,* at ¶ 5.66. To modify the noun "another person," as Defendant suggests, the proper word to use would be the adjective "knowing." *See Random House, supra,* at 1064. Therefore, based on the plain meaning, "knowingly" should only apply to "transferring, possessing or using" a fake identification.

Had Congress intended to extend the knowing requirement to the phrase "of another person," it easily could have drafted the statute to make this intention clear. For example, Congress could have drafted the statute as follows: Whoever, during and in relation to any felony violation enumerated in subsection (c), knowingly transfers, possesses, or uses, without lawful authority, a means of identification *known to belong to another actual person* . . . . *Hurtado*, 508 F.3d at 609. In the absence of this additional language, this Court should apply the plain meaning rule to the statute and determine that Defendant need only know that she possessed and used a false identification document.

B. The Plain Meaning Is Further Supported By The Legislative History, Which Also Demonstrates Congress' Concern For Victims Of Identity Theft.

Because the statute is unambiguous, it is not necessary to rely on the legislative history. *See Mendoza-Gonzalez*, 520 F.3d at 914–15. But even if the legislative history were consulted, that history supports the Government's position. *Id.* at 917. Congress was concerned with "stopping the nation-wide identity theft tidal wave by upping the ante for the thief." *Villanueva-Sotelo*, 515 F.3d at 1255 (Henderson, J., dissenting). The legislative history shows that Congress intended the term identity theft to "refer to all types of crimes in which someone wrongfully obtains and uses another person's personal data in some way that involves fraud or deception." H.R. Rep. 108–528 at 4 (2004). A Federal Trade Commission report found that "the loss to businesses and financial institutions from identity theft [is estimated] to be $47.6 billion. The costs to individual consumers are estimated to be approximately $5.0 billion." *Id.* That same report explained that "almost 10 million Americans were victims of some sort of identity theft within the last year, which means despite the attention to this type of crime . . . the incidence of this crime is increasing." *Id.*

The harm caused to victims by the unlawful use of their identification is the same regardless of whether a defendant knew that the identification belonged to an actual person. *See Villanueva-Sotelo*, 515 F.3d at 1254 n.9 (Henderson, J., dissenting). Congress' express intent to combat the growing incidence of identity theft, and the harm that this theft causes innocent victims, would be frustrated by a holding that the

---

Sidebar notes:

had wanted to extend the "knowing" requirement." Although a fact specific holding describing any important case you cite is usually required, here, on a pure issue of statutory construction the particular facts of the cases matter less.

Note that the writer offers an example of how the statute should have been drafted if Congress had intended to extend the mens rea requirement to "of another person." While it is not necessary to do so, it can be an effective argument.

The writer counters the Defendant's legislative history argument by focusing on Congress' concern for the victims.

Note that both parties found legislative history to support their arguments. This is one reason that some judges are reluctant to rely on legislative histories. When researching an issue of statutory interpretation, include research on how the relevant court approaches an issue of statutory interpretation.

Government has to prove that the Defendant knew the identification actually belonged to another person.

Requiring proof of knowledge would effectively eliminate the ability of the Government to prosecute a case against any person engaged in a fraudulent scheme who used a person's identity unless that defendant actually created the document. "It is preposterous to think that the same Congress that so plainly and firmly intended to increase the penalty . . . would then so limit its imposition as to require the Government to prove that the defendant knows he wrongfully possesses the identity 'of another person'" when that defendant is knowingly using that identification to pursue a fraudulent scheme. *Mendoza-Gonzalez*, 520 F.2d at 915–16 (quoting *Villanueva-Sotelo*, 515 F.3d at 1255 (Henderson, J., dissenting)).

The legislative history of 18 U.S.C. § 1028A shows that Congress did not intend that criminal defendants must have knowledge that the information they stole belonged to a real person. Based on the plain meaning and legislative history of the statute, this Court should deny Defendant's motion.

C. The Rule of Lenity Is Not Applicable Because § 1028A Is Unambiguous.

Although the Supreme Court has given a broader reach to the "knowing" requirement of similarly structured statutory provisions, these cases are distinguishable, and Defendant's reliance on them to establish an ambiguity is misplaced because these cases rest on a concern about criminalizing otherwise innocent conduct. *See United States v. X-Citement Video, Inc.*, 513 U.S. 64, 73 (1994) (finding that a presumption in favor of a scienter requirement should apply to each of the statutory elements that criminalize otherwise innocent conduct); *Liparota v. United States*, 471 U.S. 419, 426 (1985) (interpreting "knowing" as extending beyond the nearby verb when to do otherwise "would be to criminalize a broad range of apparently innocent conduct").

In cases involving § 1028A(a)(1), by contrast, the defendants know that they are using a means of identification to further a fraudulent scheme. *Mendoza-Gonzalez*, 520 F.3d at 917; *Hurtado*, 508 F.3d at 609–10; *Montejo*, 442 F.3d at 216. Indeed, the defendants "know[ ] from the very outset that [their] planned course of conduct is wrongful." *United States v. Feola*, 420 U.S. 671, 685 (1975). In *Feola*, the Court held that proof that the defendant knew that the victim was actually a federal officer was not necessary for a conviction under a statute prohibiting assaults on federal officers because the defendant intended to assault his victim and therefore "takes his victim as he finds him." *Id.* Similarly, here, the Defendant knowingly possessed an identification document in a name that was not her own and used that document to further a fraudulent scheme. That she now is facing an additional two-year sentence is a direct result of this illegal activity.

Here in the rule of lenity argument, you should start with your "high ground," which in this case would be that the statute is not ambiguous and the rule of lenity therefore does not apply. But in this brief, the author discussed at length in sections A and B above how the statute is unambiguous. So in this section the author decided to address first Defendant's counter-argument.

Importantly, the writer distinguishes the cases. The writer offers his own Supreme Court authority addressing the reach of a mens rea element.

Because the statute's text and legislative intent are clear, there is no need to apply the rule of lenity to construe the statute in a manner favorable to Defendant. *See Hurtado*, 508 F.3d at 610 n.8; *Montejo*, 442 F.3d at 217; *see also Salinas v. United States*, 522 U.S. 52, 66 (1997) ("The rule [of lenity] does not apply when a statute is unambiguous . . . .").

A statute is not ambiguous "merely because it [is] *possible* to articulate a construction more narrow that that urged by the Government." *Moskal v. United States*, 498 U.S. 103, 108 (1990). Rather, the rule is not applicable "unless there is a 'grievous ambiguity or uncertainty in the language and structure of the Act.'" *Chapman v. United States*, 500 U.S. 453, 463 (1991) (citations omitted). Moreover, as the Supreme Court has explained, "The rule of lenity is not invoked by a grammatical possibility. It does not apply if the ambiguous reading relied on is an implausible reading of the congressional purpose." *Caron v. United States*, 524 U.S. 308, 316 (1998). Because it is implausible to assert that Congress intended to limit the Government's ability to prosecute § 1028A(a)(1) cases to only those situations in which a defendant knew the false identification belonged to an actual person, the rule of lenity is inapplicable.

> *Here, the writer provides authority to counter Defendant's argument about the applicability of the rule of lenity.*

CONCLUSION

The Defendant's request for acquittal under Rule 29(c) of the Federal Rules of Criminal Procedure should be denied. Plain meaning analysis, legislative history, and public policy combine to support the Government's position. The Defendant's Rule 29 Motion should be denied.

Dated: January 26, 2009   Respectfully submitted,

Adam C. Toby

Adam C. Toby #45X23
Assistant U. S. Attorney
444 Federal Building
Illyria, Hosmer 1918Z
999-555-9876

The last sample trial brief includes a motion (including a notice of motion), as well as additional documents that are often required by court rules: supporting affidavits, proposed findings of fact and conclusions of law, a proposed court order, a certificate of compliance, and a certificate of service. The margin notes accompanying these sample documents provide guidance on how to draft these documents. For purposes of this sample brief, assume that the lawyer writing it was presented in 2003 with the following problem:[20]

> The lawyer's best client is Commonwealth Hospital ("Commonwealth" or "the Hospital"), located in Boom Town, Massachusetts. The Hospital treats patients whose costs are covered by private insurance and patients whose costs are covered by Medicare. In the case of the latter patients, the Hospital bills the

---

[20] The problem is based on a split of authority within the U.S. District of Massachusetts. To learn how the First Circuit ultimately ruled on this issue, *see* U.S. v. City of Woonsocket, 587 F.3d 49 (1st Cir. 2009). Note that one of the cases discussed in the briefs, U.S. v. Bank of Farmington, 166 F.3d 853 (7th Cir. 1999), was eventually overruled in Glaser v. Wound Care Consultants, Inc., 570 F.3d 907 (7th Cir. 2009).

federal government according to regulations established by the federal Department of Health and Human Services. The regulations require hospitals to bill the government only for (a) necessary services and procedures that (b) are actually provided. The regulations set a maximum fee for each service or medical procedure. The maximum fee is generally considerably lower than what the Hospital charges its private patients for the same service or procedure.

Unlike most hospitals, which usually rely on independent physicians, Commonwealth employs several of the surgeons who have privileges at the Hospital. Dr. Marcia Wellford ("Wellford") is one such employed surgeon. Over the years, Wellford and John Smith ("Smith"), who works in the Hospital billing department, have been growing quite uneasy about the Hospital's Medicare billing procedures. For the last three years, they have been secretly making copies at random of surgical and billing records relating to procedures performed on Medicare patients by employed surgeons. After examining the records, Wellford and Smith concluded that the Hospital has consistently billed the government for procedures that were either unnecessary or never performed as reported. Wellford and Smith presumed that the billing was intentional and that the purpose and effect were to evade the fee limits and overcharge the government. Wellford and Smith concluded that the Hospital was committing fraud in violation of 31 U.S.C. § 3729, also known as the federal False Claims Act.

While Wellford and Smith have been mulling over what to do with their discoveries, the *Boom Town Dispatch*, the local newspaper, published a lengthy exposé of local hospital billing practices. The article included a detailed discussion of Commonwealth's billing of Medicare, quoting a number of unnamed sources as alleging that the Hospital has routinely over billed the government. The sources gave specific alleged examples. The reporter who wrote the article has signed an affidavit that Wellford and Smith were *not* among the sources.

Shortly after the *Dispatch* story was published, and without having first notified the government of their information or intentions, Wellford and Smith brought an action under seal in federal district court in Boom Town. They sued the Hospital under 31 U.S.C. § 3730, the qui tam provision in the False Claims Act, which allows individuals with knowledge of fraud on the government to sue on behalf of the government. They complied with 31 U.S.C. § 3730(b)(2) when filing their complaint. The government, pursuant to 31 U.S.C. § 3730(b)(4)(B), declined to take over the action, leaving Wellford and Smith free to go forward as "relators."

Although the Hospital has adamantly denied any wrongdoing and is planning a vigorous defense, it takes the Complaint allegations at face value for purposes of this pre-answer motion to dismiss under Federal Rule of Civil Procedure 12(b)(1) for lack of federal subject matter jurisdiction.

UNITED STATES DISTRICT COURT
 	
FOR THE DISTRICT OF MASSACHUSETTS
 	
UNITED STATES EX REL.
MARCIA WELLFORD AND   Case No.
JOHN SMITH,   Civ. 02–65432 (JW)
        Plaintiffs,
 	
v.
 	
COMMONWEALTH   NOTICE OF MOTION
HOSPITAL, INC.,   AND MOTION
        Defendant.   TO DISMISS
                 COMPLAINT
	Case caption, including court, names of parties, case number, and document title.

TO: Plaintiff United States of America ex rel. Marcia Wellford and John Smith, and its counsel, Robert Ort, 13 Main Street, Suite 110, Boom Town, Massachusetts 01000.	Notice to other party(ies) in the case and its/their counsel.
PLEASE TAKE NOTICE that at 10:00 a.m. on [Month/Day/20XX], or as soon thereafter as counsel may be heard, Defendant will bring a Motion to Dismiss for hearing before the Honorable Judith Williams, United States District Judge, in Courtroom No. 1, fourth floor, United States Courthouse, 412 Main Street, Boom Town, Massachusetts.	Description line for the day, time, and location of the relevant hearing, and for the type of motion involved.
This Motion is made pursuant to Federal Rule of Civil Procedure 12(b)(1). The Court lacks subject matter jurisdiction over Plaintiff's Complaint because it is based upon allegations that have previously been publicly disclosed within the meaning of 31 U.S.C. § 3730(e)(4)(A).	Summary description of the basis for the motion, including a citation to the relevant procedural rule and substantive statute.
This Motion is made on the basis of the pleadings of the Parties, and the accompanying Memorandum and Affidavits in Support of the Motion.	This is a standard recitation of the items to which the court should refer in considering the motion.

Dated: March 1, 2003   Eve Johnson, #87623
                     Matters & Johnson
                     25 Winter Way
                     Boom Town, MA 01000
                     (617) 123-4567
                     ejohnson@mandj.com
 	
                     Eve Johnson
 	
                     Attorney for
                     Commonwealth
                     Hospital, Inc.
	The date of the notice.
	
	The name, attorney registration number, addresses, and telephone number of the lawyer bringing the motion, along with her signature, and the name of the moving party.

<table>
<tr>
<td>

UNITED STATES DISTRICT COURT

FOR THE DISTRICT OF MASSACHUSETTS

UNITED STATES EX REL.
MARCIA WELLFORD AND   Case No.
JOHN SMITH,   Civ. 02–65432 (JW)
         Plaintiffs,

v.

COMMONWEALTH   AFFIDAVIT OF
HOSPITAL, INC.,   LUCY SUMMER
         Defendant.

</td>
<td>

Case caption, including court, names of parties, case number, and document title.

</td>
</tr>
<tr>
<td>

Lucy Summer, being first duly sworn, states as follows:

1.   I am the Chief Medical Officer at Commonwealth Hospital, Inc. ("Commonwealth") in Boom Town, Massachusetts.

2.   I have been the Chief Medical Officer for the last five years.

3.   I submit this affidavit in support of Defendant's motion to dismiss the Plaintiff's Complaint for lack of jurisdiction.

4.   Dr. Marcia Wellford is an employed surgeon at Commonwealth. Mr. John Smith is a billing clerk at Commonwealth. Because of the confidentiality of the patient names and health information in the medical and billing records at Commonwealth, neither Dr. Wellford nor Mr. Smith is authorized to make copies of records for their own use.

Dated: [Month/Day/20XX]   *Lucy Summer*

[Notary Public stamp and signature.]

</td>
<td>

Provide a recitation that the witness is under oath.

Provide background declarations that establish the witness's qualifications to testify.

Provide a recitation of the purpose of the affidavit.

Provide whatever substantive declarations the witness needs to make.

The date and the witness's signature. The Notary attests that the witness swore to the statements in the Notary's presence.

</td>
</tr>
</table>

UNITED STATES DISTRICT COURT

FOR THE DISTRICT OF MASSACHUSETTS

UNITED STATES EX REL.
MARCIA WELLFORD AND   Case No.
JOHN SMITH,   Civ. 02–65432 (JW)
      Plaintiffs,

v.

COMMONWEALTH   AFFIDAVIT OF
HOSPITAL, INC.,   SANDY ANDREWS
      Defendant.

(See the margin notes on the previous page.)

Sandy Andrews, being first duly sworn, states as follows:

1. I am a reporter for the *Boom Town Dispatch*. I have been a reporter for the *Dispatch* since 1996.

2. I submit this affidavit in connection with the motion of Commonwealth Hospital to dismiss Plaintiff's Complaint.

3. Attached to this affidavit as Exhibit One is a true and correct copy of a newspaper article that I authored and that appeared in the *Boom Town Dispatch* on [Month/Day/20XX.]

4. I interviewed a number of sources for my article. I did not interview Dr. Marcia Wellford or Mr. John Smith, and did not otherwise obtain information from them.

Dated: [Month/Day/20XX]   *Sandy Andrews*

[Notary Public stamp and signature]

[Authors' Note: In a real case, the newspaper article would be marked and attached as Exhibit One.]

UNITED STATES DISTRICT COURT

FOR THE DISTRICT OF MASSACHUSETTS

UNITED STATES EX REL.
MARCIA WELLFORD AND   Case No.
JOHN SMITH,   Civ. 02–65432 (JW)
     Plaintiff,

v.

COMMONWEALTH
HOSPITAL, INC.,
     Defendant.

Case caption, including court, names of parties, case number, and document title. (This caption is somewhat different from the previous two samples. Many courts have their own format, which the litigants all follow.)

MEMORANDUM IN SUPPORT OF DEFENDANT'S MOTION TO DISMISS

INTRODUCTION

The Defendant, Commonwealth Hospital, Inc. ("Commonwealth" or "the Hospital"), submits this Memorandum in support of its Motion to Dismiss Plaintiff's Complaint under Federal Rule of Civil Procedure 12(b)(1).

In this case, Dr. Marcia Wellford and Mr. John Smith ("Wellford and Smith") allege, as relators on behalf of the United States, that Commonwealth has committed fraud in billing the federal government for services and procedures for Medicare patients. Commonwealth asks the Court to strike the Complaint on the ground that the allegations in it are based upon newspaper reports of the same alleged information. Thus, Wellford and Smith are not proper relators within the meaning of the federal False Claims Act, 31 U.S.C. §§ 3729, 3730.

This introductory section tells the court what the case is about, what the motion is about, what the party's position is on the motion, and what relief the party requests.

UNDISPUTED FACTS AND PROCEDURAL POSTURE

For purposes of this Motion, the following matters are undisputed.

Commonwealth is located in Boom Town, Massachusetts. Plaintiff's Complaint ("Pl.'s Compl.") ¶ 3 (Month Day, 20xx). The Hospital treats patients whose costs are covered by private insurance and patients whose costs are covered by Medicare. *Id.* at ¶ 4. In the case of the latter patients, the Hospital bills the federal government according to regulations established by the federal Department of Health and Human Services. *Id.* The regulations require hospitals to bill the government only for (a) necessary services and procedures that (b) are actually provided. *Id.* at ¶ 5. The regulations set a maximum fee for each service or medical procedure. *Id.* at ¶ 6. The maximum fee is generally lower than what the Hospital charges its private patients for the same service or procedure. *Id.*

Unlike most hospitals, which usually rely on independent physicians, Commonwealth employs several of the surgeons who have privileges at the Hospital. *Id.* at ¶ 10.

Note that there will be trial court briefs you will write from time to time where the facts are disputed. But in the present example, defense counsel wants to focus on undisputed facts to bolster the defense position that the case may be summarily and easily dismissed.

Strictly speaking for purposes of the present

Wellford is one such employed surgeon. *Id.* at ¶ 2; Affidavit of Lucy Summers ("Aff. Summers") ¶ 4. Commonwealth also employs billing personnel, one of whom is Smith. *Id.* For the last three years, Wellford and Smith have been secretly making copies at random of surgical and billing records relating to procedures performed on Medicare patients by employed surgeons at Commonwealth. Pl.'s Compl. at ¶ 13. The copying was unauthorized and violates patient confidentiality. Aff. Summers ¶ 4.

After examining the records, Wellford and Smith concluded that the Hospital was billing the government for procedures that were either unnecessary or never performed as reported. Pl.'s Compl. at ¶ 15. Wellford and Smith presumed that the billing was intentional and that the purpose and effect were to evade the fee limits and overcharge the government. *Id.* at ¶ 16. Wellford and Smith further presumed that the Hospital was committing fraud in violation of 31 U.S.C. § 3729, also known as the federal False Claims Act. *Id.* at ¶ 17.

Prior to the filing of the present lawsuit, the *Boom Town Dispatch*, the local newspaper, published a lengthy article concerning the billing practices of a number of area hospitals, including Commonwealth. *Id.* at ¶ 18; Affidavit of Sandy Andrews ("Aff. Andrews") ¶ 3, Ex. One. The article included a detailed discussion of Commonwealth's billing of Medicare. Aff. Andrews at ¶ 3, Ex. One. The article quoted a number of unnamed sources as alleging that the Hospital has routinely over billed the government. *Id.* The sources claimed to identify specific examples. *Id.* The reporter who wrote the article has signed an affidavit that Wellford and Smith were *not* among the sources. Aff. Andrews at ¶ 4. Plaintiff's Complaint allegations mirror the Dispatch article's content.

Shortly after the *Dispatch* story was published, and without having first notified the government of their information or intentions, Wellford and Smith brought an action under seal in federal district court in Boom Town. Pl.'s Compl. at ¶ 19. They sued the Hospital under 31 U.S.C. § 3730, the qui tam provision in the False Claims Act, which allows individuals with knowledge of fraud on the government to sue on behalf of the government. *Id.* at ¶ 1. They complied with 31 U.S.C. § 3730(b)(2) when filing their Complaint. *Id.* at ¶ 20. The government, pursuant to 31 U.S.C. § 3730(b)(4)(B), declined to take over the action, leaving Wellford and Smith free to go forward as "relators."

Although the Hospital has adamantly denied any wrongdoing and is planning a vigorous defense, its position for present purposes is simply that, taking the above information as given, the Court should dismiss the Complaint for lack of federal subject matter jurisdiction.

---

motion, this paragraph makes an irrelevant point. But defense counsel still choose to point it out to take away some of the luster that might otherwise attach to Wellford and Smith as "defenders of the public."

The fact description must cover the handful of key facts that drive the legal outcome from the standpoint of the writer. The existence of a prior newspaper article containing similar allegations in detail is one such key fact.

The fact that Wellford and Smith did not provide information to the government prior to filing their lawsuit is a second key fact from the Defendant's perspective.

The fact that the United States Attorney General is not bringing the case is the third key fact from the Defendant's perspective.

Conservative lawyers often insert some form of rejection of the other side's allegations into pleadings and motion papers to protect the record in case the litigation continues to go forward.

ARGUMENT

I. PLAINTIFF HAS THE BURDEN OF ESTABLISHING SUBJECT MATTER JURISDICTION OVER THE COMPLAINT.

Federal courts have limited jurisdiction. *United States ex rel. Precision Co. v. Koch Indus. Inc.*, 971 F.2d 548, 551 (10th Cir. 1992). If the defendant contests subject matter jurisdiction, the plaintiff must come forward with competent proof that jurisdiction exists. *Id.* If the Plaintiff here cannot establish jurisdiction, this Court should dismiss the Complaint.

The first discussion in a typical memorandum is the relevant burden of proof for the issue.

II. AS A MATTER OF LAW, PLAINTIFF CANNOT ESTABLISH SUBJECT MATTER JURISDICTION OVER THE COMPLAINT IN THIS CASE.

The subject matter jurisdiction provision in the federal False Claims Act provides:

This major point heading introduces the argument for the issue before the court.

(A) *No court shall have jurisdiction* over an action under this section *based upon* the *public disclosure* of allegations or transactions . . . from the *news media, unless* the action is brought by the Attorney General or the person bringing the action is an *original source* of the information. (B) For purposes of this paragraph, "original source" means an individual who has direct and independent knowledge of the information on which the allegations are based *and* has voluntarily *provided* the information to the Government *before filing* an action under this section which is based on the information.

Remember to provide the relevant rule. If the rule arises from enacted law, then begin with a quotation of the material provisions of the law. If the rule is from the common law, then provide a statement of the rule and an appropriate citation.

31 U.S.C. § 3730(e)(4) (emphasis supplied).

When a defendant contests jurisdiction under this provision in a case not brought by the Attorney General, the court must make three inquiries:

If there are discrete elements that must be addressed, break them out for the reader.

    1.   Has there been a public disclosure of the relevant allegations;

    2.   If yes, does the relator who brings the suit on behalf of the government base his or her claims upon the public disclosure; and

    3.   If yes, then is the relator an "original source" of the information within the meaning of the statute?

United States ex rel. O'Keeffe v. Sverdup Corp., 131 F. Supp. 2d 87, 91 (D. Mass. 2001).

Two of these elements are undisputed and indisputable in the present case: The allegations that Wellford and Smith have made against Commonwealth also have been made in a newspaper report that pre-dates the filing of the Complaint. And Wellford and Smith are not "original sources" within the meaning of § 3730(e)(4)(B) because they did not provide their information to the government before they filed their

Tell the court which elements are actually in dispute, and focus the court's attention on the issue that the rest of the brief will address to resolve the problem.

Complaint. Accordingly, if the Complaint is "based upon" the newspaper article, there is no subject matter jurisdiction.

A. "Based upon" means "the same as" or "substantially similar to" the allegations in the newspaper.

The most recent case in this District has held that a complaint is "based upon" prior public disclosures within the meaning of 31 U.S.C. § 3730(e)(4) if the complaint allegations are "similar to or the same as those that have been publicly disclosed." *O'Keeffe*, 131 F. Supp. 2d at 92. This is also the view of the vast majority of federal circuit courts. *See United States ex rel. Minn. Ass'n of Nurse Anesthetists v. Allina Health Sys. Corp.*, 276 F.3d 1032, 1044–47 (8th Cir. 2002); *United States ex rel. Mistick PBT v. Hous. Auth. of Pittsburgh*, 186 F.3d 376, 386–88 (3d Cir. 1999); *United States ex rel. Biddle v. Bd. of Trustees of Leland Stanford Jr. Univ.*, 161 F.3d 533, 536–40 (9th Cir. 1998); *United States ex rel. McKenzie v. BellSouth Telecomm., Inc.*, 123 F.3d 935, 940–41 (6th Cir. 1997); *United States ex rel. Findley v. FPC-Boron Employees' Club*, 105 F.3d 675, 682–85 (D.C. Cir. 1997); *Cooper v. Blue Cross and Blue Shield of Fla., Inc.*, 19 F.2d 562, 566–67 (11th Cir. 1994); *Precision Co.*, 971 F.2d at 552–53; *United States ex rel. Doe v. John Doe Corp.*, 960 F.2d 318, 324 (2d Cir. 1992). The First Circuit has not yet taken a position.

This District in *O'Keeffe* correctly summarized the two primary reasons why "based upon" means "similar to or the same." First, the public disclosure jurisdictional bar was adopted by Congress in 1986 as part of a complex balancing of competing public interests. On the one hand, Congress wanted to provide whistleblowers with incentives to come forward with valuable information concerning fraud upon the government. On the other hand, Congress sought to discourage mere parasitical suits based upon information already in the possession of federal authorities. 131 F. Supp. 2d at 91 (citing *United States ex rel. Springfield Terminal Ry. Co. v. Quinn*, 14 F.3d 645, 649 (D.C. Cir. 1994)). There is no reason to reward relators for providing information that is the same or similar to allegations already published. *O'Keeffe*, 131 F. Supp. 2d at 93 (citing *Findley*, 105 F.3d at 685).

Second, if "based upon" means only "derived from" (which is the alternative construction of the term typically proposed by plaintiffs), then the "original source" requirement in § 3730(e)(4) is rendered superfluous. By definition, if a relator's allegations are not derived from prior public disclosures, the relator has direct and independent knowledge of his claims. *O'Keeffe*, 131 F. Supp. 2d at 93. Thus, a separate original source requirement is unnecessary. But a standard rule of statutory construction is that a statute should be construed so as not to render any of its terms superfluous. *United States v. Nordic Village, Inc.*, 503 U.S. 30, 36 (1992). Thus, the fact that Congress thought it necessary to write an original source exception into § 3730(e)(4) must mean that Congress intended

---

This argument begins with the Defendant's strongest argument. Note that in this sample, the entire section (A) is used to develop the rule section.

Start with favorable authority from your own jurisdiction.

Often, string-citing merely persuasive authority from other jurisdictions is not the best use of precious space and time. However, in the present case involving an unsettled matter of law, a "weight of the authority" argument can be useful.

When possible, explain the policy bases for the relevant legal rule.

Here the writer is employing principles of statutory construction.

a broader view of the term "based upon" than simply "derived from." *O'Keeffe*, 131 F. Supp. 2d at 93.

In *O'Keeffe*, the plaintiff alleged that the defendants had falsified the results of an engineering study of the environmental impact of the proposed restoration of commuter rail service in Southeastern Massachusetts. Because both the allegedly false facts and the allegedly true facts were publicly disclosed in the documents and hearings relating to the rail project, this District ruled that the complaint was "based upon" the prior public disclosures, and granted summary judgment for the defense when plaintiff could not establish that he was an original source of the relevant information. 131 F. Supp. 2d at 96–100.

B. This Court is not bound by the limited precedent that defines "based upon" as "derived from."

Wellford and Smith asserted in a pre-trial conference that the present Complaint is not derived from the *Boom Town Dispatch* newspaper article, and that because the allegations are not so derived, this Court has subject matter jurisdiction. Further, Wellford and Smith ostensibly rely on two prior decisions of this Court. *See United States ex rel. LeBlanc v. Raytheon Co.*, 874 F. Supp. 35, 41 (D. Mass. 1995), *aff'd*, 62 F.3d 1411 (1st Cir. 1995); *United States ex rel. LaValley v. First Nat'l Bank of Boston*, 707 F. Supp. 1351, 1367 (D. Mass. 1988). Wellford and Smith also seemingly rely on the two federal circuit court opinions that have adopted the "derived from" construction of § 3730(e)(4). *See United States v. Bank of Farmington*, 166 F.3d 853, 863 (7th Cir. 1999); *United States ex rel. Siller v. Becton Dickinson & Co.*, 21 F.3d 1339, 1348 (4th Cir. 1994). But none of these cases controls the present one.

LaValley was an early case on the issue. In *LaValley*, the court first had to decide whether the 1986 False Claims Act amendments that resulted in 31 U.S.C. § 3730(e)(4)(A) and (B) should even apply retroactively to a case filed in 1985. The vast majority of the court's opinion was devoted to that question. When the court did reach the "based upon" definitional issue, it did so without the benefit of any of the circuit court precedent, all of which came after *LaValley*.

In *LeBlanc*, the court stated that it did not matter whether the plaintiff's allegations were derived from or merely similar to the prior public disclosures in the case because LeBlanc failed to establish subject matter jurisdiction under either test. Thus, the court's preference for one definition over the other was dictum. And, because the First Circuit's affirmance was an unpublished, summary one, the fact of the affirmance is of no precedential value in the present case. See 1st Cir. R. 36(c), 32.3.

Similarly, Wellford and Smith can place no reliance upon the *Bank of Farmington* case because a different panel of the Seventh Circuit more or less simultaneously concluded that when the allegations of a whistleblower plaintiff have been previously publicly disclosed, the court has jurisdiction "only if" the plaintiff is an "original source" of the facts. *United States*

Sometimes, even in questions of law, the facts of the supporting cases are important. In those situations, outline the facts in the supporting case and, if material, synthesize the patterns in the facts across the group of cases on which you rely.

Some legal writers would include a mini-conclusion for this sub-issue, to sum up the reasoning in the section. Others would not conclude until the end of the brief, on the theory that a well-framed point heading and topic sentences can replace the conclusion within a section.

Sometimes it may be appropriate to withhold a discussion of the adverse authorities for a reply brief. But we generally recommend inoculating the court against the adverse authorities in the opening brief. This recommendation particularly holds true in the present case, where two of the adverse authorities are from the controlling jurisdiction (and thus there is an obligation as an officer of the court to cite them), and the two other adverse authorities are so obvious that there is no danger of tipping off opposing counsel to anything he will not find anyway.

There are several ways to address adverse authority: Systematically go through the authorities and argue that they can be ignored, and/or that they can be

ex rel. Lamers v. City of Green Bay, 168 F.3d 1013, 1017 (7th Cir. 1999). The viability of the *Bank of Farmington* opinion is questionable even in the court that rendered it.

That only leaves the Fourth Circuit's opinion in *Siller*. But *Siller* is not binding upon this Court. Moreover, its logic has been rejected by the Second, Third, Sixth, Eighth, Ninth, Tenth, Eleventh, and D.C. Circuits, as well as implicitly by a panel of the Seventh Circuit. The *Siller* court's "derived from" construction of the term "based upon" is inconsistent with the federal courts' limited jurisdiction, which plaintiff bears the burden of establishing. It is inconsistent with Congress' decision not to create whistleblower standing for would-be plaintiffs who give the government information the government already has; and it is inconsistent with the "original source" provision in the statute, which would be superfluous under *Siller*.

C. Plaintiff's Complaint in this matter is "based upon" the prior *Boom Town Dispatch* newspaper article.

It is undisputed that the *Boom Town Dispatch* on [Month/Day/20XX] published an article concerning the billing practices of various area hospitals, including Commonwealth. Pl.'s Compl. At ¶ 18; Aff. Andrews ¶ 3, Ex. One. It is also undisputed that the article included a detailed discussion of Commonwealth's billing of Medicare. Aff. Andrews ¶ 3, Ex. One. The article identified specific alleged examples of fraudulent billing practices. *Id.* A simple facial comparison of Wellford and Smith's Complaint with the article reveals that the allegations mirror each other. Thus, by definition, Wellford and Smith's Complaint is the same as, or similar to, the publicly disclosed allegations in the newspaper article. This similarity means, as a matter of law, that the Court lacks subject matter jurisdiction in this case because Wellford and Smith are not proper plaintiffs under the federal False Claims Act.

CONCLUSION

This Court should grant Commonwealth's motion to dismiss the Complaint for lack of subject matter jurisdiction under Federal Rule of Civil Procedure 12(b)(1). If the United States believed there was good reason to pursue a claim against Commonwealth, it could have done so through the Attorney General in the manner described by the False Claims Act. But the United States did not pursue the case. Instead, Wellford and Smith are pursuing the case in the government's name. This they cannot do, for their allegations are based upon prior public disclosures within the meaning of 31 U.S.C. § 3730(e)(4).

---

distinguished, and/or that they are actually helpful, and/or that they are simply wrongly decided.

Note that in this sample, the entire section (B) is devoted to a counterargument, which has been inserted as a continuation of the rule section.

When appropriate, apply the rule to the instant facts. Note that in this sample, the application is set out in a separate section. Compare the use of the IRAC formula in the Appellate Brief template.

Provide a formal conclusion, requesting relief.

Dated: March 1, 2003

Respectfully submitted,

Eve Johnson, #87623
Matters & Johnson
25 Winter Way
Boom Town, MA 01000
(617) 123-4567
ejohnson@mandj.com

Eve Johnson

Attorneys for
Commonwealth
Hospital, Inc.

UNITED STATES DISTRICT COURT

FOR THE DISTRICT OF MASSACHUSETTS

UNITED STATES EX REL.
MARCIA WELLFORD AND
JOHN SMITH,
      Plaintiffs,

v.

COMMONWEALTH
HOSPITAL, INC.,
      Defendant.

Case No.
Civ. 02–65432 (JW)

CERTIFICATE OF
COMPLIANCE

The undersigned attorney for Defendant certifies that this Memorandum complies with the type-volume limitation of [the relevant local rule] and the type size limitation of [the relevant local rule]. The memorandum is 2,494 words long, font size 11, in Times New Roman font.

Dated: March 1, 2003

Respectfully submitted,

Eve Johnson, #87623
Matters & Johnson
25 Winter Way
Boom Town, MA 01000
(617) 123-4567
ejohnson@mandj.com

Eve Johnson

Attorneys for
Commonwealth
Hospital, Inc.

The local rules in many courts require counsel to submit certificates of compliance with type-size (font) and type-volume (word count) limitations. Most courts use word limits, rather than page limits.

The Certificate of Compliance is typically included at the end of the Memorandum in the same document. It is not a separate document.

UNITED STATES DISTRICT COURT

FOR THE DISTRICT OF MASSACHUSETTS

UNITED STATES EX REL.
MARCIA WELLFORD AND   Case No.
JOHN SMITH,   Civ. 02–65432 (JW)
       Plaintiffs,

v.

COMMONWEALTH   [Defendant's Proposed]
HOSPITAL, INC.,   Findings of Fact
       Defendant.   and Conclusions of Law

> The local rules in many district courts require counsel to submit proposed orders as part of their motion papers. Fed. R. Civ. P. 52 requires federal district courts to enter findings of fact and conclusions of law when they decide various matters.

This matter was heard before the Honorable Judith Williams on [Month/Day/20XX] at the United States Courthouse, Boom Town, Massachusetts.

Robert Ort appeared on behalf of Plaintiff. Eve Johnson appeared on behalf of Defendant.

Now, therefore, upon all of the files, records, proceedings, and arguments of counsel, the Court makes the following:

FINDINGS OF FACT

1. Commonwealth is located in Boom Town, Massachusetts. Plaintiff's Complaint ("Pl.'s Compl.") ¶ 3 (Month Day, 20xx.)

2. The Hospital treats both patients whose costs are covered by private insurance and patients whose costs are covered by Medicare. *Id.* at ¶ 4.

3. In the case of the latter patients, the Hospital bills the federal government according to regulations established by the federal Department of Health and Human Services. *Id.*

4. The regulations require hospitals to bill the government only for (a) necessary services and procedures that (b) are actually provided. *Id.* at ¶ 5.

5. The regulations set a maximum fee for each service or medical procedure. *Id.* at ¶ 6.

6. The maximum fee is generally lower than what the hospital charges its private patients for the same service or procedure. *Id.*

7. Unlike most hospitals, which usually rely on independent physicians, Commonwealth employs several of the surgeons who have privileges at the Hospital. *Id.* at ¶ 10.

8. Dr. Marcia Wellford is one such employed surgeon. *Id.* at ¶ 2; Affidavit of Lucy Summers ("Aff. Summers") at ¶ 4.

9. Commonwealth also employs billing personnel, one of whom is Mr. John Smith. *Id.*

10. For the last three years, Wellford and Smith have been secretly making copies at random of surgical and billing

> Note how closely the proposed findings and conclusions mirror the Hospital's brief.

records relating to procedures performed on Medicare patients by employed surgeons at Commonwealth. Pl.'s Compl. at ¶ 13.

11.   After examining the records, Wellford and Smith have accused the Hospital of billing the government for procedures that were either unnecessary or were actually never performed as reported. Pl.'s Compl. at ¶ 15.

12.   Wellford and Smith presume that the billing is intentional, and that the purpose and effect are to evade the fee limits and to overcharge the government. *Id.* at ¶ 16.

13.   Wellford and Smith assert that the Hospital is committing fraud in violation of 31 U.S.C. § 3729, also known as the federal False Claims Act. *Id.* at ¶ 17.

14.   Prior to the filing of the present lawsuit, the *Boom Town Dispatch*, the local newspaper, published a lengthy article concerning the billing practices of a number of area hospitals, including Commonwealth. *Id.* at ¶ 18; Affidavit of Sandy Andrews ("Aff. Andrews") at ¶ 3, Ex. One.

15.   The article included a detailed discussion of Commonwealth's billing of Medicare. Aff. Andrews ¶ 3, Ex. One.

16.   The article quoted a number of unnamed sources as alleging that the Hospital has routinely over billed the government. *Id.*

17.   The sources claimed to identify specific examples. *Id.*

18.   The reporter who wrote the article has signed an affidavit that Wellford and Smith were *not* among the sources. Aff. Andrews at ¶ 4.

19   A side-by-side comparison reveals that Plaintiff's Complaint allegations mirror the *Dispatch* article's content.

20.   Shortly after the *Dispatch* story was published, and without having first notified the government of their information or intentions, Wellford and Smith brought an action under seal in this federal district court. Pl.'s Compl. at ¶ 19.

21.   They sued the Hospital under 31 U.S.C. § 3730, the qui tam provision in the False Claims Act, which allows individuals with knowledge of fraud on the government to sue on behalf of the government. *Id.* at ¶ 1.

22.   They complied with 31 U.S.C. § 3730(b)(2) when filing their Complaint. *Id.* at ¶ 20.

23.   The government, pursuant to 31 U.S.C. § 3730(b)(4)(B), declined to take over the action, leaving Wellford and Smith free to go forward as relators.

CONCLUSIONS OF LAW

1.   Federal courts have limited jurisdiction. *United States ex rel. Precision Co. v. Koch Indus. Inc.*, 971 F.2d 548, 551

(10th Cir. 1992). If the defendant contests subject matter jurisdiction, the plaintiff must come forward with competent proof that jurisdiction exists. *Id.* If the Plaintiff in the present case cannot establish jurisdiction, this Court should dismiss the Complaint.

2.   The subject matter jurisdiction provision in the federal False Claims Act states as follows:

> (A) *No court shall have jurisdiction* over an action under this section *based upon* the *public disclosure* of allegations or transactions . . . from the *news media, unless* the action is brought by the Attorney General or the person bringing the action is an *original source* of the information. (B) For purposes of this paragraph, 'original source' means an individual who has direct and independent knowledge of the information on which the allegations are based *and* has voluntarily *provided* the information to the Government *before filing* an action under this section which is based on the information.

31 U.S.C. § 3730(e)(4) (emphasis supplied.)

3.   When a defendant contests jurisdiction under this provision in a case not brought by the Attorney General, the court must make three inquiries:

> First, has there been a public disclosure of the relevant allegations;

> Second, if yes, does the relator who brings the suit on behalf of the government base his or her claims upon the public disclosure; and

> Third, if yes, then is the relator an "original source" of the information within the meaning of the statute?

United States ex rel. O'Keeffe v. Sverdup Corp., 131 F. Supp. 2d 87, 91 (D. Mass. 2001).

4.   Two of these elements are undisputed and indisputable in the present case: The allegations that Wellford and Smith have made against Commonwealth also have been made in a newspaper report that pre-dates the filing of the Complaint. And Wellford and Smith are not "original sources" within the meaning of § 3730(e)(4)(B) because they did not provide their information to the Government before they filed their Complaint. Accordingly, if the Complaint is "based upon" the newspaper article, there is no subject matter jurisdiction.

5.   The most recent case in this District has held that a complaint is "based upon" prior public disclosures within the meaning of 31 U.S.C. § 3730(e)(4) if the complaint allegations are "similar to or the same as those that have been publicly disclosed." *O'Keeffe*, 131 F. Supp. 2d at 92. This is also the view of the vast majority of federal circuit courts. *See United States ex rel. Minn. Ass'n of Nurse Anesthetists v. Allina Health Sys. Corp.*,

276 F.3d 1032, 1044–47 (8th Cir. 2002); *United States ex rel. Mistick PBT v. Hous. Auth. of Pittsburgh*, 186 F.3d 376, 386–88 (3d Cir. 1999); *United States ex rel. Biddle v. Bd. of Trustees of Leland Stanford Jr. Univ.*, 161 F.3d 533, 536–40 (9th Cir. 1998); *United States ex rel. McKenzie v. BellSouth Telecomm., Inc.*, 123 F.3d 935, 940–41 (6th Cir. 1997); *United States ex rel. Findley v. FPC-Boron Employees' Club*, 105 F.3d 675, 682–85 (D.C. Cir. 1997); *Cooper v. Blue Cross and Blue Shield of Fla., Inc.*, 19 F.3d 562, 566–67 (11th Cir. 1994); *Precision Co.*, 971 F.2d at 552–53; *United States ex rel. Doe v. John Doe Corp.*, 960 F.2d 318, 324 (2d Cir. 1992). The First Circuit has not yet taken a position.

6. This District in *O'Keeffe* correctly summarized the two primary reasons why "based upon" means "similar to or the same." First, the public disclosure jurisdictional bar was adopted by Congress in 1986 as part of a complex balancing of competing public interests. On the one hand, Congress wanted to provide relators with incentives to come forward with valuable information concerning fraud upon the government. On the other hand, Congress sought to discourage mere parasitical suits based upon information already in the possession of federal authorities. 131 F. Supp. 2d at 91 (citing *United States ex rel. Springfield Terminal Ry. Co. v. Quinn*, 14 F.3d 645, 649 (D.C. Cir. 1994)). There is no reason to reward relators for providing information that is the same or similar to allegations already published. *O'Keeffe*, 131 F. Supp. 2d at 93 (citing *Findley*, 105 F.3d at 685).

7. Second, if "based upon" means only "derived from," then the "original source" requirement in § 3730(e)(4) is rendered superfluous. By definition, if a relator's allegations are not derived from prior public disclosures, the relator has direct and independent knowledge of his claims. *O'Keeffe*, 131 F. Supp. 2d at 93. Thus, a separate original source requirement is unnecessary. But a standard rule of statutory construction is that a statute should be construed so as not to render any of its terms superfluous. *United States v. Nordic Village, Inc.*, 503 U.S. 30, 36 (1992). Thus, the fact that Congress thought it necessary to write an original source exception into § 3730(e)(4) must mean that Congress intended a broader view of the term "based upon" than simply "derived from." *O'Keeffe*, 131 F. Supp. 2d at 93.

8. Wellford and Smith argue that the present Complaint is not derived from the *Boom Town Dispatch* newspaper article, and that because the allegations are not so derived, this Court has subject matter jurisdiction. Wellford and Smith necessarily rely on two prior decisions of this Court. *See United States ex rel. LeBlanc v. Raytheon Co.*, 874 F. Supp. 35, 41 (D. Mass. 1995), *aff'd*, 62 F.3d 1411 (1st Cir. 1995); *United States ex rel. LaValley v. First Nat'l Bank of Boston*, 707 F. Supp. 1351, 1367 (D. Mass. 1988). Wellford and Smith also rely on the two federal circuit court opinions in which the courts adopted the "derived from" construction of § 3730(e)(4). *See United States v. Bank of Farmington*, 166 F.3d 853, 863 (7th Cir. 1999); *United States ex rel. Siller v. Becton Dickinson & Co.*, 21 F.3d 1339,

1348 (4th Cir. 1994). None of these cases controls the present one.

9.   This Court grants Commonwealth's Motion to Dismiss the Complaint for lack of subject matter jurisdiction under Fed. R. Civ. P. 12(b)(1). If the United States believed there was good reason to pursue a claim against Commonwealth, it could have done so through the Attorney General in the manner described in the False Claims Act. But the United States did not pursue the case. Instead, Wellford and Smith are pursuing the case in the government's name. This they cannot do, for their allegations are based upon prior public disclosures within the meaning of 31 U.S.C. § 3730(e)(4).

LET JUDGMENT BE ENTERED ACCORDINGLY IN FAVOR OF THE DEFENDANT.

Dated: [Month/Day/20XX]

_____

United States District Judge

[Note: Under the local rules of the District of Massachusetts, court documents would be double-spaced, except for certain items such as footnotes. We single-spaced the models to save space.]

UNITED STATES DISTRICT COURT

FOR THE DISTRICT OF MASSACHUSETTS

UNITED STATES EX REL. MARCIA WELLFORD AND JOHN SMITH, Plaintiffs,	Case No. Civ. 02–65432 (JW)
v.	
COMMONWEALTH HOSPITAL, INC., Defendant.	[Defendant's Proposed] Order Dismissing Case

Defendant moved this Court for an order dismissing the case for lack of subject matter jurisdiction under Federal Rule of Civil Procedure 12(b)(1). Defendant submitted a Memorandum in Support of its Motion to Dismiss. Plaintiffs opposed the Motion. The Court agrees with the reasoning set forth in Defendant's Memorandum. Accordingly, the Court grants Defendant's Motion.

THEREFORE it is **ORDERED** this [Month/Day/20xx] that Defendant's Motion to Dismiss is granted.

Dated: [Month/Day/20XX]

_____

United States District Judge

The local rules in many district courts require counsel to submit proposed orders as part of their motion papers. These proposed orders are typically one-page documents.

UNITED STATES DISTRICT COURT

FOR THE DISTRICT OF MASSACHUSETTS

UNITED STATES EX REL.
MARCIA WELLFORD AND   Case No.
JOHN SMITH,   Civ. 02–65432 (JW)
       Plaintiffs,

v.

COMMONWEALTH   CERTIFICATE OF
HOSPITAL, INC.,   SERVICE
       Defendant.

The undersigned counsel for Defendant certifies that I have served a copy of the foregoing Notice of Motion and Motion to Dismiss Complaint, Affidavit of Lucy Summer, Affidavit of Sandy Andrews, Memorandum in Support of Defendant's Motion to Dismiss, [Defendant's Proposed] Findings of Fact and Conclusions of Law, and [Defendant's Proposed] Order Dismissing Case upon:

Robert Ott, Attorney for Plaintiffs
United States of America ex rel. Marcia Wellford and John Smith
13 Main Street, Suite 110
Boom Town, Massachusetts 01000

By delivering the listed documents to him via electronic mail on March 1, 2003.

Dated: March 1, 2003   Respectfully submitted,

Eve Johnson, #87623
Matters & Johnson
25 Winter Way
Boom Town, MA 01000
(617) 123-4567
ejohnson@mandj.com

Eve Johnson

Attorneys for
Commonwealth
Hospital, Inc.

Documents filed with the court include a certificate of service, stating that service has been made, the date of service, and the manner of service.

D. THE APPELLATE BRIEF TEMPLATE

How would you prepare an appellate brief on this issue, employing the IRAC organizational formula? A basic template is provided below in the sample excerpted brief for Appellant Commonwealth Hospital.[21] The citations generally conform to *The Bluebook.* Although we have followed a general format for briefs filed in federal circuit courts, we have, for publication-space-limitation purposes, not followed certain requirements of the Federal Rules of Appellate Procedure. For example, if this brief were filed in the First Circuit, it would have a blue cover (for appellant), the brief would be double-spaced, and the font size would be 14. When you are preparing appellate briefs, either to a federal court or a state court, make sure you follow the appropriate court rules, both the general and local rules. Our principal goal is to provide you with one way to organize a brief on this problem employing the IRAC organizational structure.

For purposes of this sample brief, assume the following additional facts occurred below:

> After a hearing, the District Court denied the Hospital's Motion to Dismiss. In denying the Motion, the court rejected the analysis in *United States ex rel. O'Keeffe v. Sverdup Corp.,* 131 F. Supp. 2d 87, 91 (D. Mass. 2001), and instead followed the earlier district court opinions in *United States ex rel. LaValley v. First Nat'l Bank of Boston,* 707 F. Supp. 1351 (D. Mass. 1988), and *United States ex rel. LeBlanc v. Raytheon Co.,* 874 F. Supp. 35 (D. Mass. 1995). Additionally, the court explicitly adopted the interpretation advanced by the Fourth Circuit in *United States ex rel. Siller v. Becton Dickinson & Co.,* 21 F.3d 1339 (4th Cir. 1994). Recognizing, however, a split within the district, as well as among the circuits, and the lack of an authoritative First Circuit opinion, the court held *sua sponte* that its " 'order involves a controlling question of law as to which there is substantial ground for difference of opinion and that an immediate appeal from the order may materially advance the ultimate termination of the litigation' " (quoting 28 U.S.C. § 1292(b)) and certified the order for interlocutory appeal. The First Circuit has accepted the appeal.

In reviewing the sample brief, note that the advocate had to consider *how* to present the arguments. In other words, the advocate had to develop a strategy. Here, the advocate had a number of things to consider. For example, if the appellate court affirms the district court, then the Hospital will be defending a multi-million dollar lawsuit—or attempting to settle—unless the Supreme Court grants certiorari and reverses. So while this is an especially important appeal for the Hospital, counsel may conclude that in presenting the arguments, the best strategy is to demonstrate that this is a relatively simple and straightforward statutory construction issue and the great weight of authority—the opinions of other circuit courts—favors the interpretation advocated by the Hospital.[22]

Additionally, counsel had to determine how much emphasis to place on the story and how much on the law. On the one hand, the Hospital is in the noble profession of healing the sick. On the other hand, the Hospital has been accused of defrauding the government, which the Hospital denies. Counsel may conclude on appeal that the best strategy is to emphasize the reasoning of other courts, rather than the particular facts of this case or the

---

[21] For a more in-depth discussion of appellate advocacy and various principles discussed below, see CLARY ET AL., ADVOCACY ON APPEAL, *supra* chapter 1, note 1, at 3–95; MARY BETH BEAZLEY, A PRACTICAL GUIDE TO APPELLATE ADVOCACY (4th ed., Wolters Kluwer 2014).

[22] There are, of course, other strategies. For example, counsel may conclude, and the Hospital may agree, that the most persuasive argument will be to emphasize the legislative history of the False Claims Act through an independent analysis, using only the opinions from other circuits as support. As an academic exercise, a legal writing professor may well expect this type of appellate brief problem to require independent research and analysis of the statute's legislative history, as well as an examination of how other circuits have decided the issue.

other cases. This can be a useful strategy with issues of first impression in general, and/or, more specifically, where the law is more favorable than the factual story may be. In other words, the "compare and contrast" analysis in these circumstances may focus on the legal reasoning of the courts in interpreting the relevant language instead of on the facts of the individual cases.

Note also some template differences between an appellate brief and a trial court brief. Appellate briefs typically require special sections such as a table of contents, a table of authorities, a recitation of the jurisdictional grounds for appeal, a formal statement of the facts and procedural posture, and a summary of the argument. The sample appellate brief includes these sections, and the margin notes provide guidance in drafting them.

One of the special sections may consist of a specific discussion of the proper standard for the appellate court to employ in reviewing a trial court's conclusions. Normally, an appellate court reviews questions of law *de novo*.[23] But the court typically reviews questions of fact only for clear error (court findings),[24] reasonable basis (jury findings),[25] or substantial evidence (agency findings).[26] And the court normally reviews discretionary matters only for abuse of discretion.[27] These standards can make a substantial difference in the likelihood of an affirmance or reversal on appeal. Accordingly, appellate courts expect a discussion of the relevant standard for the appeal in question, either as a distinct section of a brief or at the beginning of the argument section.

Another special section in an appellate brief is a formal statement of the issue(s) presented on appeal. This is a stand-alone section within the brief, not merely a discussion within the narrative introduction found in a typical trial court brief. And the section may take different forms. For example, it may consist of simple questions, or it may instead consist of "whether" statements.[28] Examples of some of these formats are included in Chapter 10.

An additional format is the three-sentence format, which is particularly suited to persuasive writing.[29] This "deep issue" format has three components: a statement of the rule, the relevant legal facts, and the question posed. The best examples of this model are limited to 75 words. The statement of the issue used in this sample brief follows the three-sentence model.

> The False Claims Act bars qui tam actions where a relator's allegations are "based upon" allegations previously disclosed publicly, unless the relator is an "original source." Relators Wellford and Smith's allegations are the same as allegations previously disclosed in a newspaper. Wellford and Smith were not the original source of that publication. Did the District Court err as a matter of law in asserting jurisdiction over this qui tam suit?

The sample appellate brief with these required sections begins on the next page.

---

[23] Bose Corp. v. Consumers Union of U.S., Inc., 466 U.S. 485, 498, 501 (1984).

[24] U.S. v. U.S. Gypsum Co., 333 U.S. 364, 395 (1948).

[25] Lavender v. Kurn, 327 U.S. 645, 652–53 (1946).

[26] F.T.C. v. Ind. Fedn. of Dentists, 476 U.S. 447, 454, 465 (1986).

[27] *E.g.* Gen. Elec. Co. v. Joiner, 522 U.S. 136, 141 (1997).

[28] For a discussion of these various formats for issue statements, see CLARY ET AL., ADVOCACY ON APPEAL, *supra* chapter 1, note 1, at 36–37.

[29] The three-sentence model is advocated by Bryan Garner. *See e.g.* BRYAN A. GARNER, THE WINNING BRIEF 77–131 (3d ed. 2014).

IN THE UNITED STATES COURT OF APPEALS

FOR THE

FIRST CIRCUIT

NO. 02–XXXX–MASS.

UNITED STATES EX REL.
MARCIA WELLFORD AND JOHN SMITH,
                Plaintiff-Appellee,

v.

COMMONWEALTH HOSPITAL, INC.,
                Defendant-Appellant.

BRIEF OF APPELLANT

COMMONWEALTH HOSPITAL, INC.

Provide the case caption, now with appropriate appellate descriptions.

Eve Johnson, #87623
Matters & Johnson
25 Winter Way
Boom Town, MA 01000
(617) 123-4567

ATTORNEY FOR APPELLANT
COMMONWEALTH HOSPITAL, INC.

Robert Ort #98709
13 Main Street, Suite 110
Boom Town, MA 01000
(617) 765-4321

ATTORNEY FOR APPELLEE
UNITED STATES EX REL.
MARCIA WELLFORD AND JOHN SMITH

Ordinarily, when there are only two sets of attorneys to be listed, the names would go side-by-side. However, to accommodate these margin notes, we have listed one name over the other.

CORPORATE DISCLOSURE STATEMENT

Commonwealth Hospital has no parent corporation and is not owned by any publicly held company.

This kind of disclosure statement is now required in the federal appellate courts.

TABLE OF CONTENTS

CORPORATE DISCLOSURE STATEMENT . . . . [insert page] TABLE OF CONTENTS TABLE OF AUTHORITIES REASONS WHY ORAL ARGUMENT SHOULD BE HEARD JURISDICTIONAL STATEMENT STATEMENT OF THE ISSUE PRESENTED FOR REVIEW STATEMENT OF THE CASE	Insert the correct page number for each section of the brief. (We have omitted them here because we have not included page numbers in the template.)

    A.   Overview

    B.   Facts

SUMMARY OF ARGUMENT

ARGUMENT

I. AS A MATTER OF LAW, THE DISTRICT COURT ERRED IN ASSERTING SUBJECT MATTER JURISDICTION IN THE QUI TAM ACTION AGAINST COMMONWEALTH HOSPITAL.	Your argument headings serve as a roadmap for the reader.

    A.   Federal Statutes Conferring Jurisdiction Are Strictly Construed.

    B.   The False Claims Act's Jurisdictional Bar Precludes Qui Tam Actions That Are Based on Allegations That Have Been Disclosed Publicly, Unless the Relator Qualifies as an "Original Source."

        1.   *"Based upon" means "the same as" or "substantially similar to" information or evidence that has been publicly disclosed.*

        2.   *Congress intended to limit federal qui tam actions that repeat information the government already possesses.*

    C.   The District Court Erred in Relying on *Siller* and Asserting Jurisdiction Over This Qui Tam Action.

CONCLUSION

CERTIFICATE OF COMPLIANCE

ADDENDUM

TABLE OF AUTHORITIES

Cases

Bailey v. United States, 516 U.S. 137 (1995) .... [insert page]

[insert remaining cases]

Statutes

28 U.S.C. § 1292(b) .... [insert page]

[insert remaining statutes]

Rules

Fed. R. Civ. P. 12(b)(1) .... [insert page]

[insert remaining rules]

Secondary Authorities

> The cases are normally listed in alphabetical order. Some courts prefer that counsel place cases in hierarchical categories (i.e., all U.S. Supreme Court cases first), and then alphabetically within each category.
>
> Statutes and court rules are normally listed in numerical order.
>
> Secondary authorities are normally listed in alphabetical order. (No secondary authorities were used in this template.)

REASONS WHY ORAL ARGUMENT SHOULD BE HEARD

This case involves an issue of first impression, requiring the Court to interpret Section 3730(e)(4) of the False Claims Act. Dr. Marcia Wellford and Mr. John Smith ("Wellford and Smith") allege as relators on behalf of the United States (collectively "Plaintiff-Appellee") that Defendant-Appellant Commonwealth Hospital, Inc. ("Commonwealth" or "the Hospital") has fraudulently billed the federal government for services and procedures on Medicare patients. The government has declined to take over the case or to intervene.

Section 3730(e)(4) requires that relators such as Wellford and Smith not base their allegations on, among other things, previously reported newspaper accounts of the same information unless they are the "original sources" of that information. The vast majority of the federal circuits have ruled that relators' allegations are "based upon" prior public disclosures within the meaning of section 3730(e)(4) if they are "substantially similar to" or the "same as" those disclosures. It is undisputed that Wellford and Smith's allegations are the same as those previously publicly disclosed.

The Hospital contends that the District Court erred as a matter of law in denying the Hospital's motion to dismiss for lack of subject matter jurisdiction under Federal Rule of Civil Procedure 12(b)(1). The Hospital requests 30 minutes for each Party to address the issue.

JURISDICTIONAL STATEMENT

This is an appeal from an Order (not yet published) dated [Month/Day/Year] issued by the Honorable Judith Williams of the United States District Court for the District of

> This section is permitted by the local rules in some courts.

> A jurisdictional statement is standard so that the appellate court

Massachusetts. The Order denied Defendant-Appellant Hospital's Motion to Dismiss for lack of subject matter jurisdiction under Federal Rule of Civil Procedure 12(b)(1).

Jurisdiction in the District Court was purportedly based on 31 U.S.C. § 3730(e)(4). Jurisdiction in this Court on appeal is invoked pursuant to 28 U.S.C. § 1292(b). The District Court certified that its Order involved a controlling question of law as to which there is substantial ground for difference of opinion and that an immediate appeal might materially advance the ultimate termination of the litigation. This Court on [Month/Day/Year] granted the Hospital's petition for immediate review.

knows the appeal is properly before it.

STATEMENT OF THE ISSUE PRESENTED FOR REVIEW

The False Claims Act bars qui tam actions where a relator's allegations are "based upon" allegations that were previously disclosed publicly, unless the relator qualifies as an "original source." Relators Wellford and Smith's allegations are the same as allegations previously disclosed in a newspaper. Wellford and Smith were not the original source of that publication. Did the District Court err as a matter of law in asserting jurisdiction over this qui tam suit?

The issue statement in this template is in the deep issue format. Note, however, that not all courts necessarily want this type of issue statement. So know your court.

Most apposite statute and cases:

31 U.S.C.§ 3730(e)(4).

United States ex rel. Minn. Ass'n of Nurse Anesthetists v. Allina Health Sys. Corp., 276 F.3d 1032 (8th Cir. 2002).

United States ex rel. Findley v. FPC-Boron Employees' Club, 105 F.3d 675 (D.C. Cir. 1997).

United States ex rel. Siller v. Becton Dickinson & Co., 21 F.3d 1339 (4th Cir. 1994).

United States ex rel. Precision Co. v. Koch Indus., Inc., 971 F.2d 548 (10th Cir. 1992).

Some courts require that counsel list the most apposite statutory and case authority with the statement of the issue. The First Circuit does not, but you may want to put in a list anyway. If you do, confine it to the three or four most important authorities.

STATEMENT OF THE CASE

A. Overview

Wellford and Smith's Complaint alleges that the Hospital has submitted false bills to the government for services to Medicare patients. The Complaint alleges that the bills violate the federal False Claims Act, 31 U.S.C. § 3729.

The Hospital denies any wrongdoing. The Hospital also contends at the threshold that the Court lacks subject matter jurisdiction over the Complaint. The District Court has denied the Hospital's Motion to Dismiss under Federal Rule of Civil Procedure 12(b)(1), but it has certified the denial for interlocutory appeal under 28 U.S.C. § 1292(b). This appeal follows this Court's grant of the Hospital's petition for immediate review.

B.   Fact Statement

For purposes of this appeal, the following matters are undisputed:

Commonwealth is located in Boom Town, Massachusetts. Plaintiff's Complaint ("Pl.'s Compl.") ¶ 3 (Month Day, 20XX.), Joint Appendix ("App.") 10. The Hospital treats patients whose costs are covered by private insurance and patients whose costs are covered by Medicare. *Id.* at ¶ 4, App. 10. In the case of the latter patients, the Hospital bills the federal government according to regulations established by the federal Department of Health and Human Services. *Id.* The regulations require hospitals to bill the government only for (a) necessary services and procedures that (b) are actually provided. *Id.* at ¶ 5, App. 10. The regulations set a maximum fee for each service or medical procedure. *Id.* at ¶ 6, App. 11. The maximum fee is generally lower than what the Hospital charges its private patients for the same service or procedure. *Id.*

Unlike most hospitals, which usually rely on independent physicians, Commonwealth employs several of the surgeons who have privileges at the Hospital. *Id.* at ¶ 10, App. 12. Wellford is one such employed surgeon. *Id.* at ¶ 2, App. 10; Affidavit of Lucy Summers ("Aff. Summers") at ¶ 4, App. 20.

Commonwealth also employs billing personnel, one of whom is Smith. *Id.* For the last three years, Wellford and Smith have been secretly making copies at random of surgical and billing records relating to procedures performed on Medicare patients by employed surgeons at Commonwealth. Pl.'s Compl. at ¶ 13, App. 13. The copying was unauthorized and violates patient confidentiality. Aff. Summers ¶ 4, App. 20.

After examining the records, Wellford and Smith assumed that the Hospital was billing the government for procedures that were either unnecessary or never performed as reported. Pl.'s Compl. at ¶ 15, App. 14. Wellford and Smith presumed that the billing was intentional, and that the purpose and effect were to evade the fee limits and to overcharge the government. *Id.* at ¶ 16, App. 14. Wellford and Smith further presumed that the Hospital was committing fraud in violation of 31 U.S.C. § 3729, also known as the federal False Claims Act. *Id.* at ¶ 17, App. 15.

Prior to the filing of the present lawsuit, the *Boom Town Dispatch*, the local newspaper, published a lengthy article concerning the billing practices of a number of area hospitals, including Commonwealth. *Id.* at ¶ 18, App. 15; Affidavit of Sandy Andrews ("Aff. Andrews") at ¶ 3, Ex. One, App. 23. The article included a detailed discussion of Commonwealth's billing of Medicare. Aff. Andrews at ¶ 3, Ex. One, App. 23. The article quoted a number of unnamed sources as alleging that the Hospital has routinely over billed the government. *Id.* The sources claimed to identify specific examples. *Id.* The reporter

Many of the facts from the District Court brief may be re-used in the First Circuit brief under the circumstances. The one major difference is in citation practice. Federal appellate courts require counsel to prepare an Appendix, preferably a Joint Appendix, that contains the relevant evidentiary material for convenient reference. Accordingly, cites must include a reference to the appropriate Appendix pages. If the briefs of the parties are submitted before the relevant Appendix or Appendices are fully prepared, there are procedures for amending the briefs to add the appropriate page references.

who wrote the article has signed an affidavit that Wellford and Smith were *not* among the sources. Aff. Andrews at ¶ 4, App. 23. Wellford and Smith's Complaint allegations mirror the *Dispatch* article's content.

Shortly after the *Dispatch* story was published, and without having first notified the government of their information or intentions, Wellford and Smith brought an action under seal in federal district court in Boom Town. Pl.'s Compl. at ¶ 19, App. 16. They sued the Hospital under 31 U.S.C. § 3730, the qui tam provision in the False Claims Act, which allows individuals with knowledge of fraud on the government to sue on behalf of the government. *Id.* at ¶ 1, App. 9. They complied with 31 U.S.C. § 3730(b)(2) when filing their complaint. *Id.* at ¶ 20, App. 16. The government, pursuant to 31 U.S.C. § 3730(b)(4)(B), has declined to take over the action, leaving Wellford and Smith free to go forward as "relators."

SUMMARY OF THE ARGUMENT

The False Claims Act's jurisdictional bar, 31 U.S.C. § 3730(e)(4), precludes qui tam suits where a relator's allegations are "based upon" the "same" allegations that were previously publicly disclosed, unless that relator is an "original source" of the relevant information. This is the view of the vast majority of federal courts that have interpreted the Act's jurisdictional bar.

Commonwealth seeks dismissal under Federal Rule of Civil Procedure 12(b)(1) of the qui tam suit brought by Wellford and Smith because Wellford and Smith cannot establish that the District Court has subject matter jurisdiction. The District Court erred in denying the dismissal for two reasons.

First, federal courts are courts of limited jurisdiction. Statutes conferring jurisdiction on federal courts are to be strictly construed. The District Court liberally construed the False Claims Act's jurisdictional bar so as to permit qui tam actions where a relator's allegations are the same as allegations that have been previously publicly disclosed, even when the relator is not an original source, so long as the relator did not "derive" his or her allegations from the public disclosure. That liberal construction flies in the face of the limited jurisdiction principle.

Second, if "based upon" means only "derived from," as the District Court ruled, then the "original source" provision is rendered impermissibly superfluous. The "derived from" construction violates the standard rule of statutory interpretation that a statute should be construed so as not to render any of its terms superfluous. The District Court's construction is inconsistent with Congress' intent to preclude qui tam actions that simply repeat allegations that have already been publicly disclosed.

It is undisputed that Wellford and Smith's allegations are the same as the allegations that were previously publicly

Most appellate courts require a summary of the argument. A good rule of thumb is that an appellate court should be able to read your Statement of the Case/Facts, as well as your Summary of the Argument, and know in a nutshell (a) exactly what you want it to do, (b) why that is the right thing to do, and (c) how the court can get to the desired result.

Note that the Summary of the Argument is not the place for all of the technical citations. It is the overall road map to the argument that will follow thereafter.

disclosed in the *Dispatch*. It is also undisputed that Wellford and Smith are not "original sources." Thus, the District Court should have dismissed Wellford and Smith's Complaint for lack of subject matter jurisdiction.

ARGUMENT

I. **AS A MATTER OF LAW, THE DISTRICT COURT ERRED IN ASSERTING SUBJECT MATTER JURISDICTION IN THE QUI TAM ACTION AGAINST COMMONWEALTH HOSPITAL.**

This Court has yet to consider the parameters of the federal False Claim Act's jurisdictional bar, but most of the other circuits have addressed the issue. Although the circuit courts are split, they are not split evenly. *See United States v. LaFortune*, 192 F.3d 157, 160 (1st Cir. 1999) (noting a split among the circuits was not evenly divided and adopting the majority view). The vast majority of courts have ruled that when a relator's allegations are the same as or similar to allegations that have already been publicly disclosed, then the relator cannot demonstrate that the court has jurisdiction unless the relator qualifies as an "original source." The courts have based their rulings on the text of the statute, canons of statutory interpretation, and the legislative history.

This Court reviews the District Court's failure to dismiss for lack of subject matter jurisdiction involving a pure question of law *de novo*. *Gonzalez v. United States*, 285 F.3d 281, 287 (1st Cir. 2002).

A. Federal Statutes Conferring Jurisdiction Are Strictly Construed.

Jurisdiction in federal court is never presumed for the reason that federal courts have limited jurisdiction. *Viqueira v. First Bank*, 140 F.3d 12, 16 (1st Cir. 1998). If a statute confers jurisdiction on the federal courts, as does the False Claims Act, then the court must strictly construe the jurisdictional provision. *United States ex rel. Precision Co. v. Koch Indus., Inc.*, 971 F.2d 548, 552 (10th Cir. 1992). Where doubts persist, the court must rule *against* federal jurisdiction. *Id.*

Accordingly, the District Court impermissibly interpreted the jurisdictional bar of the False Claims Act as broadly conferring the court with jurisdiction any time a relator's allegations are not "derived from" the publicly disclosed allegations.

B. The False Claims Act's Jurisdictional Bar Precludes Qui Tam Actions That Are Based on Allegations That Have Been Publicly Disclosed, Unless the Relator Qualifies as an "Original Source."

Interpreting the jurisdictional bar of the False Claims Act first requires an examination of the relevant text. *Brady v. Credit Recovery Co.*, 160 F.3d 64, 66 (1st Cir. 1998). If the proposed meaning renders the provision ambiguous, or leads to

---

As with the trial brief, the major point heading introduces the arguments. When there is only one issue, and thus one major point heading, the writer can choose whether to use a roman numeral before the point heading.

Where there is more than one argument, the introduction also signals the discrete substantive arguments that follow, as set forth under the minor point headings. After the introduction, identify the standard of review on appeal.

The minor point heading introduces the discrete argument or part of the argument being made. Most often, it is advisable to begin with more general propositions, then move to the more specific. Note the basic IRAC structure. Here, the application and conclusion are combined.

unreasonable results, then the Court must look to canons of statutory construction and the legislative history. *Id.*

The subject matter jurisdiction provision in the False Claims Act states:

(A) *No court shall have jurisdiction* over an action under this section *based upon* the *public disclosure* of allegations or transactions . . . from the *news media, unless* the action is brought by the Attorney General or the person bringing the action is an *original source* of the information. (B) For purposes of this paragraph, 'original source' means an individual who has direct and independent knowledge of the information on which the allegations are based *and* has voluntarily *provided* the information to the Government *before filing* an action under this section which is based on the information.

31 U.S.C. § 3730(e)(4) (emphasis supplied).

When a defendant contests jurisdiction under this provision in a case not brought by the Attorney General, the court must make the following inquiries:

> 1. Has there been a public disclosure of the relevant allegations?
>
> 2. If yes, does the relator who brings the suit on behalf of the government base his or her claims upon the public disclosure?
>
> 3. If yes, then is the relator an "original source" of the information within the meaning of the statute?

Minn. Ass'n of Nurse Anesthetists v. Allina Health Sys. Corp., 276 F.3d 1032, 1042 (8th Cir. 2002).

Two of these elements, 1 and 3, are undisputed and indisputable in the present case: The allegations that Wellford and Smith have made against the Hospital also have been made in a newspaper report that pre-dates the filing of their Complaint. And Wellford and Smith are not "original sources" within the meaning of § 3730(e)(4)(B) because they did not provide their information to the government before they filed their Complaint. Accordingly, if the Complaint is "based upon" the newspaper article, there is no subject matter jurisdiction.

The False Claims Act does not define "based upon." And a straight textual reading of the jurisdictional bar does not resolve the ambiguity. If "based upon" means merely "derived from," as the lower court ruled, then the "original source" provision is superfluous, which violates a fundamental principle of statutory construction. *See Brady*, 160 F.3d at 67 (interpreting a statutory provision and stating that one interpretation would render another provision "impermissibly

---

Margin notes:

When appropriate, break apart the elements for the reader.

Note that the writer in this appellate setting now cites to the opinions of other circuits, rather than to a lower court opinion within the circuit.

Where appropriate, apply the rule to the facts and dispense with those elements that are not at issue. Focus the court's attention on the disputed element.

Provide the Court with the "crux" of the problem. Set the stage for more development of the rule section—here, how other courts have interpreted the critical language. Note how the writer signals a

superfluous") (citing *Bailey v. United States*, 516 U.S. 137, 145 (1995)).

counterargument that will be fleshed out in subsequent sections.

1. ***"Based upon" means "the same as" or "substantially similar to" information or evidence that has been publicly disclosed.***

The most recent circuit to interpret the jurisdictional bar of the False Claims Act ruled that a qui tam action is "based upon" a public disclosure if the relator's allegations and the publicly disclosed allegations are the same. *Minn. Ass'n of Nurse Anesthetists*, 276 F.3d at 1047. This is also the view of the vast majority of federal circuit courts. *See United States ex rel. Mistick PBT v. Hous. Auth. of Pittsburgh*, 186 F.3d 376, 386–88 (3d Cir. 1999); *United States ex rel. Biddle v. Bd. of Trustees of Leland Stanford Jr. Univ.*, 161 F.3d 533, 536–40 (9th Cir. 1998); *United States ex rel. McKenzie v. BellSouth Telecomm., Inc.*, 123 F.3d 935, 940–41 (6th Cir. 1997); *United States ex rel. Findley v. FPC-Boron Employees' Club*, 105 F.3d 675, 682–85 (D.C. Cir. 1997); *Cooper v. Blue Cross and Blue Shield of Fla., Inc.*, 19 F.3d 562, 566–67 (11th Cir. 1994); *Precision Co.*, 971 F.2d at 552–53; *United States ex rel. Doe v. John Doe Corp.*, 960 F.2d 318, 324 (2d Cir. 1992).

Note that the writer often refers to the relevant section of the statute not by its numerical designation, but by its function—a jurisdictional bar, which is consistent with the advocate's overall theme.

In *Minnesota Association of Nurse Anesthetists*, the relators brought a qui tam action against various hospitals and anesthesiologists, alleging that the defendants defrauded the government by overcharging for their services. In adopting the majority rule, the Eighth Circuit reasoned that "based upon" means the "same as" because any other construction would render the "original source" provision of the jurisdictional bar meaningless. 276 F.3d at 1047.

Begin to synthesize the cases—in the present context, the reasoning is more important than a factual analysis of each case. On other occasions, the factual story in each case will be vital. For brevity, we have omitted part of the case summary in this model. However, in constructing such a summary, be careful not to merely present a case digest. Instead, weave the analysis by staying focused on the common thread—here, that the "original source" provision has no effect if "based upon" does not mean the "same as" or "similar to." Then briefly state the pattern you have synthesized from the cases.

Similarly, in *Mistick*, the relator alleged that the defendants, a city housing authority and an architectural firm, defrauded the government by making false claims to the Department of Housing and Urban Development. In adopting the majority view, the court reasoned that an alternative construction to "based upon" would render the "original source" provision superfluous. 186 F.3d at 386.

And in . . .

. . .

The majority rule recognizes that it is impermissible to render one part of a statute superfluous when there is another construction that provides coherency and consistency and effects Congress' intent. *See United States v. Nordic Village, Inc.*, 503 U.S. 30, 36 (1992) (stating the "settled rule" is that a statute "must, if possible, be construed in such a fashion that every word has some operative effect"). The most coherent reading of the False Claims Act gives operative effect to the "original source" provision and equates "based upon" with "the same as" or "substantially similar to."

2. *Congress intended to limit federal qui tam actions that repeat information the government already possesses.*

Congress initially enacted the qui tam provisions of the False Claims Act of 1863 to encourage private citizens to bring suit against those who defrauded the government. *Findley*, 105 F.3d at 679 (providing an in-depth discussion of the legislative history). As an inducement, the Act permitted a successful qui tam relator to collect one-half of what was recovered. *Id.*

The inducement worked. As government spending increased, especially in the 1930s and 1940s, qui tam litigation increased—"opportunistic private litigants chased after generous case bounties" by bringing parasitic lawsuits copied directly from publicly disclosed information. *Id.* at 679–80. The Act provided no effective mechanism to prevent these parasitic suits. As a result, the government gained no new information and recovered less. *Id.* at 680.

These parasitic suits reached their nadir when the Supreme Court allowed a qui tam action where the relator simply copied the allegations in his complaint directly from an indictment for criminal fraud. *Id.* (citing and discussing *United States ex rel. Marcus v. Hess*, 317 U.S. 537 (1943)). Congress reacted and amended the Act in 1943, barring "qui tam suits that were 'based upon evidence or information in the possession of the United States . . . at the time such suit was brought.'" *Id.* (quoting 57 Stat. 608). Thus, qui tam actions were barred if the evidence or information was already in possession of the government, even if the relator was the one who informed the government. *Id.*

Predictably, the pendulum swung to the other extreme. In 1984, the Seventh Circuit ruled that the State of Wisconsin was precluded from proceeding in a qui tam action because the government was already in possession of the evidence. Yet it was Wisconsin that exposed the fraud and reported it to the government. *Id.* (citing and discussing *United States ex rel. Wis. v. Dean*, 729 F.2d 1100 (7th Cir. 1984)). Thus, "[q]ui tam actions under the FCA had gone in forty years from unrestrained profiteering to a flaccid enforcement tool." *Doe*, 960 F.2d at 321 (recounting the legislative history of the False Claims Act).

Congress reacted once again and amended the Act, precluding qui tam actions if the relator's allegations were based upon transactions or allegations that had been publicly disclosed, unless the attorney general brought the action or the relator was an "original source." *Findley*, 105 F.3d at 681.

Preventing parasitic lawsuits was not Congress' only concern.

From its inception, the qui tam provisions of the [False Claims Act] were designed to inspire whistleblowers to come forward promptly with information concerning fraud so that the government can stop it and recover ill-gotten gains.

The legislative history provides additional support for the interpretation being advocated.

Note that although the writer has chosen not to delve deeply into the legislative history, some context is important to develop the rule explanation. Here, the writer is deliberately relying on the D.C. Circuit's discussion of the legislative history because of its depth and breadth.

As a general rule, long quotes from opinions are not helpful. But here, the advocate chose to rely on the court's language to impress upon the Court that Congress intended more than just

Once the information is in the public domain, there is less need for a financial incentive to spur individuals into exposing frauds. Allowing qui tam suits after that point may either pressure the government to prosecute cases when it has good reasons not to or reduce the government's ultimate recovery.

Id. at 686; *see also Biddle*, 161 F.3d at 538–39.

Indeed, nowhere in the legislative history is there evidence that Congress intended "based upon" to mean something other than repeating, or "parroting," information already available to the government. *See Findley*, 105 F.3d at 684–85. Where a relator's allegations merely repeat publicly disclosed information, and the relator does not qualify as an "original source," the court lacks jurisdiction.

> *Conclude the rule section with a description of what the rule means.*

In this case, it is undisputed that the *Dispatch* published an article concerning the billing practices of various area hospitals, including Commonwealth. Pl.'s Compl. at ¶ 18, App. 15; Aff. Andrews ¶ 3, Ex. One, App. 23. It is undisputed that the article was published before Wellford and Smith brought this qui tam action. *Id.* And it is undisputed that the article included a detailed discussion of Commonwealth's billing of Medicare. Aff. Andrews ¶ 3, Ex. One, App. 23. The article identified specific alleged examples of fraudulent billing practices. *Id.* A simple facial comparison of Wellford and Smith's Complaint with the article reveals that the allegations mirror each other. Thus, by definition, the allegations in the Complaint are the same as or similar to the publicly disclosed allegations in the newspaper article. This similarity means, as a matter of law, that the lower court lacked subject matter jurisdiction in this case because Wellford and Smith are not proper plaintiffs under the False Claims Act. To decide otherwise, as the lower court did, impermissibly renders the "original source" provision meaningless and fails to effect Congress' intent in enacting the jurisdictional bar to the False Claims Act.

> *Apply the reasoning to the instant facts.*

> *Provide, if helpful, a brief conclusion.*

C. The District Court Erred in Relying on *Siller* and Asserting Jurisdiction Over This Qui Tam Action.

Only one circuit has advanced the minority view of what "based upon" means. In *United States ex rel. Siller v. Becton Dickinson & Co.*, 21 F.3d 1339 (4th Cir. 1994), the court ruled that "based upon" means "derived from." The court further explained that a "relator's action is 'based upon' a public disclosure of allegations only where the relator has actually derived from that disclosure the allegations upon which his qui tam action is based." *Id.* at 1348.

Every other circuit to consider the meaning of "based upon" has explicitly or implicitly rejected the *Siller* court's interpretation because it violates the canons of statutory construction and fails to effect Congress' intent. *See, e.g., United States ex rel. Mistick PBT v. Hous. Auth. of Pittsburgh*, 186 F.3d

> *This minor point heading introduces the key counterargument and refutation. In the trial brief, the writer chose to weave the counterargument addressing the adverse authority within the rule section. Here, the writer provides a discrete argument that follows the IRAC formula.*

preventing parasitic lawsuits.

376, 386–88 (3d Cir. 1999). (One panel of the Seventh Circuit adopted the *Siller* court's interpretation; but another panel almost simultaneously concluded that, when the allegations of a relator have been previously publicly disclosed, the court has jurisdiction "only if" the relator is an "original source" of the facts. *Compare United States v. Bank of Farmington*, 166 F.3d 853, 863 (7th Cir. 1999) *with United States ex rel. Lamers, v. City of Green Bay*, 168 F.3d 1013, 1017 (7th Cir. 1999)).

The *Siller* court relied principally on an isolated textual reading of the "based upon" clause. In doing so, it created a construction that is inconsistent with the federal courts' limited jurisdiction; is inconsistent with the "original source" provision; and is inconsistent with Congress' intent to preclude relator standing for would-be plaintiffs who parrot information the government already has.

In relying on *Siller*, the District Court similarly violated canons of statutory interpretation, adopting a construction that leads to unreasonable results.

The District Court's reliance on two prior decisions within the District was also misplaced. In *United States ex rel. LaValley v. First National Bank of Boston*, 707 F. Supp. 1351, 1367 (D. Mass. 1988), the court first had to decide whether the 1986 False Claims Act amendments that resulted in 31 U.S.C. § 3730(e)(4)(A) and (B) should even apply retroactively to a case filed in 1985. The vast majority of the court's opinion was devoted to that question. When the court did reach the "based upon" definitional issue, it did so without the benefit of any of the later circuit court precedent.

Similarly, in *United States ex rel. LeBlanc v. Raytheon Co.*, 874 F. Supp. 35, 41 (D. Mass. 1995), *aff'd*, 62 F.3d 1411 (1st Cir. 1995), the court stated that it did not matter whether the plaintiff's allegations were derived from or merely similar to the prior public disclosures in the case because LeBlanc failed to establish subject matter jurisdiction under either test. Thus, the court's preference for one definition over the other was dictum. And, because the First Circuit's affirmance was an unpublished, summary one, the fact of the affirmance is of no precedential value in the present case. *See* 1st Cir. R. 36(c), 32.3.

The District Court should have followed the reasoning of the court in *United States ex rel. O'Keeffe v. Sverdup Corp.*, 131 F. Supp. 2d 87 (D. Mass. 2001). In that case, the plaintiff alleged that the defendants had falsified the results of an engineering study of the environmental impact of the proposed restoration of commuter rail service in Southeastern Massachusetts. Because both the allegedly false facts and the allegedly true facts were publicly disclosed in the documents and hearings relating to the rail project, the court ruled that the complaint was "based upon" the prior public disclosures, and granted summary judgment for the defense when the plaintiff could not establish that he was an original source of the relevant information. *Id.* at 100.

The writer chose to briefly, but strongly, summarize the weaknesses in the adverse authority rather than synthesize the reasoning of the other cases rejecting this interpretation. Either strategy, depending upon the circumstances, may be effective.

Here, the writer must also address the split among the judges within the District.

The *O'Keeffe* court reviewed the split among the federal circuits, adopted the majority view, and explicitly rejected the reasoning of *LeBlanc* and *LaValley*. *Id.* at 92–93. The court correctly summarized the two primary reasons why "based upon" means "similar to or the same." First, Congress amended the public disclosure jurisdictional bar in 1986 as part of a complex balancing of competing public interests. On the one hand, Congress wanted to provide inside whistleblowers with incentives to come forward with valuable information concerning fraud upon the government. On the other hand, Congress sought to discourage suits based upon information already in the possession of federal authorities. *Id.* at 91 (citing *United States ex rel. Springfield Terminal Ry. Co. v. Quinn*, 14 F.3d 645, 649 (D.C. Cir. 1994)).

Second, if "based upon" means only "derived from," then the "original source" requirement is rendered superfluous. By definition, if a relator's allegations are not derived from prior public disclosures, the relator has direct and independent knowledge of his claims. *Id.* at 93. The fact that Congress thought it necessary to write an original source exception into § 3730(e)(4) must mean that Congress intended a broader view of the term "based upon" than simply "derived from." *Id.*

CONCLUSION

[For all of the above reasons, the Court should reverse the ruling of the District Court and dismiss the Complaint for lack of subject matter jurisdiction.]

[This Court should reverse the ruling of the District Court and dismiss the Complaint for lack of subject matter jurisdiction. The relators have based their Complaint upon publicly disclosed allegations. The Complaint is merely parasitical in that it is based upon information the Government already has. 31 U.S.C. § 3730(e)(4) bars the Complaint.]

Dated: April 1, 2003

Respectfully submitted,

Eve Johnson, #87623
Matters & Johnson
25 Winter Way
Boom Town, MA 01000
(617) 765-4321
ejohnson@mandj.com

Eve Johnson

Attorney for Appellant
Commonwealth Hospital,
Inc.

CERTIFICATE OF COMPLIANCE

[as to the length of the brief]

Two types of conclusion are possible. One is an abbreviated form, that can be desirable to avoid repetition in an otherwise short brief. The other is a longer, more descriptive form that can be a useful bookend to the initial Summary of the Argument in an otherwise long brief. Reasonable lawyers may disagree over which form of conclusion to use. Part of the answer depends upon the audience. If the relevant judge or judges like to jump to the end of a brief for the punch line before they read the full brief, then opt for the longer, more descriptive form.

Attach these items to the brief.

ADDENDUM [containing relevant district court opinion and any other material required]	

E. ONE MORE ETHICAL CONSIDERATION

In representing clients, there is a general rule that prohibits an attorney from "conduct involving dishonesty, fraud, deceit or misrepresentation."[30] This broadly worded rule governs lawyers' conduct and applies to the drafting of documents submitted to the court. It also applies to a lawyer's interactions with third parties during a lawyer's representation of a client. Preserve your reputation as an honest and forthright person. Be mindful of your role as an officer of the court and as an administrator of justice.

---

[30] MODEL RULES OF PROF'L CONDUCT R. 8.4(b) (2016).

CHAPTER 12

Oral Argument

Once a brief is submitted to a trial or appellate court, the litigants typically are given an opportunity for oral argument on the issues presented. (We say typically because oral argument is not an automatic right, and there are courts that decline to grant it.)

The purpose of oral argument is to leave the court with an impression of why you should win and to answer the court's questions about how the court can reach the result you want. There simply will not be time for much more. As a result, we encourage a simplified approach.

LEARNING OBJECTIVES

1.   Students will learn how to prepare and present a formal oral argument before a court.

2.   Students will learn how to listen and engage with judges to communicate and advocate in support of a legal position.

A.   ETHICAL CONSIDERATIONS

Oral argument allows the attorneys in the case before the court to engage in a dialogue with the bench (the judge or panel of judges). It affords an attorney the opportunity to eloquently explain the case, wisely answer questions, and masterfully explain away opposing counsel's arguments. It is, however, by its nature adversarial. The judges may disagree with the attorney's presentation of the law or facts, and opposing counsel will argue vehemently against the attorney's presentation of the law and facts. Despite the intense conversation that may occur, the attorney must not offer any false evidence[1] or mislead the court,[2] and must avoid any conduct that is prejudicial to the administration of justice.[3]

B.   A WAY TO PREPARE THE ARGUMENT

There are many ways to prepare to deliver an oral argument. The following is one efficient methodology that works. First, divide an 8½-inch by 14-inch legal-sized manila folder into four columns. Second, place in the first column your outline for opening the argument. Third, place in the second and third columns the key material you need to talk about on the (let's say for convenience) two issues in the matter. Finally, place in the fourth column the four or five hardest questions you expect the court to ask and the short-hand bullet points for your answers.

---

[1]   MODEL RULES OF PROF'L CONDUCT R. 3.3(a)(3) (2016).

[2]   MODEL RULES OF PROF'L CONDUCT R. 8.4(c) (2016).

[3]   *Id*. at 8.4(d).

In practice, this approach might look like the following chart for Defendant's counsel in the context of the Commonwealth Hospital Motion to Dismiss presented in Chapter 11.

OPENING 30 SECONDS	FIRST ISSUE	SECOND ISSUE	HARD QUESTIONS
May it please the Court	Public disclosures	Original source	Hard question 1:
I am John Doe	Statute language states:	Statute language states:	Answer:
Lawyer for Commonwealth Hospital			Hard question 2:
Case about prevention of parasitical suits	Legislative history provides:	Legislative history provides:	Answer:
Motion to dismiss	Key case says:	Key case says:	Hard question 3:
Two issues:			Answer:
One—public disclosures	Hot three facts:	Hot three facts:	Hard question 4:
Two—not original source	•	•	Answer:
	•	•	
Result: no subject matter jurisdiction	•	•	Hard question 5:
Grant motion			Answer:
	Result: Defendant wins	Result: Defendant wins	

There are several advantages to this approach: There are no pages to shuffle. There are no note cards to re-arrange after they get mixed up or fall on the floor of the courtroom. There is not enough room to write out or type full sentences in the columns, so the advocate will not be tempted to simply read the argument. The advocate can organize the material into blocks for convenient reference even if the court wants to focus on Issue 2 before Issue 1, or hard question 5 ahead of hard question 1. In short, this approach puts you, the advocate, in a flexible position to present the building blocks that form your argument.

C. A WAY TO BEGIN THE ARGUMENT

Once prepared with an outline, you need to be ready to begin the argument in a strong position. One simple way to launch an argument to the court is to proceed as follows.

"May it please the Court."	The first example is the traditional opening. The second example may be used in a trial court setting if you have appeared in front of the judge before.
[Less formal alternative: "Good morning/afternoon, your Honor."]	
"I am [insert your name]."	
"I represent [insert the name of your client(s)] in this matter."	
[Less formal alternative: "I am here today on behalf of [insert the name of your client]."]	If you are co-counsel with another lawyer and will be splitting the argument, then you may substitute "My co-counsel [name co-counsel] and I represent [client]."
"This case is about [complete the sentence with your theme]."	Note: The insert is a theme, not a legal position. The legal position follows afterwards. The theme evokes loyalty, responsibility, freedom, or the like.
"There are [insert the correct number—assume two for now] issues before the Court today. The first is [identify]. The second is [identify]."	
"The Court should [insert what you want the court to do] on the first issue for the following 1/2/3 reasons. The Court should [insert what you want the court to do] on the second issue for the following 1/2/3 reasons."	Also tell the Court which issue you will address and which issue your co-counsel will address, if you are splitting oral argument.
[Then explain the argument in more detail, answer the court's questions, and sit down.]	

In practice, this template might play out something like this in the context of one of the motions to dismiss presented in Chapter 11.

> *Good morning, your Honor. I am Eve Johnson, appearing for Defendant Commonwealth Hospital. This case is about preventing parasitical lawsuits in federal court. Before this Court today is Commonwealth's Motion to Dismiss Plaintiffs' Complaint. The issue is whether the Court has subject matter jurisdiction over Plaintiffs' "whistleblower" allegations of Medicare fraud. The answer is no for two reasons: One, Plaintiffs ground their complaint on public disclosures already in the possession of the federal government. Two, Plaintiffs are not the original source of those disclosures. The relevant statute, 31 U.S.C. § 3730(e)(4), precludes Plaintiffs from free riding on the prior disclosures of other persons as a basis for their complaint. So we ask the Court to grant our Motion to Dismiss.*

On appeal, the argument would look like this if Defendant won below and is now the Respondent.

> *May it please the Court. I am Eve Johnson, appearing for Defendant Commonwealth Hospital. This case is about preventing parasitical lawsuits in federal court. Before the Court today is Plaintiffs' appeal from the district court's order granting Commonwealth's Motion to Dismiss Plaintiffs' Complaint. The issue is whether the Court has subject matter jurisdiction over Plaintiffs' "whistleblower" allegations of Medicare fraud. The answer is no for two reasons: One, Plaintiffs ground their complaint on public disclosures already in the possession of the federal government. Two, Plaintiffs are not the original source of those disclosures. The relevant statute, 31 U.S.C. § 3730(e)(4), precludes Plaintiffs from free riding on the prior disclosures of other persons as a basis for their complaint. So the district court properly granted our motion to dismiss for lack of subject matter jurisdiction as a matter of law. This Court should affirm the dismissal.*

In both settings, you have told the court who you are, who your client is, what matter is before the court, what you will be arguing, what you want the court to do, and why the court should do what you request. The court now knows in the first thirty seconds of your argument everything it needs to know to rule in your client's favor. Now all you have to do is flesh out the arguments in more detail, answer the court's questions, and sit down.

D. A WAY TO APPROACH THE MIDDLE OF THE ARGUMENT

Once you have successfully launched the argument, the question is how to proceed through the balance of your time. With the caveat that every argument will have its own twists and turns, depending on the subject matter of the issues before the court and the individual judge or judges presiding, it is safe to say that some substantive and methodological matters will routinely surface. They include the following.

1. **The standard to be applied to the issues.** Every court will want to know the standard that it should apply to the matters before it. If you are before the court on a motion to dismiss, then the relevant standard is whether the complaint as a matter of law fails to state a claim upon which relief may be granted. If you are before the court on a summary judgment motion, then the relevant standard is whether the material facts are undisputed and there is only one possible outcome on the relevant issue when the law is applied to those undisputed material facts. If you are before the court on a preliminary injunction, then the relevant standard is whether the court should use its discretion to preserve the status quo in the case pending fuller proceedings. In the end, the question is whether the standard is met; so the court will care what the standard is. Tell the court.

2. **The standard to be applied to review another court's ruling.** Suppose you are on appeal. Now the appellate court will want to know not only what standard the district court applied to the issues before it, but also what standard the appellate court should use to review the district court's actions. Classically, appellate courts review district court conclusions of law *de novo*, district court exercises of discretion for abuse, and district court findings of fact for clear error.[4] Those are quite different review standards. Tell the court in your argument which one applies to which issue.

3. **The procedural posture in which issues are coming before the court.** Every court will want to know how the issues before it are surfacing at the present time. The procedural posture of the case, as well as of the specific issues involved in the oral argument, helps determine the answers to the two questions listed above about the appropriate standard the court should apply. Is the case in a pre-trial stage? Has there been any discovery of facts? Has there been a trial? Was there a jury? All of these things, and more, potentially matter. Tell the court what it needs to know about them.

4. **The nature of the court's task in the matter before it.** A district court's job is to decide the issues before it and thus render justice as between the parties to the specific dispute. When the district court acts, it applies the law as found in the existing mandatory authority in the jurisdiction. The district court takes that authority as given. Sometimes, of course, there is no controlling authority, and the court will look to persuasive authority.

An intermediate court of appeals is an error-correcting court. When the intermediate appellate court acts, it applies the law as found in the existing mandatory authority in the jurisdiction. The court takes that authority as given. Its job is to review, under the proper *de novo*, abuse of discretion, or clear error standard, what a district court did and to determine

---

[4] For a more extended discussion of standards of review, consult BRADLEY G. CLARY, SHARON REICH PAULSEN & MICHAEL J. VANSELOW, ADVOCACY ON APPEAL 50–53 (3d ed. West 2008).

if the district court correctly acted. Again, the intermediate court may have to consult persuasive authority from other jurisdictions.

The highest-level court of appeals, whether denominated as a "supreme court" or something else, is not simply an error-correcting court. When a supreme court acts on a matter of common law in its jurisdiction, it makes that common law. Or it decides whether the jurisdiction's enacted law conforms to the state's or to the United States' constitution. The highest-level court then is in part a policy-making court.

These roles matter for purposes of your oral argument. A district court may think a particular law is "wrong" from a policy standpoint, but can do little about that. So it is primarily interested in what the mandatory authority *is* rather than what it should be. That is not to say you should ignore policy arguments in a district court setting, merely that in the end the district court cannot make policy. By contrast, you should be thinking about policy questions in arguments to the jurisdiction's highest court because that court wants to know what policy effects will result from a particular decision.

5.   Consider the slippery slopes. Particularly in the jurisdiction's highest court, but in other courts as well, the judges are looking over their shoulders at the next cases coming down the line. "If we decide this case the way counsel advocates, what will we have to do with the next variation of this same issue that comes before us?" Be sensitive to that concern. Give the court comfort that the sound decision you request in the present matter will also lead to sound decisions in other, subsequent matters.

6.   Answer questions directly. Try to answer the court's questions directly. If the question calls for a yes or a no answer, give one. ("Yes, your Honor, because . . . ." OR "No, your Honor, because . . . .") If the question cannot be answered with a simple yes or no, then say so and explain why. ("Yes in part, your Honor, as to X, but the rest of the answer depends on the following . . . .") If you don't respond yes or no to the court's question, then you look evasive even if that is not your intention.

7.   Simplify. The best oral arguments take complex positions and simplify them so the court understands the essentials. (In effect, but not literally, you say, "Here's what the Court really needs to know.") Then you may work in the details that give flavor to the argument. But if you cannot tell the court in a few simple sentences what the debate really comes down to, the argument will be much harder for the court to follow.

The above advice might play out as follows in connection with the Commonwealth Hospital's motion.

Court: Ms. Johnson, we are here on your motion to dismiss?

Counsel: Yes, your Honor. The complaint fails to state a claim as a matter of law.

Court: Why?

Counsel: Because Plaintiffs claim to be whistleblowers, but their allegations are very similar to a newspaper report that pre-dates the complaint. The Plaintiffs are just free riding on the report. Allowing Plaintiffs to free ride on published information for whistleblower claims opens the courthouse doors to frivolous litigation.

Court: But the Plaintiffs say they are not basing their complaint on the newspaper report because their claims are not derived from disclosures in the report.

Counsel: That is what Plaintiffs argue, your Honor. But that is not the legal test. The legal test as adopted in the majority of circuits is that a plaintiff's complaint is "based upon" the report for 31 U.S.C. § 3730(e)(4) purposes as long as the allegations are similar to those in a public disclosure. That test is met here. And that test makes sense because there is a separate "original source" requirement in the statute that would be superfluous if Plaintiffs were correct that "based upon" only means "derived from."

Court: There is no First Circuit binding opinion.

Counsel: That's correct, your Honor.

Court: Tell me why then I should ignore this district's own LeBlanc opinion. That case goes against you?

Counsel: Ostensibly yes, your Honor, but what actually happened in LeBlanc is that the court did not think it mattered whether plaintiff's allegations were derived from or merely similar to the prior public disclosures in that case because plaintiff failed under either test. The First Circuit affirmed the LeBlanc opinion, but in an unpublished opinion that had no precedential value when decided. If faced with the question now, we are saying the First Circuit would agree with the majority of circuit court precedent.[5]

Turning to the second component of the argument, your Honor—the question as to whether the Plaintiffs are original sources of information provided to the government in advance of the complaint—the answer is that they are not because of three indisputable facts. . . .

This is the kind of dialogue you should expect and *welcome*. Oral argument is a conversation with the court, not a speech or lecture.

E. A WAY TO APPROACH THE CONCLUSION OF THE ARGUMENT

Once the body of the argument is concluded, you need to find a way to finish. If the argument is rigidly timed, and you have used your full time, then it is appropriate to say, "I see my time is up. Thank you, your Honor(s)," and sit down.

Suppose alternatively that the argument is rigidly timed, and as the red light goes on you are about to answer a judge's question. Then it is appropriate to say, "I see my time is up, your Honor. May I have a moment to answer your question?" If the court says yes, then go ahead and answer the question, but do not take more than a few moments to answer the question and conclude. If the court says no, then say thank you, and sit down.

What if you actually have time left when you have reached a high point on which to conclude the argument? That is not a problem. In our experience, courts appreciate lawyers who make their points and conclude early. If you do wish to insert a conclusion, then remind the court what you want it to do and why the court should do that. ("Your Honor, we request that you grant the motion to dismiss. The complaint does not state a claim for relief because Plaintiffs are not proper whistleblowers under the statute as a matter of law.") Do not feel obligated to go into an elaborate re-summarization of your argument. The re-summarization will simply sound repetitive and take away any advantage you achieved by making the body of the argument succinct. And avoid the temptation to fill the time with "additional" points. You may find that you say something you later regret.

In the end, relax and have fun with the oral argument experience. Welcome the dialog with the court.

---

[5]   Authors' Note: In fact, the First Circuit subsequently rendered two decisions on this issue. These opinions are U.S. v. City of Woonsocket, 587 F.3d 49 (1st Cir. 2009), and U.S. ex rel. Duxbury v. Ortho Biotech Products, L.P., 579 F.3d 13 (1st Cir. 2009). In *Woonsocket*, the First Circuit adopted the majority view. 587 F.3d at 57.

Quick Reference Index

References are to Pages

Add your own quick references: